T0135106

Communications in Computer and Information Science 1857

Editorial Board Members

Joaquim Filipe ⓘ, *Polytechnic Institute of Setúbal, Setúbal, Portugal*
Ashish Ghosh ⓘ, *Indian Statistical Institute, Kolkata, India*
Raquel Oliveira Prates ⓘ, *Federal University of Minas Gerais (UFMG), Belo Horizonte, Brazil*
Lizhu Zhou, *Tsinghua University, Beijing, China*

Rationale

The CCIS series is devoted to the publication of proceedings of computer science conferences. Its aim is to efficiently disseminate original research results in informatics in printed and electronic form. While the focus is on publication of peer-reviewed full papers presenting mature work, inclusion of reviewed short papers reporting on work in progress is welcome, too. Besides globally relevant meetings with internationally representative program committees guaranteeing a strict peer-reviewing and paper selection process, conferences run by societies or of high regional or national relevance are also considered for publication.

Topics

The topical scope of CCIS spans the entire spectrum of informatics ranging from foundational topics in the theory of computing to information and communications science and technology and a broad variety of interdisciplinary application fields.

Information for Volume Editors and Authors

Publication in CCIS is free of charge. No royalties are paid, however, we offer registered conference participants temporary free access to the online version of the conference proceedings on SpringerLink (http://link.springer.com) by means of an http referrer from the conference website and/or a number of complimentary printed copies, as specified in the official acceptance email of the event.

CCIS proceedings can be published in time for distribution at conferences or as post-proceedings, and delivered in the form of printed books and/or electronically as USBs and/or e-content licenses for accessing proceedings at SpringerLink. Furthermore, CCIS proceedings are included in the CCIS electronic book series hosted in the SpringerLink digital library at http://link.springer.com/bookseries/7899. Conferences publishing in CCIS are allowed to use Online Conference Service (OCS) for managing the whole proceedings lifecycle (from submission and reviewing to preparing for publication) free of charge.

Publication process

The language of publication is exclusively English. Authors publishing in CCIS have to sign the Springer CCIS copyright transfer form, however, they are free to use their material published in CCIS for substantially changed, more elaborate subsequent publications elsewhere. For the preparation of the camera-ready papers/files, authors have to strictly adhere to the Springer CCIS Authors' Instructions and are strongly encouraged to use the CCIS LaTeX style files or templates.

Abstracting/Indexing

CCIS is abstracted/indexed in DBLP, Google Scholar, EI-Compendex, Mathematical Reviews, SCImago, Scopus. CCIS volumes are also submitted for the inclusion in ISI Proceedings.

How to start

To start the evaluation of your proposal for inclusion in the CCIS series, please send an e-mail to ccis@springer.com.

Inseop Na · Go Irie

Editors

Frontiers of Computer Vision

29th International Workshop, IW-FCV 2023
Yeosu, South Korea, February 20–22, 2023
Revised Selected Papers

 Springer

Editors
Inseop Na
Chonnam National University
Yeosu, Korea (Republic of)

Go Irie
Tokyo University of Science
Tokyo, Japan

ISSN 1865-0929 ISSN 1865-0937 (electronic)
Communications in Computer and Information Science
ISBN 978-981-99-4913-7 ISBN 978-981-99-4914-4 (eBook)
https://doi.org/10.1007/978-981-99-4914-4

© The Editor(s) (if applicable) and The Author(s), under exclusive license
to Springer Nature Singapore Pte Ltd. 2023

This work is subject to copyright. All rights are reserved by the Publisher, whether the whole or part of the material is concerned, specifically the rights of translation, reprinting, reuse of illustrations, recitation, broadcasting, reproduction on microfilms or in any other physical way, and transmission or information storage and retrieval, electronic adaptation, computer software, or by similar or dissimilar methodology now known or hereafter developed.
The use of general descriptive names, registered names, trademarks, service marks, etc. in this publication does not imply, even in the absence of a specific statement, that such names are exempt from the relevant protective laws and regulations and therefore free for general use.
The publisher, the authors, and the editors are safe to assume that the advice and information in this book are believed to be true and accurate at the date of publication. Neither the publisher nor the authors or the editors give a warranty, expressed or implied, with respect to the material contained herein or for any errors or omissions that may have been made. The publisher remains neutral with regard to jurisdictional claims in published maps and institutional affiliations.

This Springer imprint is published by the registered company Springer Nature Singapore Pte Ltd.
The registered company address is: 152 Beach Road, #21-01/04 Gateway East, Singapore 189721, Singapore

Preface

We are pleased to publish the post proceedings of the 29th International Workshop on Frontiers of Computer Vision (IW-FCV 2023), which was held in Yeosu, South Korea, from February 20 to 22, 2023. This workshop is an annual event that brings together researchers in the field of computer vision and artificial intelligence to share their research results. The workshop was started 29 years ago as a way to strengthen networking and share research results between Japanese and Korean researchers, and it has since grown in scope and influence, so from 2017, the workshop became an international event. Unfortunately, the workshop was not held in on-site format for the past three years due to the COVID-19 pandemic. However, this year, the pandemic situation has improved and the workshop was held on-site in Yeosu. We are very proud of the fact that we have continued the tradition built up by our seniors by continuing this workshop for 29 years despite the difficult environment.

The main topics covered in this workshop include, but are not necessarily limited to, basic theories related to image processing, computer vision, image media, and human interface, as well as all research areas in applied fields such as autonomous vehicle driving, robot automation, and image content recognition. Recently, topics related to applications in the medical, bio, and entertainment fields applying artificial intelligence are also frequently included.

We were concerned that many researchers would not be able to participate in the workshop due to the previous two online workshops and concern over the spread of the pandemic. However, we received 72 papers from authors in 8 countries. Each paper was reviewed by two reviewers, and the feedback from the reviewers was used to select the papers to be presented. After the workshop, the top 18% of the papers, 13 full papers, were published in CCIS based on the review results, on-site presentation evaluation, and PC member evaluation.

We would like to express our sincere gratitude to all the members of the various committees who worked hard to plan and operate the workshop. We would also like to thank the Korean Society of Computer Vision (KCVS), the Korean Society of Smart Media (KISM), the Jeollanam-do Tourism Organization, Yeosu City, the National Program of Excellence in Software at Chonnam National University, and the Culture Technology Institute at Chonnam National University for their co-hosting and financial support. We would also like to thank the Springer staff for their hard work in editing and publishing the proceedings. Finally, we would like to express our deepest gratitude to all the authors who submitted and presented their papers despite the difficult circumstances.

Thank you.

June 2023

Chilwoo Lee
Kazuhiko Sumi
In Seop Na
Go Irie

Organization

General Chairs

Chilwoo Lee   Chonnam National University, South Korea
Kazuhiko Sumi   Aoyama Gakuin University, Japan

Program Chairs

Inseop Na   Chonnam National University, South Korea
Go Irie   Tokyo University of Science, Japan

Financial Chair

Daejin Kim   Chonnam National University, South Korea

Publication Chair

Hieyong Jeong   Chonnam National University, South Korea

Publicity Chair

Kyungbaek Kim   Chonnam National University, South Korea

Local Arrangement Chair

Chunseong Shin   Chonnam National University, South Korea

Web Chair

Inseop Na   Chonnam National University, South Korea

Steering Committee

Yoshimitsu Aoki	Keio University, Japan
Hiroyasu Koshimizu	YYC-Solution, Japan
Takio Kurita	Hiroshima University, Japan
Chikahito Nakajima	CRIEPI, Japan
Makoto Niwakawa	Meidensha, Japan
Rin-ichiro Taniguchi	Kyushu University, Japan
Kazuhiko Yamamoto	Gifu University, Japan
Jun-ichiro Hayashi	Kagawa University, Japan
Kazuhiko Sumi	Aoyama Gakuin University, Japan
Kanghyun Jo	University of Ulsan, South Korea
Soon Ki Jung	Kyungpook National University, South Korea
Chilwoo Lee	Chonnam National University, South Korea
Weon-Geun Oh	ETRI, South Korea
Jong-Il Park	Hanyang University, South Korea
Inseop Na	Chonnam National University, South Korea
Hieyong Jeong	Chonnam National University, South Korea
Kiryong Kwon	Bukyung National University, South Korea

Program Committee

Kyoung Ho Choi	Mokpo National University, South Korea
Kaushik Deb	Chittagong University of Engineering and Technology, Bangladesh
Van-Dung Hoang	Quangbinh University, Vietnam
Md Zahidul Islam	Islamic University, Kushtia, Bangladesh
Moon-Ho Jeong	Kwangwoon University, South Korea
Hyun-Deok Kang	UNIST, South Korea
Jaeil Kim	Kyungpook National University, South Korea
Soo Hyung Kim	Chonnam National University, South Korea
Wonjun Kim	Konkuk University, South Korea
My Ha Le	Ho Chi Minh City University of Education, Vietnam
Chul Lee	Dongguk University, South Korea
Jae-Ho Lee	ETRI, South Korea
Suk Hwan Lee	Tong Myong University, South Korea
Soon-Yong Park	Kyungpook National University, South Korea
Hoang-Hon Trinh	Ho Chi Minh City University of Technology, Vietnam
Ming-Hsuan Yang	University of California at Merced, USA

Byoung-Ju Yun   Kyungpook National University, South Korea
Wahyono   Gadja Mada University, Indonesia
Kwanghee Won   South Dakota State University, USA
Takayuki Fujiwara   Hokkaido Information University, Japan
Yoshinori Kuno   Saitama University, Japan
Hidehiro Ohki   Oita University, Japan
Hideo Saito   Keio University, Japan
Atsushi Shimada   Kyushu University, Japan
Kenji Terada   Tokushima University, Japan
Yasutomo Kawanishi   Nagoya University, Japan
Takayoshi Yamashita   Chubu University, Japan
Hironobu Fujiyoshi   Chubu University, Japan
Kengo Terasawa   Future University Hakodate, Japan
Toru Tamaki   Hiroshima University, Japan
Diego Thomas   Kyushu University, Japan
Maiya Hori   Kyushu University, Japan
Michihiro Mikamo   Kagoshima University, Japan
Kazuhiko Sumi   Aoyama Gakuin University, Japan
Hiroshi Tanaka   Fujitsu Laboratories Ltd., Japan
Keiji Yanai   University of Electro-Communications, Japan
Hitoshi Habe   Kindai University, Japan
Shuichi Akizuki   Chukyo University, Japan
Masakazu Iwamura   Osaka Prefecture University, Japan
Gou Koutaki   Kumamoto University Japan
Masashi Nishiyama   Tottori University, Japan
Wataru Ohyama   Saitama Institute of Technology, Japan
Takahiro Okabe   Kyushu Institute of Technology, Japan
Tsubasa Minematsu   Kyushu University, Japan

Reviewers

Hiroaki Aizawa   Kanghyun Jo
Shuichi Akizuki   Soonki Jung
Jun Fujiki   Naoshi Kaneko
Takayuki Fujiwara   Gou Koutaki
Ryosuke Furuta   Takio Kurita
Hitoshi Habe   Chilwoo Lee
Vandung Hoang   Sang Hwa Lee
Maiya Hori   Seokju Lee
Hae-Gon Jeon   Suk-Hwan Lee
Hieyong Jeong   Tsubasa Minematsu

Yu Mitsuzumi
Minoru Mori
Katsuyuki Nakamura
Kazuaki Nakamura
Masashi Nishiyama
Wataru Ohyama
Takahiro Okabe
Yuji Oyamada
Hanhoon Park
Takashi Shibata

Inwook Shim
Yongqing Sun
Toru Tamaki
Yukinobu Taniguchi
Kengo Terasawa
Diego Thomas
Xiaomeng Wu
Yota Yamamoto
Keiji Yanai
Inseop Na

Contents

Multi-attributed Face Synthesis for One-Shot Deep Face Recognition

Muhammad Shaheryar(✉) ⓘ, Lamyanba Laishram ⓘ, Jong Taek Lee ⓘ,
and Soon Ki Jung ⓘ

School of Computer Science and Engineering, Kyungpook National University,
Daegu, Republic of Korea
{shaheryar,yanbalaishram,jongtaeklee,skjung}@knu.ac.kr

Abstract. Nothing is more unique and crucial to an individual's identity than their face. With the rapid improvement in computational power and memory space and recent specializations in deep learning models, images are becoming more essential than ever for pattern recognition. Several deep face recognition models have recently been proposed to train deep networks on enormously big public datasets like MSCeleb-1M [8] and VG-GFace2 [5], successfully achieving sophisticated performance on mainstream applications. It is particularly challenging to gather an adequate dataset that allows strict command over the desired properties, such as hair color, skin tone, makeup, age alteration, etc. As a solution, we devised a one-shot face recognition system that utilizes synthetic data to recognize a face even if the facial attributes are altered. This work proposes and investigates the feasibility of creating a multi-attributed artificial face dataset from a one-shot image to train the deep face recognition model. This research seeks to demonstrate how the image synthesis capability of the deep learning methods can construct a face dataset with multiple critical attributes for a recognition process to enable and enhance efficient face recognition. In this study, the ideal deep learning features will be combined with a conventional one-shot learning framework. We did experiments for our proposed model on the LFW and multi-attributed synthetic data; these experiments highlighted some insights that can be helpful in the future for one-shot face recognition.

Keywords: Deep Learning · Computer Vision · One-Shot Face recognition · Siamese Networks · Image Classification

1 Introduction

The practical significance and great theoretical interest from cognitive scientists have been precisely the reason why facial recognition systems have been the target of such great curiosity and attention for the past few decades, making it impossible to disregard their importance as a non-contact verification method. It has expanded its usage in a variety of digital media, including video indexing,

© The Author(s), under exclusive license to Springer Nature Singapore Pte Ltd. 2023
I. Na and G. Irie (Eds.): IW-FCV 2023, CCIS 1857, pp. 1–13, 2023.
https://doi.org/10.1007/978-981-99-4914-4_1

video analytics, and security departments. Face identification and face verification are often two sub-tasks that make up face recognition. Three phases are involved in each task: face detection, feature extraction, and classification.

Fig. 1. Examples of Face images in the Smoking Gun's mug shot collection [24].

It is pretty daunting to build a face recognizer, especially with a small dataset. Even though there has been a significant advancement in face detection, problems still prevent the technology from being as accurate as a human. Early research created shallow models with basic facial features, while contemporary face recognition methods are considerably improved and powered by deep CNNs.

A deep convolutional network promises to attain greater accuracy using a straightforward classification approach, but it requires a lot of memory to train. One of the significant challenges is the very volatile and unbalanced amount of training data, where certain classes in the dataset may have a lot of photos. In contrast, others may have relatively few, affecting the quality of the results severely. The latest expansion of methods based on deep learning, including generative adversarial networks (GANs) [10,15], can solve the problem of varying dataset sizes by producing realistic facial images while accepting appropriate control parameters. Additionally, there are other issues, such as various humans having remarkably similar appearances and the fact that the faces of the same person may look very different due to lighting, position, and age variations. Although other deep network approaches can also handle variations in pose, lighting, and facial expressions, their requirement of a significant quantity of annotated data to train the system will always be a considerable drawback. Since GANs continue to be successful in producing artificial data for computer vision tasks [26], a new field of biometric research is beginning to explore how synthetic face images might be produced and utilized to train FR models. Face attribute adjustment is possible with the encoder-decoder architecture by decoding the encoder's latent space representation based on the given attributes. Compared to other synthetic data generation challenges, this research challenges assigning an identity to the synthetically generated faces to render them usable while ensuring variations within identity.

The fundamental pillar of this research is developing a hybrid approach for one-shot face recognition that, while sustaining the true identity, allows for an accurate modification of 14 various multi-attributes of any specified face. One can utilize our strategy to increase the variety of single faces in a dataset and strengthen face recognition algorithms. This one-shot-based deep face recognition (OS-DFR) method is distinct from typical face synthesizing methods and seeks to learn the synthetic features without giving the original characteristics. Motivated by the ATTGAN [10]'s success in generating realistic facial attributes, OS-DFR integrates the two tasks, one-shot synthetic face generation and face recognition. According to the statistical link between synthetic characteristics and face identification, this method successfully achieves the aim of deep face recognition. It is crucial when only one sample is available for a particular person. Face images generated from the "MugShots" for evaluating the performance of a recognition job and benchmarking are soon to be proposed as our dataset that includes unconstrained face images. The key contributions to this work are:

- We provided a technique for multi-attributed face synthesis for one-shot face recognition, employing synthetic data to replace augmentation approaches for development of realistic and feature enriched images of a person. To the best of our knowledge, this is the first instance of one-shot facial recognition using multi-attributed synthetic data.
- We empirically verified the effectiveness of the approach for multi-attributed synthetic data for face recognition in the real world.

The remainder of the paper is organized as follows: In Sect. 2, prior studies on the creation of synthetic data, one-shot face recognition, and the use of synthetic data for deep neural network training are reviewed. A thorough explanation of the suggested technique, including an explanation of the network and the created synthetic dataset, is given in Sect. 3. The outcomes of our methodology are presented in Sect. 4, along with experimental settings and details. The ideas and algorithms created in this study are summarized in Sect. 5, which is then followed by a brief discussion of prospective future work.

2   Related Work

The majority of this section covers the current status of one-shot learning in the literature. The most recent low-shot learning work [23,29] also garners a lot of interest in the broader image recognition scenario. The authors divided the ImageNet data2 into the base and low-shot (referred to as new in [23]) classes, and the goal is to recognize images from both the base and low-shot classes. Their benchmark job is quite similar to one-shot face recognition but in the broader image recognition domain. Since the domain is really distinct from ours, their approach is pretty different from ours.

Overall, one-shot learning remains an unresolved issue. A natural source of information is obtained from new data in numerous ways through "data manufacturing" [2]. There have been several works that tackle this issue in recent years. With little data, transfer learning is a viable method that encourages the usage of deep CNNs in several disciplines. [13,17] shows that by leveraging information from similar tasks with more enormous datasets, CNN-based transfer learning can produce superior classification results in our work with limited datasets (target domain). In their research [7,9], the authors proposed CNN-based novel frameworks. The primary focus of their framework was to address an issue in one-shot learning by constructing generative models to build samples to solve the underrepresented classes' problems.

Bromley et al. [4] suggested the idea of Siamese Networks for the signature verification problem, and [16] demonstrated the application of deep convolutional Siamese networks for one-shot tasks with exceptional accuracy. The approach of deep attribute encoding of faces for one-shot face recognition was proposed in another work [14]. They honed a deep CNN for face recognition using particular features of human faces, such as the face's shape, hair, and gender. One-shot face recognition using mix method of Siamese neural network and deep feature encoding was proposed in [6]. [19] demonstrated the application of deep convolutional Siamese networks for one-shot tasks with substantial accuracy. By relying on a similarity function [8,9] based on pairs of images, this network seeks to build a deep relevant feature representation. In fact, the neural network learns to distinguish between two inputs associated with distinct classes rather than explicitly learning to categorize its input. Moreover, this network focuses on learning embeddings for the similar classes samples and we can learn semantic similarities. In order to construct a trustworthy face recognition system, the method we propose in this study integrates the concept of Deep Convolutional Siamese Networks and synthetic data generation.

The use of synthetic data in face recognition has gained popularity in recent times. The behavior of face image quality generated by [15] has been examined in [31]. Furthermore, Shen et al. [22] concluded that synthetic face images could deceive humans. The excellent quality images that GANs and their various variations [15,19,25,27] can create have attracted more and more attention. To address the insufficient dataset, images generated by MorphGan [20] can severely assist with their data augmentation. There is a spike and improvement in performance by up to 9% by merely augmenting the faces with new expressions and poses - consequently addressing the issue of limited datasets. It is, however, limited to the head and expression of the face image. Three methods based on meta-learning, disentangling, and filtering were described by Zhai et al. [30] to lessen the modal difference between synthetic and real data. Then, they trained face recognition model using a hybrid of a synthetic and real dataset. Recent work proposed in the field of face recognition using synthetic data [3] has come to light, where the authors examine the viability of training face recognition algorithms using a synthetically created face dataset and raise a variety of privacy, legal, and ethical issues in relation to the gathering, use, and sharing of real biometric data.

Face recognition is abstracted into two phases. Extraction of facial features is the first phase, and estimation of the person's identification from the extracted face features is the second. Face recognition has recently paced due to the rapid development of deep convolutional neural networks and put great emphasis on learning a clear facial feature space where faces of the same person are close to each other and faces of different people are far apart. This representative technique aimed to learn the discriminative face representations directly from the original picture space. In limited circumstances, face recognition performance has significantly increased. In order to obtain the SOTA accuracy of 97.35%, DeepFace {[23] introduced classification loss and three-dimensional normalized alignment processing in 2014 on the LFW dataset [12]. FaceNet [21] achieved 99.63% on LFW using the triplet loss function in 2015. However, there are significant problems for the use of the face recognition system in genuine unconstrained scenarios [18]. One of the most significant issues is that the quality of the input facial image might impact the system's accuracy. Even ArcFace, which is extremely strong, can only attain an accuracy of 63.22% on the RealWorld Masked Face Recognition Dataset (RMFRD) [28]. This result is based on [11], which was obtained when ArcFace was not retrained on this dataset. As a result, how to improve facial recognition in unconstrained real-world settings is now the most pressing topic.

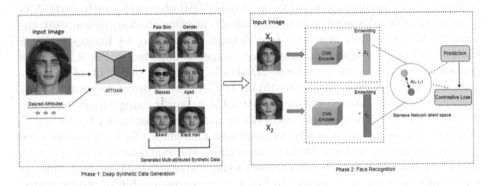

Fig. 2. Overview of the proposed approach. On the left, ATTGAN [10] is used to create synthetic face dataset from the one-shot image with multi attributes. The identity label is assigned to each generated synthetic images. The learning strategy is shown on the right, where the face recognition will be trained on the synthetic dataset using Contrastive loss. The trained model will be used for better face recognition.

3 One-Shot Synthetic Face Recognition

Deep learning algorithms requiring hundreds or thousands of images to bear effective results have always been one of their vast drawbacks. This section describes the method for creating and using synthetic face images to train a Face recognition model that accounts for the various subject variables, such as hair color, age, mustache etc. Two distinct phases will comprise the One-Shot based synthetic face recognition. Overall architecture can be shown in Fig. 2. In this section, we outline these processes as well as our suggested technique for one-shot face recognition using synthetic data.

3.1 Deep Synthetic Data Generation

The primary objective of our generative model is to provide valuable auxiliary data for the one-shot classes in order to facilitate one-shot deep face recognition. We can span the feature space for these classes by doing this. We initially generated multi-attributed synthetic face data from one mugshot face image (Fig. 1). This step utilizes an Attribute GAN (AttGAN) [10] due its high reliability in altering attributes to the generated image. The attribute classification constraint, the reconstruction loss, and the adversarial loss are combined to generate a unified AttGAN. With the knowledge of the omitted characteristics preserved, this enables alteration of the desired attributes. Overall, the encoder and decoder network's objectives are as follows:

$$\min_{G_{enc}, G_{dec}} L_{enc,dec} = \lambda_1 L_{rec} + \lambda_2 cls_g + L_{adv_g} \tag{1}$$

These hyper parameters λ_1, λ_2 and λ_3 are used to balance the losses.

The code for AttGAN implemented in machine learning framework Tensorflow [1] is publicly accessible at https://github.com/LynnHo/AttGAN-Tensorflow. For additional information about implementation, please visit the website. We create our synthetic face dataset by creating 14 images for each individual from a mugshot one-shot face image, as depicted in Fig. 3. We have generated 14 images with multiple attributes from just one shot of the person. Another important characteristic of AttGAN is its direct applicability for attribute intensity control. Although AttGAN is taught using binary attribute values $(0/1)$, its basic principle may still be used when testing with continuous attribute values. So, additionally, we produced nine photos for each feature with varying intensities, and we obtained more than 50+ synthetic face images with actual attributes for a single person from a single shot image. With a continuous input value between $[0, 1]$, as seen in Fig. 4, the progressive shift of the generated images is natural and smooth.

3.2 Face Recognition

The convolutional Siamese network utilized in this research is constructed to learn properties of the input images independent of previous domain knowledge using very few samples from a given distribution. One-shot learning can be accomplished using a Siamese network design [6]. The twin networks' shared weights, which need fewer training parameters and reduce the possibility of overfitting, were another factor in the decision to utilize this model. For the investigation, a small labeled support set of classes used for train, test and validation.

In addition to this, several approaches may be investigated while taking into account the loss functions. One that is highly popular uses the softmax loss, whose goal is to increase the probability associated with the correct class. This straightforward strategy, however, has poor feature derivation performance for the face recognition task. To acquire highly discriminative deep features for face recognition, Euclidean-distance-based loss is preferred because of the maximization of inter-class variance and minimization of intra-class variance. It is the main reason we choose Contrastive loss function shown in Eq. 2

$$L = (1 - Y) \frac{1}{2} (D_w)^2 + (Y) \frac{1}{2} \{\max (0, n - D_w)\}^2 \qquad (2)$$

where $m > 0$ represents margin, D_w is the distance function between two samples, and Y stands for the output label. The Siamese network produces a distance value. We measured the distance between two image's feature embeddings using the Euclidean distance.

The core idea in this phase is to learn discriminative facial characteristics with a wide gap across classes throughout the training phase. A neural network (with a certain structure) is trained for this phase under a specified loss function, which controls how the network's parameters vary. After getting optimal feature representation from input images, it can be used to perform face verification. The significant conclusions will be how helpful the first step in producing synthetic face characteristics will be for computer vision in the future. The testing data is supplied to the Siamese Network during the testing phase in order to extract facial features, which are then utilized to compute the euclidean distance to conduct face verification and identification. A benefit of this strategy is that by creating synthetic data, the Siamese Network can distinguish between several people who have multiple attributes and can become more resilient to high-level feature fluctuation. The time- and space-complexity of the network can be a drawback.

4 Evaluation Experiments

We carried out assessment studies utilizing two publicly available datasets to assess the efficacy of the proposed OS-DFR approach.

4.1 Datasets

First dataset mugshots (citation: [24] for the initial experiments Due to the scant amount of annotation available for these images, we used some of the dataset's image samples to train the ATTGAN. Since a mugshot is a photographic portrait of a person from the shoulders up and we have just one image of each person, there is a good chance that ATTGAN hasn't been trained on it yet, which is why we chose these mugshot face images. In all of our experiments, 14 attributes that have a significant visual impact are used. These are "Bags Under Eyes," "Bald," "Bangs," "Black Hair," "Blond Hair," "Brown Hair," "Bushy Eyebrows," "Eyeglasses," "Gender," "Mouth Open," "Mustache," "No Beard," "Pale Skin," and "Age," which cover the majority of the attributes used in the previous works depicted in Fig. 3.

Moreover, we have also used the attribute intensity control characteristic of ATTGAN and generated multiple synthetic images for single attributes shown in Fig. 4.

Fig. 3. Editing results of the Facial attributes on the custom one-shot dataset: the first is the original image, and the rest 14 images result from multi-attributed synthetic face images generated by ATTGAN [10].

Fig. 4. Illustration of pale skin with several degrees of intensity.

4.2   Network Settings

The network was implemented using PyTorch. On a batch size of 16, we trained networks for 30 epochs. Rmsprop was used as the optimizer, with a learning rate of 0.001. The NVIDIA Titan Xp with 12 GB of RAM was used to train and test the system. Two convolutional layers with kernel sizes of 11×11 and 7×7 make up the Siamese network. 2D max pooling immediately follows each layer.

4.3   Results

The network showed poor performance in our initial tests while trying to deal with 5, 10 and 15-way one-shot recognition. After epochs and network layer settings we achieve the highest accuracy of 78% as shown in Fig. 7. We tried our experiments with the following settings: Table 1 shows the appropriate resultant

Table 1. Performance based on the characteristics of the training and the testing set.

Experiment Data Set	Train accuracy		Val accuracy		Test accuracy	
	LFW	Combined	Synthetic	LFW	Synthetic	Combined
5-Way Task	98%	93%	65%	73%	65.66%	78%
10-Way Task	99%	94%	67%	77%	68%	72.50%
15-Way Task	96.50%	91%	68%	75%	62.29%	66%

performances. It is clear from that table that the verification work becomes more challenging the more dissimilar the training and testing sets are.

There are some serious takeaways from the results. It can be seen that the performance of the model is strongly dependent on how different the images are in both the training and validation sets. If we take an example of just identifying the person from the face that is already present in the database, then the trained model on multi-attributed synthetic data would be enough to support that case (Fig. 5).

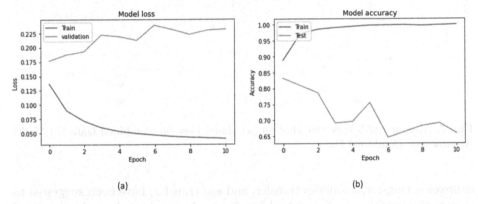

(a)   (b)

Fig. 5. 10-Way One shot on LFW & Synthetic Test Data (a) Model Loss (b) Model Accuracy.

It is demonstrated in Fig. 6 as an ablations study the accuracy of 10-way shot when the model was solely testes on synthetic dataset.

This particular Siamese network was chosen since it is a basic net that was trained using a contrastive loss with feature normalization at the end and no final linear layer following the computation of feature distance.

5   Limitations and Discussion

Face data augmentation is the most complicated of the other data augmentation techniques. Several techniques, including pose transfer, hairdo transfer,

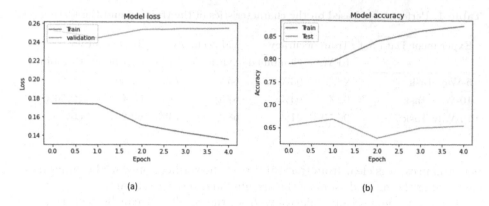

(a)

(b)

Fig. 6. 10-Way One shot on Synthetic Test Data.

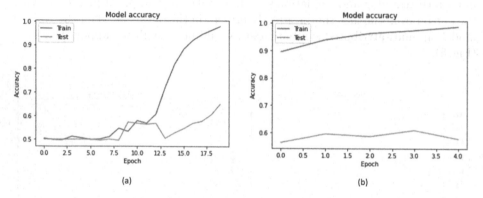

(a)

(b)

Fig. 7. Accuracy of 5-Way One shot on (a) Model Loss on Combined Data (b) Model Accuracy on Combined Data.

expression transfer, cosmetics transfer, and age transfer, have been suggested to change the appearance of an actual face image. In the meantime, the simulated virtual faces can also be improved to match the realism of the genuine ones. We proposed a one-shot synthetic data generation for deep face recognition in this work. The model is based on the image generation capability of GANs, whereby we try to use the data variance of the base set to synthesize more efficient augmented data for one-shot face recognition. The idea was built to aid researchers in making efficient facial recognition technology and minimizing the impact of the obstacle of limited data. Our solution can also identify a person who keeps changing their facial appearance. Our architecture shares the same constraints and is based on synthetic image generation with multiple attributes. Any new findings that enhance the image generation capability with multiple attributes should directly be applicable to our technique. Our approach, irrespective of the current limitations, has shed some light that, with the help of computer graphics, will allow for efficient training and recognition of facial models from just one-shot face images. Future research plan is to use more efficient GAN network for generating high quality multi-attributed synthetic face images and train a deeper face recognition system.

Acknowledgement. This study was supported by the BK21 FOUR project (AI-driven Convergence Software Education Research Program) funded by the Ministry of Education, School of Computer Science and Engineering, Kyungpook National University, Korea (4199990214394) and was also supported by Institute of Information & communications Technology Planning & Evaluation (IITP) grant funded by the Korea government (MSIT) (No. 2019-0-00203, Development of 5G-based Predictive Visual Security Technology for Preemptive Threat Response) and also by the MSIT(Ministry of Science and ICT), Korea, under the Innovative Human Resource Development for Local Intellectualization support program (IITP-2022-RS-2022-00156389) supervised by the IITP (Institute for Information & communications Technology Planning & Evaluation).

References

1. Abadi, M., et al.: {TensorFlow}: a system for {Large-Scale} machine learning. In: 12th USENIX Symposium on Operating Systems Design and Implementation (OSDI 2016), pp. 265–283 (2016)
2. Bart, E., Ullman, S.: Cross-generalization: learning novel classes from a single example by feature replacement. In: 2005 IEEE Computer Society Conference on Computer Vision and Pattern Recognition (CVPR 2005), vol. 1, pp. 672–679. IEEE (2005)
3. Boutros, F., Huber, M., Siebke, P., Rieber, T., Damer, N.: Sface: privacy-friendly and accurate face recognition using synthetic data. arXiv preprint arXiv:2206.10520 (2022)
4. Bromley, J., Guyon, I., LeCun, Y., Säckinger, E., Shah, R.: Signature verification using a "siamese" time delay neural network. Adv. Neural Inf. Process. Syst. **6** (1993)
5. Cao, Q., Shen, L., Xie, W., Parkhi, O.M., Zisserman, A.: Vggface2: a dataset for recognising faces across pose and age. In: 2018 13th IEEE International Conference on Automatic Face & Gesture Recognition (FG 2018), pp. 67–74. IEEE (2018)
6. Chanda, S., GV, A.C., Brun, A., Hast, A., Pal, U., Doermann, D.: Face recognition-a one-shot learning perspective. In: 2019 15th International Conference on Signal-Image Technology & Internet-Based Systems (SITIS), pp. 113–119. IEEE (2019)
7. Guo, Y., Zhang, L.: One-shot face recognition by promoting underrepresented classes. arXiv preprint arXiv:1707.05574 (2017)
8. Guo, Y., Zhang, L., Hu, Y., He, X., Gao, J.: MS-Celeb-1M: a dataset and benchmark for large-scale face recognition. In: Leibe, B., Matas, J., Sebe, N., Welling, M. (eds.) ECCV 2016. LNCS, vol. 9907, pp. 87–102. Springer, Cham (2016). https://doi.org/10.1007/978-3-319-46487-9_6
9. Hariharan, B., Girshick, R.: Low-shot visual recognition by shrinking and hallucinating features. In: Proceedings of the IEEE International Conference on Computer Vision, pp. 3018–3027 (2017)
10. He, Z., Zuo, W., Kan, M., Shan, S., Chen, X.: Attgan: facial attribute editing by only changing what you want. IEEE Trans. Image Process. **28**(11), 5464–5478 (2019)

11. Huang, B., et al.: When face recognition meets occlusion: a new benchmark. In: ICASSP 2021–2021 IEEE International Conference on Acoustics, Speech and Signal Processing (ICASSP), pp. 4240–4244. IEEE (2021)
12. Huang, G.B., Mattar, M., Berg, T., Learned-Miller, E.: Labeled faces in the wild: a database for studying face recognition in unconstrained environments. In: Workshop on Faces in 'Real-Life' Images: Detection, Alignment, and Recognition (2008)
13. Huang, Z., Pan, Z., Lei, B.: Transfer learning with deep convolutional neural network for sar target classification with limited labeled data. Remote Sens. 9(9), 907 (2017)
14. Jadhav, A., Namboodiri, V.P., Venkatesh, K.S.: Deep attributes for one-shot face recognition. In: Hua, G., Jégou, H. (eds.) ECCV 2016. LNCS, vol. 9915, pp. 516–523. Springer, Cham (2016). https://doi.org/10.1007/978-3-319-49409-8_44
15. Karras, T., Laine, S., Aila, T.: A style-based generator architecture for generative adversarial networks. In: Proceedings of the IEEE/CVF Conference on Computer Vision and Pattern Recognition, pp. 4401–4410 (2019)
16. Koch, G., Zemel, R., Salakhutdinov, R., et al.: Siamese neural networks for one-shot image recognition. In: ICML Deep Learning Workshop, Lille, vol. 2 (2015)
17. Li, X., Pang, T., Xiong, B., Liu, W., Liang, P., Wang, T.: Convolutional neural networks based transfer learning for diabetic retinopathy fundus image classification. In: 2017 10th International Congress on Image and Signal Processing, Biomedical Engineering and Informatics (CISP-BMEI), pp. 1–11. IEEE (2017)
18. Masi, I., Wu, Y., Hassner, T., Natarajan, P.: Deep face recognition: a survey. In: 2018 31st SIBGRAPI Conference on Graphics, Patterns and Images (SIBGRAPI), pp. 471–478. IEEE (2018)
19. Mokhayeri, F., Kamali, K., Granger, E.: Cross-domain face synthesis using a controllable gan. In: Proceedings of the IEEE/CVF Winter Conference on Applications of Computer Vision, pp. 252–260 (2020)
20. Ruiz, N., Theobald, B.J., Ranjan, A., Abdelaziz, A.H., Apostoloff, N.: Morphgan: one-shot face synthesis gan for detecting recognition bias. arXiv preprint arXiv:2012.05225 (2020)
21. Schroff, F., Kalenichenko, D., Philbin, J.: Facenet: a unified embedding for face recognition and clustering. In: Proceedings of the IEEE Conference on Computer Vision and Pattern Recognition, pp. 815–823 (2015)
22. Shen, B., RichardWebster, B., O'Toole, A., Bowyer, K., Scheirer, W.J.: A study of the human perception of synthetic faces. In: 2021 16th IEEE International Conference on Automatic Face and Gesture Recognition (FG 2021), pp. 1–8. IEEE (2021)
23. Taigman, Y., Yang, M., Ranzato, M., Wolf, L.: Deepface: closing the gap to human-level performance in face verification. In: Proceedings of the IEEE Conference on Computer Vision and Pattern Recognition, pp. 1701–1708 (2014)
24. The smoking gun (1997). http://www.thesmokinggun.com/mugshots
25. Viazovetskyi, Y., Ivashkin, V., Kashin, E.: StyleGAN2 distillation for feed-forward image manipulation. In: Vedaldi, A., Bischof, H., Brox, T., Frahm, J.-M. (eds.) ECCV 2020. LNCS, vol. 12367, pp. 170–186. Springer, Cham (2020). https://doi.org/10.1007/978-3-030-58542-6_11
26. Wang, Q., Gao, J., Lin, W., Yuan, Y.: Learning from synthetic data for crowd counting in the wild. In: Proceedings of the IEEE/CVF Conference on Computer Vision and Pattern Recognition, pp. 8198–8207 (2019)
27. Wang, T.C., Liu, M.Y., Zhu, J.Y., Tao, A., Kautz, J., Catanzaro, B.: High-resolution image synthesis and semantic manipulation with conditional gans. In:

Proceedings of the IEEE Conference on Computer Vision and Pattern Recognition, pp. 8798–8807 (2018)

28. Wang, Z., et al.: Masked face recognition dataset and application. arXiv preprint arXiv:2003.09093 (2020)

29. Wu, Y., Liu, H., Fu, Y.: Low-shot face recognition with hybrid classifiers. In: Proceedings of the IEEE International Conference on Computer Vision Workshops, pp. 1933–1939 (2017)

30. Zhai, Z., et al.: Demodalizing face recognition with synthetic samples. In: Proceedings of the AAAI Conference on Artificial Intelligence, vol. 35, pp. 3278–3286 (2021)

31. Zhang, H., Grimmer, M., Ramachandra, R., Raja, K., Busch, C.: On the applicability of synthetic data for face recognition. In: 2021 IEEE International Workshop on Biometrics and Forensics (IWBF), pp. 1–6. IEEE (2021)

Efficient Multi-Receptive Pooling
for Object Detection on Drone

Jinsu An[1], Muhamad Dwisnanto Putro[2], Adri Priadana[1],
and Kang-Hyun Jo[1(✉)]

[1] Department of Electrical, Electronic and Computer Engineering, University of
Ulsan, Ulsan, South Korea
jinsu5023@islab.ulsan.ac.kr, priadana3202@mail.ulsan.ac.kr,
acejo@ulsan.ac.kr
[2] Department of Electrical Engineering, Universitas Sam Ratulangi, Manado,
Indonesia
dwisnantoputro@unsrat.ac.id

Abstract. Object detection is the most fundamental and important research in computer vision to discriminate the location and class of the object in the image. This technology has been continuously researched for the past few years. Recently, with the development of hardware such as GPU computing power and cameras, object detection technology is gradually improving. However, there are many difficulties in utilizing GPUs on low-cost devices such as drones. Therefore, efficient deep learning technology that can operate on low-cost devices is needed. In this paper, we propose a deep learning model to enable real-time object detection on a low-cost device. We experiment to reduce the amount of computation and improve speed by modifying the CSP Bottleneck and SPPF parts corresponding to the backbone of YOLOv5. The model has been trained on MS COCO and VisDrone datasets, and the mAP values are measured at 0.364 mAP and 0.19 mAP, which are about 0.07 and 0.04 higher than Refinedetlite and Refinedet, respectively. The speed is 23.010 frames per second on the CPU configuration, which is enough for real-time object detection.

Keywords: Object Detection · Drone Vision · Convolutional Neural Network (CNN) · Efficient Module · Attention Modules

1 Introduction

Nowadays, drone technology has developed rapidly and guided to widespread use for many purposes. Drones, equipped with cameras, can capture images or videos and generate a variety of beneficial application scenarios, such as video surveillance [2], monitoring [11,34], tracking [41] and searching [31,33]. A drone even can enter difficult or dangerous areas that are impossible for humans to perform these works. This approach can also reduce the possibility of risks incurred.

Advances in computer vision have dramatically enhanced drone vision technology. Many works, such as object detection and classification, can be conducted

© The Author(s), under exclusive license to Springer Nature Singapore Pte Ltd. 2023
I. Na and G. Irie (Eds.): IW-FCV 2023, CCIS 1857, pp. 14–25, 2023.
https://doi.org/10.1007/978-981-99-4914-4_2

based on video captured by the drone to support the intelligence system. It leads the drone to localize and classify the objects based on its vision with high accuracy. It can even perform over enormous areas because the drone can capture extensive coverage only in a short period. It pushes drone vision technology to become increasingly popular.

Recently, the rapid development of Convolutional Neural Networks (CNNs) has improved object detection and classification tasks, providing improved results. Many researchers are developing deeper networks to achieve higher performance [20,28,30]. Unfortunately, it guides the architecture to produce enormous parameters and operate inefficiently. A drone practically uses a low-cost device to run its system. Therefore, it requires an efficient model to perform, especially in real-time.

The field of object detection has evolved over the past 20 years. It is generally divided into two methods. It is a traditional image processing method and a deep learning method. The deep learning method is also divided into two types, one-stage, and two-stage. The network proposed in this paper is an Improved one-stage YOLO (You Only Look Once) network. One-stage based YOLO has been presented as superior real-time object detection and brought much attention. YOLOv5 [12] appeared, which applies a Cross Stage Partial (CSP) [36] block with a bottleneck mechanism to make the network more efficient. This method offers many types based on size, which have various performances. Although the framework provides small versions with fewer parameters, the detector still suffers from infeasible results.

CNN architecture creates feature maps at different levels in each layer. The initial layer creates low-level features representing simple shapes, and as the layer deepens, mid and high-level features representing complex features are extracted. In general, small, medium, and large size objects are detected using low, mid, and high-level features. However, even when detecting large objects, for example, low-level features that respond strongly to edges or small instances are needed. We also need a high-level feature that captures the context of the image to detect small objects. To this end, it is possible to more accurately localize by effectively utilizing low, medium, and large features. In order to detect an object, these various feature information are essential. The existing Feature Pyramid Network (FPN) goes through more than 100 layers to deliver low-level information to high-level, but about 10 layers are sufficient in PANet. The detector used in YOLOv5 is applied to three layers of 80, 40, and 20 sizes of PANet. This layer is upsampled from the last layer of the backbone feature map and merged with the previous level feature map of the same size.

In this work, we adjusted the C3 and SPPF [10] layers to operate the object detection algorithm in real-time, the number of parameters of the network must be reduced. The C3 layer and SPPF layer used in the original YOLOv5 are lightened, and the C3 layer is composed of a bottleneck and 3 convolution layers as CSP bottleneck with 3 convolutions. The C3 layer is lightened by adjusting the convolution of the C3 layers from three to two and changing the order of the concatenation and addition operations of the feature map.

The SPPF layer consists of two convolution layers and three max-pooling layers. To lighten the layer, we reduced one max-pooling layer and added an addition operation. The contributions of this work are summarized as follows:

1. A real-time object detection method is proposed to localize the specific object quickly that can be operated on a low-cost device.
2. A new structure of the convolutional block is introduced by modifying the fusion operation on the CSP bottleneck module.
3. SPPF layer is improved to be more efficient. It supports the network to operate on a low-cost device without compromising its accuracy.

2   Related Work

CNN architectures as a backbone have been employed and developed to perform object detection and classification. It has offered outstanding results in extracting features equipped with many techniques to predict object locations with various sizes. Faster R-CNN [30] came to refine the previous version, R-CNN [9] and Fast R-CNN [8], proposed a Region Proposal Network (RPN) to locate the Region of Interest (RoI) and identify the class of objects. Another work, RetinaNet, offered a novel loss called Focal Loss to deal with the class imbalance problem. Meantime, YOLOv3 [25], YOLOv4 [3], and YOLOv5 [12] utilized the Feature Pyramid Network (FPN) [18] strategy to combine features with various levels.

Many researchers designed various efficient CNN architectures as a backbone to perform object detection. Fast-PdNet [27] offered a lightweight CNN architecture with multi-level contextual blocks that produce fewer parameters than general detectors. The detector is specially designed to perform person detection in supporting assistive robots. Another work [1] adjusted C3 module with a residual bottleneck mechanism on YOLOv5 [12] to make the model more efficient.

Several works modified the YOLO framework to perform efficient object detection applied in supporting drone vision. Pruned-YOLOv3/v5 [39] proposed an iterative channel pruning mechanism to design a lightweight network for YOLOv3 and YOLOv5. It gains a satisfactory balance between efficiency and accuracy on MS-COCO and VisDrone datasets. ECAP-YOLO [13], modified from YOLOv5 [12], offered an efficient channel attention pyramid method to deal with small object problems in aerial images. SPB-YOLO [38] also adjusted YOLOv5 [12] with Strip Bottleneck (SPB) module to build an efficient real-time detector for a drone. It achieves a good trade-off between speed and accuracy.

3   The Proposed Method

The proposed architecture has two main modules as shown in Fig. 1. Both are used in the backbone of YOLOv5, which corresponds to the baseline. The first is Efficient Residual Bottleneck (ERB), and the second is Efficient Multi-Receptive Pooling (EMRP).

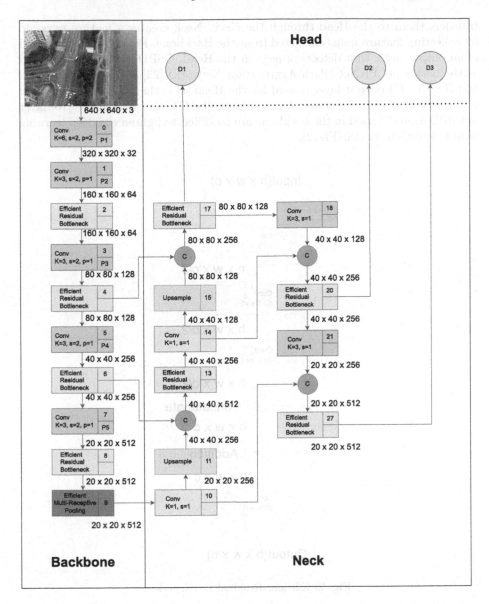

Fig. 1. The proposed architecture. A backbone module is used to extract object features with the proposed efficient methods. Besides, the PANet (Neck) and detection (Head) modules help the detector identify the location of the object in multi-scale variants.

3.1   The Backbone

The framework of YOLOv5 has three main components. It consists of Backbone, Neck, and Head. The Backbone extracts the features of the image and transfers them to the Head through the Neck. Neck creates a feature pyramid by collecting feature maps extracted from the Backbone. Finally, it is composed of an output layer that detects objects in the Head. CSPDarknet53 [35] is used as the backbone, PANet (Path Aggregation Network) [23] is used for the Neck, and $B \times (5 + C)$ output layer is used for the Head. B is the number of bounding boxes, and C is the class score. Among them, the C3 layer and SPPF [10] layer of CSPDarknet53 used in the backbone are modified to lighten the deep learning object detection model (Fig. 2).

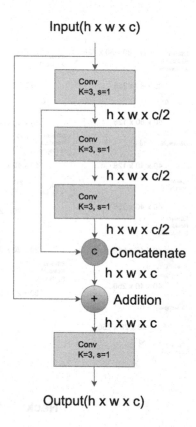

Fig. 2. Efficient Residual Bottleneck.

3.2 Efficient Residual Bottleneck

Efficient Residual Bottleneck (ERB) is an improved layer of the C3 layer used in YOLOv5. The C3 layer is CSP Bottleneck with 3 convolutions and consists of a bottleneck and 3 convolution layers. In order to operate the object detection algorithm in real-time on drones using low-cost devices, the number of parameters of the deep learning object detection network must be reduced. To decrease the number of parameters, the convolution of the C3 layer is adjusted from three to two, and the order of concatenation and addition operations of the feature map is changed. The proposed network offers an improved backbone that extracts the object features and discriminates the essential elements from the background. It applies a set of convolution layers sequentially using an efficient module. Light blocks apply residual techniques to maintain the quality of the feature map to push high performance in the final prediction. To avoid gradient performance degradation and prevent saturation of the training process, SiLU activation and Batch Normalization are employed sequentially in each convolution operation.

3.3   Efficient Multi-Receptive Pooling

Improved from [10], the efficient multi-receptive pooling is introduced to capture the difference of spatial information that employs a cascade pooling and a simple convolution. It applies convolutional and two sequential pooling to provide various receptive areas. It can increase the options of feature selection from multi-perspective combinations. It uses simple convolution to obtain one spatial area. Two pooling with window size of 5×5 is employed sequentially to capture the maximum value of the features. Combining features from different receptive areas will increase the variety of information so that the network will learn more about the feature type. Then, it applies a convolution operation to mix the various information. The residual technique is used in this module to ensure that the different feature pooling results obtain the expected quality and reduce the error rate of the filtering process (Fig. 3).

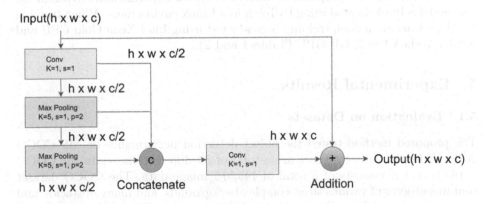

Fig. 3. Efficient Multi-Receptive Pooling, less complexity by double receptive pooling & addition path ways.

3.4 Loss Function

In YOLOv5, IoU loss, binary cross-entropy, and confidence loss were used as loss functions. Bounding-box regression is the most widely used method in object detection algorithms used to predict the position of an object to be detected using a bounding box. This method aims to correct the position of the predicted bounding box. Bounding box regression uses an overlapping region of the box of the real object and the predicted box location, called Intersection over Union (IOU). First, the IoU loss evaluates the difference between the predicted box position and the actual object's box's intersection, centroid distance, and aspect ratio. Second, we apply a confidence loss to evaluate whether or not there is an object in each cell. Finally, we use binary cross-entropy to measure the probability error of the predicted object class. Binary cross entropy is very effective for training models to solve many classification problems simultaneously. Combining the above three loss functions, the multi-box loss is expressed as:

$$
L_{MB} = \lambda_{coord} \sum_{g=1}^{G^2} \sum_{a=1}^{A} g_{ga}^{obj} L_{coord} + lambda_{obj} \sum_{g=1}^{G^2} \sum_{a=1}^{A} 1_{ga}^{obj} L_{obj}
$$
$$
+ lambda_{cls} \sum_{g=1}^{G^2} \sum_{a=1}^{A} 1_{ga}^{obj} L_{cls}
$$

$$(1)$$

4   Implementation Details

In this section, experiments with MS COCO [22] and VisDrone [41] datasets are described through the proposed architecture. As an experimental environment, the model is implemented using PyTorch in a Linux environment. When training the deep learning model, training is conducted using Intel Xeon Gold CPU and Nvidia Tesla V100 32 GB GPU (Tables 1 and 2).

5   Experimental Results

5.1   Evaluation on Datasets

The proposed method tested the object detection performance on MS COCO 2017, VisDrone dataset. There are a total of 80 different classes in the COCO dataset, and it consists of a total of 143,575 image data. The COCO dataset contains objects of various sizes, complex backgrounds, and many obstacles, and the proposed model is trained with 118,287 image data. The model is evaluated with 5000 images, and the model is tested with the remaining 20,288 images. The VisDrone dataset consists of 288 video clips (261,908 images) and 10,209 static photos were collected from multiple cameras mounted on drones and has a total of 10 classes (pedestrian, people, bicycle, car, van, truck, tricycle, awning-tricycle, bus, motor). Among them, the proposed model is trained with 6,471 image data, and the model is evaluated with 1,610 images and tested with 548

Table 1. Detection Result Comparisons on MS COCO Dataset, where Time@CPU1 and Time@CPU2 mean Running Time Tested on Intel I7-6700@3.40 GHZ and Intel I5 6600@3.30 GHZ, respectively.

Model	mAP 0.5:.95	Backbone	Time@CPU1	Time@CPU2
SSD [24]	0.193	MobileNet	128 ms	-
SSDLite [32]	0.222	MobileNet	125 ms	-
SSDLite [32]	0.221	MobileNetV2	120 ms	-
Pelee [37]	0.224	PeleeNet	140 ms	-
Tiny-DSOD [15]	0.232	DDB-Net+D-FPN	180 ms	-
SSD [24]	0.251	VGG	1250 ms	-
SSD [24]	0.28	ResNet101	1000 ms	-
YOLOv3 [29]	0.282	DarkNet53	1300 ms	-
RefineDetLite [7]	0.268	Res2NetLite72	130 ms	-
RefineDetLite++ [7]	0.296	Res2NetLite72	131 ms	-
YOLOv5s-ERB	**0.367**	**Improved CSPDarknet53**	-	43 ms
YOLOv5s-ERB_wosppf	**0.334**	**Improved CSPDarknet53**	-	36 ms
YOLOv5s-ERB_conv3	**0.366**	**Improved CSPDarknet53**	-	40 ms
YOLOv5s-ERB_EMRP	**0.364**	**Improved CSPDarknet53**	-	-

Table 2. Detection Result Comparisons on VisDrone Dataset.

Model	mAP 0.5:.95	Backbone
Cascade R-CNN+ [5]	0.183	SEResNeXt-50
EnDet	0.178	ResNet101-fpn
DCRCNN [6]	0.178	ResNeXt-101
Cascade R-CNN++ [5]	0.177	ResNeXt-101
ODAC	0.174	VGG
DA-RetianNet [26]	0.171	ResNet101
MOD-RETINANET	0.169	ResNet50
DBCL	0.168	Hourglass-104
ConstraintNet	0.161	Hourglass-104
CornetNet* [14]	0.174	Hourglass-104
Light-RCNN* [16]	0.165	ResNet101
FPN* [19]	0.165	ResNet50
Cascade R-CNN* [4]	0.161	ResNeXt-101
DetNet59* [17]	0.153	ResNet50
RefineDet* [40]	0.149	ResNet101
RetinaNet* [21]	0.118	ResNet101
YOLOv5s-ERB	**0.195**	**Improved CSPDarknet53**
YOLOv5s-EMRP	**0.193**	**Improved CSPDarknet53**
YOLOv5s-ERB_EMRP	**0.190**	**Improved CSPDarknet53**

images. An object detection model is evaluated through a dataset by extracting and learning the features of various objects included in the dataset. To evaluate the model, we use Average Precision (AP) to measure the accuracy of the predicted bounding box, derive AP for each class, and finally calculate the mean Average Precision (mAP) value for all classes. As a result, the mAP values of the proposed method are calculated as 0.364 and 0.190, respectively.

Fig. 4. Visualization of the Detection Result on VisDrone dataset.

6   Conclusion

This paper proposes efficient residual bottleneck and efficient multi-receptive pooling for a deep learning algorithm capable of real-time object detection. In order to reduce the complexity, the existing CSP Bottleneck and SPPF are improved. And the proposed network is trained on MS COCO and VisDrone datasets. The mAP value on the MS COCO dataset is measured at 0.364, and when compared to RefineDetLite++, the performance increased by about 0.07 mAP difference. The mAP value on the VisDrone dataset is measured at 0.190, and when compared to RefineDet+, the value is about 0.04 mAP higher. In the future, we plan to use the additional detector to increase the object detection rate. As the number of layers in the network increases, the number of parameters required for computation increases. It is expected that the method proposed in this paper can be used to reduce the number of parameters and increase the object detection rate by using additional detectors (Fig. 4).

Acknowledgement. This work was supported by the National Research Foundation of Korea (NRF) grant funded by the government (MSIT). (No. 2020R1A2C2008972).

References

1. An, J., Putro, M.D., Jo, K.H.: Efficient residual bottleneck for object detection on CPU. In: 2022 International Workshop on Intelligent Systems (IWIS), pp. 1–4. IEEE (2022)
2. Bera, B., Das, A.K., Garg, S., Piran, M.J., Hossain, M.S.: Access control protocol for battlefield surveillance in drone-assisted IoT environment. IEEE Internet Things J. **9**(4), 2708–2721 (2021)
3. Bochkovskiy, A., Wang, C.Y., Liao, H.Y.M.: YOLOv4: optimal speed and accuracy of object detection. arXiv preprint arXiv:2004.10934 (2020)
4. Cai, Z., Vasconcelos, N.: Cascade R-CNN: delving into high quality object detection. CoRR abs/1712.00726 (2017). arXiv:1712.00726
5. Cai, Z., Vasconcelos, N.: Cascade R-CNN: high quality object detection and instance segmentation. IEEE Trans. Pattern Anal. Mach. Intell. **43**(5), 1483–1498 (2021). https://doi.org/10.1109/TPAMI.2019.2956516
6. Chakraborty, S., Aich, S., Kumar, A., Sarkar, S., Sim, J.S., Kim, H.C.: Detection of cancerous tissue in histopathological images using dual-channel residual convolutional neural networks (DCRCNN). In: 2020 22nd International Conference on Advanced Communication Technology (ICACT), pp. 197–202 (2020). https://doi.org/10.23919/ICACT48636.2020.9061289
7. Chen, C., Liu, M., Meng, X., Xiao, W., Ju, Q.: RefineDetLite: a lightweight one-stage object detection framework for CPU-only devices. CoRR abs/1911.08855 (2019). arXiv:1911.08855
8. Girshick, R.: Fast R-CNN. In: 2015 IEEE International Conference on Computer Vision (ICCV), pp. 1440–1448. IEEE (2015)
9. Girshick, R., Donahue, J., Darrell, T., Malik, J.: Rich feature hierarchies for accurate object detection and semantic segmentation. In: 2014 IEEE Conference on Computer Vision and Pattern Recognition, pp. 580–587. IEEE (2014)
10. He, K., Zhang, X., Ren, S., Sun, J.: Spatial pyramid pooling in deep convolutional networks for visual recognition. IEEE Trans. Pattern Anal. Mach. Intell. **37**(9), 1904–1916 (2015)
11. Ikshwaku, S., Srinivasan, A., Varghese, A., Gubbi, J.: Railway corridor monitoring using deep drone vision. In: Verma, N., Ghosh, A. (eds.) Computational Intelligence: Theories, Applications and Future Directions - Volume II. Advances in Intelligent Systems and Computing, vol. 799, pp. 361–372. Springer, Singapore (2019). https://doi.org/10.1007/978-981-13-1135-2_28
12. Jocher, G., Stoken, A., Borovec, J.: ultralytics/yolov5: v3.0. https://doi.org/10.5281/zenodo.3983579

13. Kim, M., Jeong, J., Kim, S.: ECAP-YOLO: efficient channel attention pyramid yolo for small object detection in aerial image. Remote Sens. **13**(23), 4851 (2021)
14. Law, H., Deng, J.: CornerNet: detecting objects as paired keypoints. CoRR abs/1808.01244 (2018). arXiv:1808.01244
15. Li, Y., Li, J., Lin, W., Li, J.: Tiny-DSOD: lightweight object detection for resource-restricted usages. CoRR abs/1807.11013 (2018). arXiv:1807.11013
16. Li, Z., Peng, C., Yu, G., Zhang, X., Deng, Y., Sun, J.: Light-head R-CNN: in defense of two-stage object detector. CoRR abs/1711.07264 (2017). arXiv:1711.07264
17. Li, Z., Peng, C., Yu, G., Zhang, X., Deng, Y., Sun, J.: DetNet: a backbone network for object detection. CoRR abs/1804.06215 (2018). arXiv:1804.06215
18. Lin, T.Y., Dollár, P., Girshick, R., He, K., Hariharan, B., Belongie, S.: Feature pyramid networks for object detection. In: 2017 IEEE Conference on Computer Vision and Pattern Recognition (CVPR), pp. 936–944. IEEE (2017)
19. Lin, T., Dollár, P., Girshick, R.B., He, K., Hariharan, B., Belongie, S.J.: Feature pyramid networks for object detection. CoRR abs/1612.03144 (2016). arXiv:1612.03144
20. Lin, T.Y., Goyal, P., Girshick, R., He, K., Dollár, P.: Focal loss for dense object detection. IEEE Trans. Pattern Anal. Mach. Intell. **42**(2), 318–327 (2018)
21. Lin, T., Goyal, P., Girshick, R.B., He, K., Dollár, P.: Focal loss for dense object detection. CoRR abs/1708.02002 (2017). arXiv:1708.02002
22. Lin, T.-Y., et al.: Microsoft COCO: common objects in context. In: Fleet, D., Pajdla, T., Schiele, B., Tuytelaars, T. (eds.) ECCV 2014. LNCS, vol. 8693, pp. 740–755. Springer, Cham (2014). https://doi.org/10.1007/978-3-319-10602-1_48
23. Liu, S., Qi, L., Qin, H., Shi, J., Jia, J.: Path aggregation network for instance segmentation. In: 2018 IEEE/CVF Conference on Computer Vision and Pattern Recognition, pp. 8759–8768. IEEE (2018)
24. Liu, W., et al.: SSD: single shot multibox detector. CoRR abs/1512.02325 (2015). arXiv:1512.02325
25. Murthy, C.B., Hashmi, M.F.: Real time pedestrian detection using robust enhanced YOLOv3. In: 2020 21st International Arab Conference on Information Technology (ACIT), pp. 1–5. IEEE (2020)
26. Pasqualino, G., Furnari, A., Signorello, G., Farinella, G.M.: An unsupervised domain adaptation scheme for single-stage artwork recognition in cultural sites. Image Vis. Comput. **107**, 104098 (2021). https://doi.org/10.1016/j.imavis.2021.104098
27. Putro, M.D., Nguyen, D.L., Priadana, A., Jo, K.H.: Fast person detector with efficient multi-level contextual block for supporting assistive robot. In: 2022 IEEE 5th International Conference on Industrial Cyber-Physical Systems (ICPS), pp. 1–6. IEEE (2022)
28. Redmon, J., Divvala, S., Girshick, R., Farhadi, A.: You only look once: unified, real-time object detection. In: 2016 IEEE Conference on Computer Vision and Pattern Recognition (CVPR), pp. 779–788. IEEE (2016)
29. Redmon, J., Farhadi, A.: YOLOv3: an incremental improvement. CoRR abs/1804.02767 (2018). arXiv:1804.02767
30. Ren, S., He, K., Girshick, R., Sun, J.: Faster R-CNN: towards real-time object detection with region proposal networks. IEEE Trans. Pattern Anal. Mach. Intell. **39**(6), 1137–1149 (2016)
31. Sambolek, S., Ivasic-Kos, M.: Automatic person detection in search and rescue operations using deep CNN detectors. IEEE Access **9**, 37905–37922 (2021)

32. Sandler, M., Howard, A.G., Zhu, M., Zhmoginov, A., Chen, L.: Inverted residuals and linear bottlenecks: mobile networks for classification, detection and segmentation. CoRR abs/1801.04381 (2018). arXiv:1801.04381

33. Sibanyoni, S.V., Ramotsoela, D.T., Silva, B.J., Hancke, G.P.: A 2-D acoustic source localization system for drones in search and rescue missions. IEEE Sens. J. 19(1), 332–341 (2018)

34. Sun, W., Dai, L., Zhang, X., Chang, P., He, X.: RSOD: real-time small object detection algorithm in UAV-based traffic monitoring. Appl. Intell. 52(8), 8448–8463 (2022). https://doi.org/10.1007/s10489-021-02893-3

35. Wang, C.Y., Liao, H.Y.M., Wu, Y.H., Chen, P.Y., Hsieh, J.W., Yeh, I.H.: CSPNet: a new backbone that can enhance learning capability of CNN. In: 2020 IEEE/CVF Conference on Computer Vision and Pattern Recognition Workshops (CVPRW), pp. 1571–1580. IEEE (2020)

36. Wang, C., Liao, H.M., Yeh, I., Wu, Y., Chen, P., Hsieh, J.: CSPNet: a new backbone that can enhance learning capability of CNN. CoRR abs/1911.11929 (2019). arXiv:1911.11929

37. Wang, R.J., Li, X., Ao, S., Ling, C.X.: Pelee: a real-time object detection system on mobile devices. CoRR abs/1804.06882 (2018). arXiv:1804.06882

38. Wang, X., Li, W., Guo, W., Cao, K.: SPB-YOLO: an efficient real-time detector for unmanned aerial vehicle images. In: 2021 International Conference on Artificial Intelligence in Information and Communication (ICAIIC), pp. 099–104. IEEE (2021)

39. Zhang, J., Wang, P., Zhao, Z., Su, F.: Pruned-YOLO: learning efficient object detector using model pruning. In: Farkaš, I., Masulli, P., Otte, S., Wermter, S. (eds.) ICANN 2021. LNCS, vol. 12894, pp. 34–45. Springer, Cham (2021). https://doi.org/10.1007/978-3-030-86380-7_4

40. Zhang, S., Wen, L., Bian, X., Lei, Z., Li, S.Z.: Single-shot refinement neural network for object detection. CoRR abs/1711.06897 (2017). arXiv:1711.06897

41. Zhu, P., et al.: Detection and tracking meet drones challenge. IEEE Trans. Pattern Anal. Mach. Intell. 44(11), 7380–7399 (2021)

Rough Target Region Extraction
with Background Learning

Ryo Nakamura[1]($\boxtimes$), Yoshiaki Ueda[2], Masaru Tanaka[3], and Jun Fujiki[1]

[1] Fukuoka University, 8-19-1 Nanakuma, Jonan-ku, Fukuoka 814-0180, Japan
sd210501@cis.fukuoka-u.ac.jp fujiki@fukuoka-u.ac.jp
[2] Ryukoku University, 1-5 Yokotani, Seta Oe-cho, Otsu, Shiga 520-2194, Japan
uedayos@rins.ryukoku.ac.jp
[3] Fukuoka, Japan

Abstract. Object localization is a fundamental and important task in computer vision, that is used as a pre-processing step for object detection and semantic segmentation. However, fully supervised object localization requires bounding boxes and pixel-level labels, and these annotations are expensive. For this reason, Weakly Supervised Object Localization (WSOL) with image-level (weak) supervision has been the focus of much research in recent years. However, WSOL requires a large dataset to detect the region of an object in images with high performance. When the large dataset is unavailable, it is difficult to localize the image with high performance. This paper proposes a method for extracting target regions using small amounts of target and background images with image-level labels. The proposed method enables the detection of object locations with high performance using relatively less training images by classifying multiple patches cut from the image. This object localization method differs from the typical WSOL method that takes a single image as input and detects the location of an object because it assumes a small patch of area as input. The label of the patch cropped from the image must be labeled with the ground truth. However, the proposed method uses labels attached to images because ground truth labeling is costly. Instead, in the proposed method, the network learns by learning many "background" labeled background patches, and learns to induce the network to classify the mislabeled background patches that resemble ground truth as background. We call this key idea Decision-Boundary Induction(DBI). Moreover, learning many background patches for such a DBI is what we call background learning. In our experiments, we verified that decision boundaries are induced, and accordingly, we could roughly extract the target region. Also, we showed that the Loc. Acc. is higher than that of WSOL.

Keywords: Weakly supervised object localization · Patch-based training · Background learning · Noisy label training

Prof. Masaru Tanaka deceased in June 2021.

© The Author(s), under exclusive license to Springer Nature Singapore Pte Ltd. 2023
I. Na and G. Irie (Eds.): IW-FCV 2023, CCIS 1857, pp. 26–42, 2023.
https://doi.org/10.1007/978-981-99-4914-4_3

1   Introduction

Object localization is a fundamental and important task in computer vision and is used as preprocessing for object detection [1–6], semantic segmentation [7–10], etc. For this, methods of deep learning, such as convolutional neural networks (CNN), are widely used. To achieve high accuracy, these need labeled training datasets, which include pixel-level labels and bounding boxes of target objects. When we carry out pixel-level labeling, it often becomes a burden compared to image-level labeling (i.e., labeling each image individually).

As a methodology to overcome such problems, Weakly Supervised Object Localization (WSOL) [11–18] has received recent attention from researchers in the field. This approach aims for high-accuracy object localization, requiring only training datasets consisting of image-level labels, and thus we can save time and human resources despite the high accuracy. Typically, WSOL estimates regions in the images, which are recognized to be important for the classification of images. The regions are then used in object localization. This procedure requires large datasets, which contribute significantly to the total cost due to their size. This implies that we have to label many images to use WSOL, which would also be a heavy task.

To overcome this challenge, we propose a novel method for identifying the location of the target object to be recognized (see Fig. 1). The method comprises two parts, which are explained below: The first part involves randomly cutting out small parts from images, each referred to as a 'atch,' and classifying them into two categories with attached labels: 'foreground' (target) and 'background.' More specifically, all patches from an image will be labeled as the common name of an object (e.g., 'cat,' 'dog,' 'horse,' 'owl,' and so on) if the object in the consideration is in the image, and they will be labeled as 'background' otherwise. An image showing a cat might contain a background area. It's important to note that all patches from the image are labeled as 'cat,' even if the patch does not contain any part of the cat. In such a case, the false labels of the patches will be called 'label noises.' On the other hand, all patches from an image showing no objects in consideration are assigned with 'background,' in coincidence with the true label. Therefore one can easily collect a large dataset consisting of truly-labeled patches, namely the ones with 'background' labels, since it is easy to prepare images showing no objects.

The second part involves a method we call 'background learning.' This method enables our model to discern which labels should be attached to new patches by training it with a large dataset of patches correctly labeled 'background' and a relatively smaller dataset containing label noises. We refer to the process of assigning new patches to either the true target or true background as 'object localization.' This process is facilitated by the network trained using our background learning method. It would be natural to design all patches with label noises, and the ones with background labels should be similar to each other. The true labels of such patches are both 'background.' The main ingredients in the dataset are cut out from background images, which is why we call the method 'background learning'.

All patches in the labeled training dataset for background learning are classified into three categories, as shown in Fig. 2:

28   R. Nakamura et al.

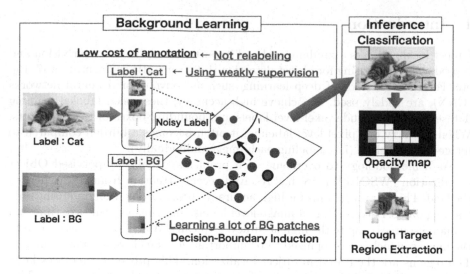

Fig. 1. Overview of proposal method: We consider the task of classifying randomly cropped multiple small patches from an image as whether they are in the target or background (BG). In order to classify patches with high accuracy, it is necessary to attach ground truth to the patches. However, in background learning, we do not provide the ground truth. Instead, the network induces the decision boundary to classify patches of label noise as background by learning many background patches cropped from the background image. Note that label noise is the background patch labeled with the target label. In inference, the background learning network roughly extracts the target region by outputting the backgroundness (sigmoid value) of patches in the target image as a sliding window formula.

- One category consists of patches showing (a part of) objects (thus, these are cut out from images showing objects).
- Another category is label-noises, which consist of patches cut out from images showing objects (and thus labeled as the target), but the patches themselves show no parts of the object.
- The last category consists of patches cut out from background images (images showing no objects), which are truly labeled as 'background.'

In this paper, each state of the classes is said to be positive (i.e., showing objects), false positive (i.e., showing no object but cut out from an image showing objects), and negative (i.e., cut out from a background image), respectively. With these terminologies, background learning is a method to determine whether the states of patches showing objects are positive or false positive. Equivalently, it is a method to detect false positives (or extract positives) among states of patches showing objects.

For our experiments, we prepared 240 images showing one of cats, dogs, horses, or owls and 240 background images. We trained networks by WSOL and our background learning separately. As a result, we showed that our background learning successfully extracted target regions (regions lying in positive patches).

For the object localization task, we showed that the performance of background learning is superior to WSOL in the sense of Localization Accuracy (Loc. Acc.).

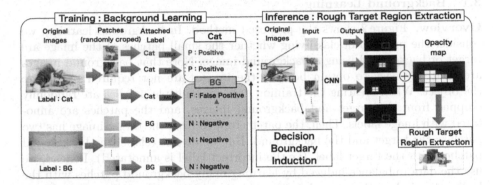

Fig. 2. Explanation of rough target area extraction with background learning. In background learning, a large amount of training data is prepared by randomly cropping multiple small-area patches from the image. Then, annotations to patches are not annotated with the correct labels, instead using image labels, which does not increase the annotation cost. In fully supervised learning, a patch of F is classified as a "cat," but learning a large number of patches of N that resemble F induces it to be classified as a "background (Decision-Boundary Induction). For rough target extraction, CNN with background training is used to output target patches using the sliding window method to generate a targetness map of the corresponding patch region.

2   Related Work

Weakly Supervised Object Localization(WSOL) aims to learn to localize the object using only image-level labels. A popular method for WSOL is Class Activation Map (CAM) [11], which generates localization maps by aggregating deep feature maps using fully connected layers by class. Hwang and Kim [19] simplify the network structure of CAM by removing the last unnecessary fully connected layer. CAM methods are simple and effective, but they can only classify the small classification region of the object. In order to improve the activation map of CAM, HaS [17] and CutMix [16] adopted the region dropout-based strategy from the input image so that the network focuses on the more related region of the object. ADL [12] focuses on the problem that learning while deleting classifiable regions with high performance requires high computational resources and eliminates feature maps corresponding to discriminable regions to localize objects with a lightweight model that is efficient and has low network parameters.

3 Rough Target Region Extraction with Background Learning

3.1 Background Learning

Overview. Figure 2 shows the proposed method. In background learning, we consider the problem of classifying whether the small patches of the image are target or background using a background image. Note that background images are relatively easy to obtain because the images are not required to include the object. When creating the training dataset, multiple patches are randomly cropped from the target and background images, and the patches are annotated with image labels. Then, the patch cropped from the target image has two patches: the target and the background. But we do not relabel the background patches with the target label. (i.e.the incorrect label is annotated). Instead, we use the data imbalance induced by learning many background patches with the F. We then induce the network to classify the mislabeled background patches as background (We call this induction DBI: Decision-Boundary Induction).

Define Target/Background. In this paper, "target" and "background" mean the target object to be extracted and the non-target object to be extracted. In a specific example, if the target is the cat, the cat's area in the image represents the target, and the other image areas represent the background. Therefore, if an image contains a cat and a dog, the cat area would be the target, while the other dog and background areas would be the background.

About the Type of Patches to be Cropped. The cropped patch from the image is a small area image of the target or background image. The size of the small area is an optional parameter. Also, the number of patches to be cropped is an optional parameter. We use image labels to label the patches. Therefore, cropped patches have three types of patterns, as shown in Fig. 2. The first is a positive (P) patch that includes the target region cropped from the target image. (P) patches are labeled with the target label. The second is a false positive (F) patch that does not include the target region cropped from the target image. (F) patches are labeled with the target label. Not labeling (F) patches with ground truth are to avoid labeling costs. The third is a negative (N) patch cropped from the background image. (F) patches are labeled with the background label.

Background Learning Purpose (Decision-Boundary Induction). The purpose of background learning is to induce the "background" classification result of the network when inputting the F patch. Therefore, we induce the classification of the network by training a large amount of N patch on it, causing bias in the learning. In fully supervised learning, the network learns that background F patches labeled as targets are to be classified as backgrounds based on their labels. However, to classify it as "background," we need to relabel F with a background label. But relabeling increases the annotation cost. Therefore we want to train the network to correctly classify P, F, and N patches into target and background patches without relabeling. In this paper, the problem of classifying such P, F, and N patches is called the PFN classification problem. Then, we use the imbalance of the number of training data, i.e., the property of [20] (Decision-Boundary Induction), which induces the class with the largest number of training data to be classified.

Training. For learning patches with label noise such as PFN, we use fully supervised learning, which is widely used in deep learning. In this learning, the error function is optimized to classify the patches so that they correctly answer the label of the image to be cropped, without relabeling. In the paper, binary cross-entropy is used for the error function and Stochastic Gradient Descent (SGD) for optimization.

Fig. 3. Sample image of the dataset used in the experiments.

3.2   Rough Target Region Extraction

The CNN with background training roughly calculates the target region by the following procedure. First, the target image is slided window by a specified step width (in this paper, 8 pixels in height and width), and the backgroundness of each patch is output. Next, for each pixel in the target image, add the final output c, which is the output of the sigmoid function. When this score is calculated for all pixels, the maximum value is M, and the minimum value is m. The "Targetness" is defined as follows for each pixel.

$$\text{Targetness} = \frac{c - m}{M - m} \in [0, 1] \tag{1}$$

In this paper, we consider the targetness to be the probability that each pixel is in the region to be classified. The target region can be visualized as an opacity map by using the targetness as the value of α channel, representing the opacity (see Fig. 2).

4   Experiments

4.1   Experimental Setting

Data Collection. In order to verify the effectiveness of decision-boundary induction, we prepare the dataset, which includes target (cat, dog, owl, horse) images with forest and playground background regions and background images with a different scene from the target backgrounds. Since there are no publicly available open datasets with such limited backgrounds, we collected 240 targets and 480 backgrounds (240 treated as background areas of targets and 240 treated as background images) from Fricker, manually generated masks of targets and background areas, and used the masks to composite them with targets and background images to construct a data set (see Fig. 3).

Table 1. Performance evaluation of rough target region extraction with background learning with Loc. Acc.: The result that performs well in comparing background patches is assumed to be bold.

Model	Target	BG: Forest		BG: Playground	
		TG:BG=1:1	TG:BG=1:2	TG:BG=1:1	TG:BG=1:2
VGG16	Cat	0.81	**0.98**	0.90	**0.91**
	Dog	0.61	**0.93**	**0.83**	0.79
	Owl	**0.85**	0.81	**0.76**	0.75
	Horse	**0.78**	0.53	**0.75**	0.55
	Avg.	0.76	**0.81**	**0.81**	0.75
ResNet50	Cat	0.88	**0.90**	0.88	**0.90**
	Dog	**0.96**	0.90	**0.86**	0.76
	Owl	**0.83**	0.76	**0.83**	0.80
	Horse	0.53	**0.81**	**0.78**	0.57
	Avg.	0.80	**0.84**	**0.84**	0.76

Create Train/Test Dataset. The training dataset is a two-category dataset of target and background images, each with 240 images (a total of 480 images). The test dataset uses target images from the training dataset and Ground truth masks labeled with targets at the pixel level to measure the performance of extracting target regions from the target images in the training dataset. This mask can compare target region extraction performance and extract patches related to PFN from the mask information. Note that the masks containing the target and background merge with the background and evaluate target area extraction performance, but not for training.

Experiment Details. We use the VGG16 [21] and ResNet50 [22] models in this experiment. We train the models with the binary cross-entropy loss for 150 epochs using SGD with a learning rate of 0.01. The mini-batch size is 64 for the WSOL methods and 512 for our method. The reason for this is to align the updates of the network parameters. HaS [17] and Cutmix [16] are localized with CAM [11]. In the proposed method, 8 patches are randomly cropped with size $48 \times 48 \times 3$ch from a single image ($256 \times 256 \times 3$ch).

Evaluation. In the evaluation of target area extraction, we evaluate the performance of target area extraction on trained data rather than on the performance of target area extraction on unlearned target images. The number of target images used is 240, the same as the number of training data. We use the localization accuracy metric (Loc. Acc.) to evaluate the roughness of the target region extraction. Loc. Acc. is a metric that calculates the proportion of images with an Intersection over Union (IoU) of 40% or higher. The threshold value of IoU when calculating Loc. Acc. is [0.05, 0.15, ... 0.95], and the best value is used as the experimental result.

4.2 Evaluation of the Effectiveness of Decision-Boundary Induction

We show through experiments that Decision-Boudary Induction can be used by adjusting the amount of background patches in the dataset, and that the use of DBI can lead to improved performance in target region extraction. For this experiment, we conducted the following on datasets with one and two times the ratio of background patches to target patches.

- Quantitative evaluation of the extraction performance of the target region by Loc. Acc.
- Qualitative evaluation visualizing relative frequencies of background-ness of patches of PFN.
- Qualitative evaluation to compare target area extraction results

Evaluation of Target Area Extraction Performance with Background Learning. Table 1 shows the results of Loc. Acc. for each condition when the background patches are trained with the ratio of background patches $1\times$ and $2\times$ compared to the target patches and the target regions are extracted. Cat results showed that the Loc. Acc. was higher in all cases when the background was learned $2\times$. Dog's results show that for VGG16, the Loc Acc is higher when the background is trained $2\times$ only when the background region is Forest, and $1\times$ is higher for all other cases. In the Owl results, the Loc. Acc. was higher when the background was trained 1× for VGG16, ResNet50, and the background was Forest and Playground. In the Horse results, the Loc. Acc. was higher when the background region was Forest, the Loc. Acc. was higher when the background region was Playground and the Loc. Acc. was higher when the background region was Playground. As shown above, it can be confirmed that adjusting the number of background patches according to the target and the model used contributes to the performance improvement of Loc. Acc.

We consider the bias of the background pattern of the image to be related to the reason that Forest and Playground did better with 2× background patches and 1× background patches, respectively. In the case of Forest, since F contains many similar patterns, such as diverse leaves and trees, it is necessary to learn many N to induce identification. On the other hand, Playground contains many instances of playground equipment, trees, sand, etc., and the patterns are distributed, so the discrimination induction works effectively with a relatively small number of N images.

Comparison by Backgroundness Relative Frequency Graph for Each Patch. Figure 4 is the result of visualizing the sigmoid (backgroundness) of P, F, and N patches as relative frequencies (see Fig. 4.) when background learning is performed using Forest as the background on ResNet50, which had high Loc. Acc. in Table 1. In this experiment, for patches, P is defined as if the target is included in 10% or more of the patches cropped from the target image, and F is defined as otherwise. The data for each PFN is 200, for a total of 600. We denote patches extracted from the image containing the region to be identified as X and patches extracted from the background image as Y to clarify the training data structure used for background training in the graph. The CNN trained with X and Y is denoted as Model(X,Y).

The Fig. 4 shows that the relative frequencies of F and N above 0.8 of the sigmoid are higher when the targets are Cat and Dog by learning the background patches twice. In Table 1, we can verify that Loc. Acc. is also high following the results. On the other hand, when the target is Owl, learning as 2x background patches did not increase the relative frequencies of backgroundness of F and N above 0.8. We consider that one of the reasons why the owl case has not worked is that the features of the forest and the Owl are similar. Owls are mimic animals as they hide and hunt in the forest. Therefore, as a result, we consider that learning to classify the P, F, and N patches became difficult, the learning was unstable, and thus the hypothetical results were not observed.

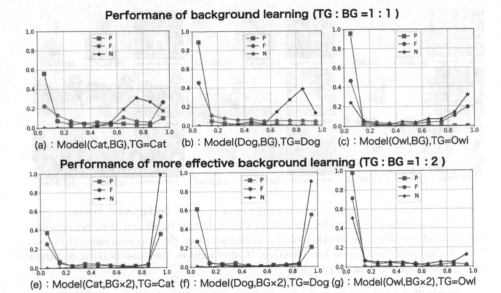

Fig. 4. Relative frequency graph of backgroundness of P, F, and N patches (This experiment uses ResNet50 and Forest background region). The horizontal axis represents the backgroundness (sigmoid value of the background class), and the vertical axis represents the relative frequency. We used forest for the background and ResNet50 for the network.

Comparison by Target Area Extraction Map. Figure 5 shows the target region extracted image using the trained network of (a)–(h) in Fig. 4. (a)–(d) are the target region extraction images when the number of target patches and background patches are the same. (e)–(h) are the target region extraction images when more background patches are trained. The Cat, Dog, and Horse results show that when the background is trained strongly, the regions are extracted to remove the background region. On the other hand, the Owl results show that when the background is learned too much, the target region is extracted in such a way that the backgroundness body region of the Owl is removed. The effectiveness of can also be verified through qualitative results on the amount of background patches (Fig. 4).

4.3 Comparison of Target Region Extraction Performance

We compare the proposed method with the WSOL method by Loc. Acc. to show that the proposed method can extract the target region with a smaller amount of images than the WSOL method (The results are shown in Table 2). Avg. in the table is the average of Loc. Acc. for the four targets (Cat, Dog, Owl, and Horse). For each model and target, the highest value of Loc. Acc. is indicated by bold and the second highest by underline.

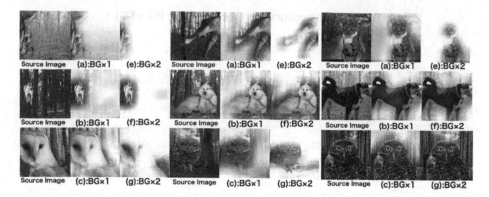

Fig. 5. The results of extracting the target region when background learning: (a)–(h) are the results of the model learned in Fig. 4. It can be shown that background learning induces the classification of the background in the target image. However, if the background learning is too effective, it also induces the classification of target regions that look like the background.

Table 2. Loc. Acc. comparison on a dataset where the background region.

Model	Method	Forest					Playground				
		Cat	Dog	Owl	Horse	Avg	Cat	Dog	Owl	Horse	Avg.
VGG16	CAM [11]	0.83	0.58	0.67	0.42	0.62	0.72	0.57	0.68	0.51	0.62
	ADL [12]	0.73	0.75	0.67	0.38	0.63	0.74	0.60	0.69	0.46	0.62
	HaS [17]	0.70	0.65	0.78	0.55	0.67	0.86	0.64	0.68	0.46	0.66
	Cutmix [16]	0.89	0.65	0.73	0.44	0.68	0.88	0.76	0.69	0.46	0.70
	Ours(BG×1)	0.81	0.61	**0.85**	**0.78**	0.76	0.90	**0.83**	**0.76**	**0.75**	**0.81**
	Ours(BG×2)	**0.98**	**0.93**	0.81	0.53	**0.81**	**0.91**	0.79	0.75	0.55	0.75
ResNet50	CAM [11]	0.66	0.66	0.75	0.44	0.63	0.85	0.72	0.74	0.50	0.70
	ADL [12]	0.85	0.73	0.71	0.55	0.71	0.89	0.81	0.78	0.62	0.78
	HaS [17]	0.70	0.59	0.68	0.52	0.62	0.72	0.66	0.69	0.54	0.65
	Cutmix [16]	0.70	0.50	0.66	0.47	0.58	0.86	0.66	0.74	0.53	0.70
	Ours(BG×1)	0.88	**0.96**	**0.83**	0.53	0.80	0.88	**0.86**	**0.83**	**0.78**	**0.84**
	Ours(BG×2)	**0.90**	0.90	0.76	**0.81**	**0.84**	0.90	0.76	0.80	0.57	0.76

In the results of Forest in Table 2, our method has the highest Loc. Acc. for all targets in VGG16 and ResNet50, where we adjusted the number of background patches and used DBI effectively. Avg. results show that our method occupies at least the top two positions. It is interesting to note that the results show a higher Avg. than WSOL, even though the parameters for the amount of background patch are roughly chosen.

The Playground results in Table 2 also show that when DBI is used effectively, our method has the highest Loc. Acc. for all targets in VGG16 and ResNet50. The difference from Forest results was that ResNet50 had the second-best per-

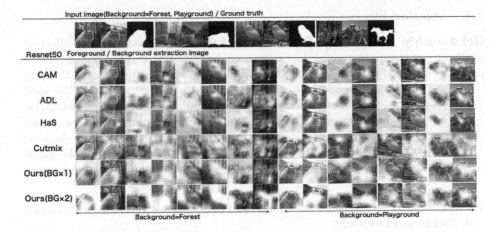

Fig. 6. Visualization results of target region extraction for existing WSOL methods and our method. We use ResNet50 for the network.

Table 3. The relationship between patch size and the performance of target area extraction with background learning. We study the relationship between the patch size {32, 48, 64, 96, 128}pixels.

Patch size	Forest				Playground			
	Cat		Dog		Cat		Dog	
	VGG16	ResNet50	VGG16	ResNet50	VGG16	ResNet50	VGG16	ResNet50
32	0.954	**0.979**	**0.914**	**0.902**	0.786	0.942	**0.967**	0.7
48	**0.958**	0.975	0.858	0.793	**0.962**	**0.979**	0.931	**0.943**
64	0.967	0.975	0.846	0.846	0.958	0.975	0.894	0.923
96	0.913	0.86	0.7	0.663	0.942	0.876	0.801	0.7
128	0.786	0.777	0.627	0.570	0.847	0.802	0.570	0.542

formance with ADL of Avg. The reason for this is the difference in the features of the background since there are more variations of objects, such as playground equipment, the ground, and trees, in the Playground than in the Forest. This can be considered to increase the learning of the target object.

Figure 6 shows the results of the visualization images where each target is extracted using WSOL and our method. The images extracted by CAM and ADL, among the conventional WSOL methods compared, tended to be extracted for frequently appearing parts, such as cat's whiskers, dog's face, owl's face, and horse's feet. Region dropout-based methods that mask part of the image, such as HaS and Cutmix, increased the target area to be extracted, but Cutmix also tends to extract more background areas as foreground, and HaS tended to extract some parts of the body as targets, but still tended to extract parts that appeared frequently.

4.4 Ablation Study

Relationship Study with Patch Size (Table 3). We studied the effect of patch size on the extraction of the target area. Specifically, we changed the size of patches extracted from images in {32, 64, 96, 128} and studied the relationship between Loc. Acc. We used VGG16 and ResNet50 as the networks. We used VGG16 and ResNet50 as the network and cat and dog as the target images. Then, we used the forest and playground as the background. The background patch is cropped twice as many times as the target patch to create the dataset. The results are shown in Table 3. The experimental results show that the patch sizes with the highest Loc. Acc. were 32 for the forest and 48 for the playground.

Table 4. Study of Background Patch Ratio and Performance of Target Area Extraction with Background Learning.

Patch size	Forest				Playground			
	Cat		Dog		Cat		Dog	
	VGG16	ResNet50	VGG16	ResNet50	VGG16	ResNet50	VGG16	ResNet50
BG×1.0	0.93	0.9	0.923	0.846	0.934	**0.979**	0.902	**0.947**
BG×2.0	0.95	0.954	0.914	0.902	**0.962**	**0.979**	0.931	0.943
BG×4.0	**0.983**	**0.975**	**0.971**	**0.951**	0.925	0.917	**0.939**	0.906

We consider the reason that the accuracy increases as the patch size decreases is because the proportion of patches that contain the target decreases. Background learning aims to DBI a background patch F with a target label by learning many N true background patches. Therefore, the smaller the F patches are, the more likely they produce DBI. Therefore, the smaller the patch size, the higher Loc. Acc. However, if the patch size is too small, DBI will also occur in the body of the target image, as shown by the owl in Fig. 5, so a moderately small patch is important for target area extraction.

Also, patch size differs depending on the background because of the background's complexity. The forest has a bias toward trees, leaves, and other patterns that appear in the background. Small patches will cause pattern bias in the clipped patches when there are many background patterns. Since it is difficult to perform DBI on a background with few patterns, we believe that increasing the size of the patch increases the number of patterns in the image and reduces pattern bias, which is effective in improving accuracy.

Study of Relationships with Background Patches Ratio (Table 4). We studied the relationship between the ratio of background patches to target patches and the performance of target region extraction. Changing the ratio of each patch is equivalent to adjusting the strength of the DBI effect. Specifically, we changed the proportion of background patches by {1.0, 2.0, 4.0} and studied the relationship between Loc. Acc. We used VGG16 and ResNet50 as the network and cat and dog as the target images are cat and dog. Then, we used the forest and playground as the background. The patch size is 32 × 32. The results are shown in Table 4. The results for forest show that increasing the ratio of background patches results in a better Loc. Acc. In the playground, no consistent trend was found comparing the models.

In the forest results, the DBI works correctly and improves accuracy. On the other hand, the playground results showed some variation depending on the model and target. We consider this because the patch size of 32 × 32 is relatively small, and the image does not contain a variety of background patterns. If there is a large piece of playground equipment in the background image, a large percentage of the image will contain the equipment if the patches are cut out randomly. If the patch size is large, a sandbox and playground equipment appear as patterns in the patch, which can be classified as background because it contains equipment frequently appearing as background. However, if the patch size is small, the number of patches containing only playground equipment patterns increases, making it difficult to distinguish other patterns from the background, in our opinion.

4.5 Limitation

Our proposed method can extract the target region with higher performance than the conventional method in a situation where only a small number of images are available, but it has some challenges.

First, it is not easy to classify the target body and background in the patch input. Figure 4 shows the relative frequency of the PFN backgroundness when the synthetic data is background trained. Comparing background learning and the effect of background learning enhancement, the backgroundness of most F improved, but the backgroundness of some P also increased. A possible reason for the increased backgroundness of P is that P has patches of the target body, which are not discernable from the background patches, so the DBI is also working on the patches of the body. This problem represents the limitation of learning only patches. To deal with this problem, it is necessary to incorporate a mechanism that can determine the target's body from the target's structural information based on the relationship of the positions of the cropped patches.

Second, there is a need to establish clear indicators for use in selecting background images for background studies. In the background learning, F and P classification results are decided by the background image prepared as the dataset. One approach to effectively DBI F is to use a large background image, but this approach is likely to cause an unbalance in the number of images in the target and background images, and thus DBI for P as well. Currently, we perform background learning by preparing random background images, but to perform DBI effectively, it is important to incorporate a mechanism to select an effective N for DBI. Due to the lack of a clear metric for background images, we consider it difficult to apply the method to large datasets with target images from diverse backgrounds in the current situation.

5 Conclusions

In this paper, we proposed the patch-based rough target region extraction method to extract target object regions with a relatively small number of images and a small annotation cost. The proposed method learns the network to robustly classify whether a small patch in the image is the target or background by using the method we call background learning. Also, the trained network is used to localize objects by determining whether the small areas of the image are targets or backgrounds. There are two important aspects to classifying target and background patches with fewer training images and less annotation cost. First, we do not use a single image to train the network but rather assume small patches randomly cropped from multiple images as input. This assumption is data efficient and enables the neural network to be trained by cropping many patches from several training images. Second, even if background images have noisy labels, background learning can improve classification robustness. Background learning is a method of classifying target and background patches by learning many background patches of ground truth cropped from background images, even when the labeling of patches cropped from the target image is done roughly. Using this learning, we provide a more robust classification of patches without using the cost of relabeling. For patch-based rough target area extraction, we calculate the backgroundness of the patch by inputting a small region of the image in a sliding window to the network. The result is calculated as the map of backgroundness, and the maps are merged by averaging the maps of backgroundness calculated for all regions. In our experiments, we verified that DBI works and improves the performance of target region extraction on an ideal dataset with similar background images and target object backgrounds. In addition, we verified that our method could extract target regions with higher Loc Acc than the existing WSOL method, although limited.

Acknowledgments. I am grateful to Associate Professor Takafumi Amaha of Fukuoka University for advice on writing the paper. I would like to take this opportunity to thank him.

References

1. Wang, C., Ren, W., Huang, K., Tan, T.: Weakly supervised object localization with latent category learning. In: Fleet, D., Pajdla, T., Schiele, B., Tuytelaars, T. (eds.) ECCV 2014. LNCS, vol. 8694, pp. 431–445. Springer, Cham (2014). https://doi.org/10.1007/978-3-319-10599-4_28
2. Song, H.O., Girshick, R., Jegelka, S., Mairal, J., Harchaoui, Z., Darrell, T.: On learning to localize objects with minimal supervision. In: Proceedings of the 31st International Conference on International Conference on Machine Learning, ICML 2014, vol. 32, pp. 1611–1619. JMLR.org (2014)
3. Cinbis, R., Verbeek, J., Schmid, C.: Multi-fold MIL Training for weakly supervised object localization (2014). https://doi.org/10.1109/CVPR.2014.309

4. Oquab, M., Bottou, L., Laptev, I., Sivic, J.: Is object localization for free? - weakly-supervised learning with convolutional neural networks (2015). https://doi.org/10.1109/CVPR.2015.7298668

5. Liang, X., Liu, S., Wei, Y., Liu, L., Lin, L., Yan, S.: Towards computational baby learning: a weakly-supervised approach for object detection (2015). https://doi.org/10.1109/ICCV.2015.120

6. Teh, E.W., Rochan, M., Wang, Y.: Attention networks for weakly supervised object localization. In: Wilson, R.C., Hancock, E.R., Smith, W.A.P. (eds.) Proceedings of the British Machine Vision Conference (BMVC), pp. 52–15211. BMVA Press (2016). https://doi.org/10.5244/C.30.52

7. Simonyan, K., Vedaldi, A., Zisserman, A.: Deep inside convolutional networks: Visualising image classification models and saliency maps. CoRR abs/1312.6034 (2013)

8. Pathak, D., Krahenbuhl, P., Darrell, T.: Constrained convolutional neural networks for weakly supervised segmentation. In: ICCV, pp. 1796–1804 (2015)

9. Kolesnikov, A., Lampert, C.H.: Seed, expand and constrain: three principles for weakly-supervised image segmentation. In: Leibe, B., Matas, J., Sebe, N., Welling, M. (eds.) ECCV 2016. LNCS, vol. 9908, pp. 695–711. Springer, Cham (2016). https://doi.org/10.1007/978-3-319-46493-0_42

10. Khoreva, A., Benenson, R., Omran, M., Hein, M., Schiele, B.: Weakly supervised object boundaries. In: CVPR, pp. 183–192 (2016)

11. Zhou, B., Khosla, A., Lapedriza, A., Oliva, A., Torralba, A.: Learning deep features for discriminative localization (2016). https://doi.org/10.1109/CVPR.2016.319

12. Choe, J., Lee, S., Shim, H.: Attention-based dropout layer for weakly supervised single object localization and semantic segmentation. IEEE Trans. Pattern Anal. Mach. Intell. **43**(12), 4256–4271 (2021). https://doi.org/10.1109/TPAMI.2020.2999099

13. Wei, Y., Feng, J., Liang, X., Cheng, M.-M., Zhao, Y., Yan, S.: Object region mining with adversarial erasing: a simple classification to semantic segmentation approach (2017). https://doi.org/10.1109/CVPR.2017.687

14. Bae, W., Noh, J., Kim, G.: Rethinking class activation mapping for weakly supervised object localization. In: Vedaldi, A., Bischof, H., Brox, T., Frahm, J.-M. (eds.) ECCV 2020. LNCS, vol. 12360, pp. 618–634. Springer, Cham (2020). https://doi.org/10.1007/978-3-030-58555-6_37

15. Zhang, C.-L., Cao, Y.-H., Wu, J.: Rethinking the route towards weakly supervised object localization (2020). https://doi.org/10.1109/CVPR42600.2020.01347

16. Yun, S., Han, D., Chun, S., Oh, S.J., Yoo, Y., Choe, J.: CutMix: regularization strategy to train strong classifiers with localizable features (2019). https://doi.org/10.1109/ICCV.2019.00612

17. Singh, K.K., Lee, Y.J.: Hide-and-seek: forcing a network to be meticulous for weakly-supervised object and action localization (2017). https://doi.org/10.1109/ICCV.2017.381

18. Rahimi, A., Shaban, A., Ajanthan, T., Hartley, R., Boots, B.: Pairwise similarity knowledge transfer for weakly supervised object localization. In: Vedaldi, A., Bischof, H., Brox, T., Frahm, J.-M. (eds.) ECCV 2020. LNCS, vol. 12369, pp. 395–412. Springer, Cham (2020). https://doi.org/10.1007/978-3-030-58586-0_24

19. Hwang, S., Kim, H.-E.: Self-transfer learning for weakly supervised lesion localization. In: Ourselin, S., Joskowicz, L., Sabuncu, M.R., Unal, G., Wells, W. (eds.) MICCAI 2016. LNCS, vol. 9901, pp. 239–246. Springer, Cham (2016). https://doi.org/10.1007/978-3-319-46723-8_28

20. Chawla, N., Japkowicz, N., Kołcz, A.: Editorial: special issue on learning from imbalanced data sets. SIGKDD Explor. **6**, 1–6 (2004). https://doi.org/10.1145/1007730.1007733
21. Simonyan, K., Zisserman, A.: Very deep convolutional networks for large-scale image recognition. In: ICLR (2015)
22. He, K., Zhang, X., Ren, S., Sun, J.: Deep residual learning for image recognition. In: CVPR (2016)

Dynamic Circular Convolution for Image Classification

Xuan-Thuy Vo, Duy-Linh Nguyen, Adri Priadana, and Kang-Hyun Jo[✉]

Department of Electrical, Electronic and Computer Engineering, University of Ulsan,
Ulsan 44610, South Korea
xthuy@islab.ulsan.ac.kr, {ndlinh301,priadana3202}@mail.ulsan.ac.kr,
acejo@ulsan.ac.kr

Abstract. In recent years, Vision Transformer (ViT) has achieved an outstanding landmark in disentangling diverse information of visual inputs, superseding traditional Convolutional Neural Networks (CNNs). Although CNNs have strong inductive biases such as translation equivariance and relative positions, they require deep layers to model long-range dependencies in input data. This strategy results in high model complexity. Compared to CNNs, ViT can extract global features even in earlier layers through token-to-token interactions without considering geometric location of pixels. Therefore, ViT models are data-efficient and data-hungry, in another work, learning data-dependent and producing high performances on large-scale datasets. Nonetheless, ViT has quadratic complexity with the length of the input token because of the natural dot product between query and key matrices. Different from ViTs-and-CNNs-based models, this paper proposes a Dynamic Circular Convolution Network (DCCNet) that learns token-to-token interactions in Fourier domain, relaxing model complexity to $O(Nlog(N))$ instead of $O(N^2)$ in ViTs, and global Fourier filters are treated dependently and dynamically rather than independent and static weights in conventional operators. The token features, dynamic filters in spatial domain are transformed to frequency domain via Fast Fourier Transform (FFT). Dynamic circular convolution, in lieu of matrix multiplication in Fourier domain, between Fourier features and transformed filters are performed in a separable way along channel dimension. The output of circular convolution is revered back to spatial domain by Inverse Fast Fourier Transform (IFFT). Extensive experiments are conducted and evalued on large-scaled dataset ImageNet1k and small dataset CIFAR100. On ImageNet1k, the proposed model achieves 75.4% top-1 accuracy and 92.6% top-5 accuracy with the budget 7.5M paramaters under similar setting with ViT-based models, surpassing ViT and its variants. When fine-tuning the model on smaller dataset, DCCNet still works well and gets the state-of-the-art performances. Both evaluating the model on large and small datasets verifies the effectiveness and generalization capabilities of the proposed method.

Keywords: Vision Transformer · Dynamic Global Weights · Fourier Transform · Image Classification

© The Author(s), under exclusive license to Springer Nature Singapore Pte Ltd. 2023
I. Na and G. Irie (Eds.): IW-FCV 2023, CCIS 1857, pp. 43–55, 2023.
https://doi.org/10.1007/978-981-99-4914-4_4

1 Introduction

In the view of understanding involved visual data, the model compresses high dimension of image data to lower spaces and keeps informative features through processing layer-by-layer of the model. The way the model compresses and extracts the features relies on what the image encompasses. As we interpret datas, one point in the image contains two components: content (intensity values) $c \in \mathbb{R}^3$ and geometric information $w \in \mathbb{R}^2$. The image is interpreted as $I \in \mathbb{R}^{5 \times N}$, where $N = H \times W$ is number of pixels in the image. With the formulation of convolution, CNNs aggregate information of local windows to the center of the local windows in the sliding manner and also capture the relative position w_{i-j} inside local window. General speaking, CNN models [8,13,20] can extract helpful features that the image contains and result in translation equivariance and locality. Otherwise, Transformer invented by [32] views a sentence as a sequence of words (tokens) and compute word-to-word relationship and dynamically aggregate these features by global multi-head self-attention blocks for machine translation. With the success of Transformer in both general modeling capabilities and scalable models, ViT [5] tries to adapt self-attention operation in computer vision. Each image is separated into a sequence of patches (tokens), and the model learns an affinity matrix of token-to-token similarity. The ViT only considers content-to-content relationships from the input images or input features and can fail to capture positional information. The lack of geometric w_{i-j} results in weak inductive biases. The model needs a lot of data to compensate for the absence of w_{i-j}.

In terms of model complexity, the convolution operation is more efficient than the self-attention block. To extract global features, CNN-based models stack a series of convolution layers with residual connections that create a large computational cost. At the heart of Transformer, self-attention operation requires quadratic complexity with the lengths of input tokens and the model is not acceptable to adapt self-attention operation at earlier layers. Especially for downstream tasks, these networks perform predictions on the input features with high resolution. With the bottleneck computation of ViT, many methods try to reduce the cost $O(N^2)$ to $O(N)$ [22], sub-sample the query, key, and value matrices [33,34], and compute attention in local windows mimicking convolution [18,19]. Another line of research is to enhance the weak inductive biases of the transformer. The affinity matrix is supplemented with positional information such as absolute positional embedding [32], relative positional embedding [2,4,19,23]. Other works [14,15,21,22] attempt to combine the strengths of convolution and self-attention operations to build hybrid networks. They inherit the strong inductive biases of CNNs and the strong modeling of ViTs, and deliver better performance than pure CNNs and ViTs.

On the research trend of Transformer, this paper develops a new operator, dubbed Dynamic Circular Convolution (DCC), which can extract and aggregate global features by performing the circular convolution between reweighted global Fourier kernels and Fourier transformed features. The reweighting coefficients are generated conditioned on the input features and are dynamically adopted according to the content of the input. The DCC layers are used to replace self-attention blocks in ViT, called DCCNet. Our proposed DCCNet brings four benefits: (1) Global features are extracted in one layer; (2) the content and geometric information of the input image are utilized when computing circular convolution; (3) the generated weights are input-dependent instead of input-independent in conventional convolution; and (4) the complexity is $O(N(logN))$ rather than $O(N^2)$ in Transformer.

To verify the effectiveness of the proposed method, we conduct the experiments on the large dataset Imagenet1k, and small dataset CIFAR100. As a result, the DCCNet surpasses the baseline ViT and its variant by a clear margin under the same setting and budget (7.5M parameters and 1.2 GFLOPs).

2   Related Works

In this section, we briefly review some related works about Convolutional Neural Networks, Vision Transformer and its variant, and Fourier transform in computer vision.

CNNs: In 2012, with the development of parallel hardware computation, AlexNet [13] successfully train the convolution networks on large datasets and open new directions in Computer Vision. VGG [28] enlarge the network depth by stacking a sequence of plain 3×3 convolutions. Even though VGGNet achieves the large improvement on large-scale ImageNet dataset, the model causes vanishing gradient problem when the depth beyond 19 layers. ResNet [8] proposes residual blocks that can eliminate vanishing gradient and number of layers are stacked up to 1000 layers. From that event, many works are introduced to improve the baseline ResNet such as dense connection [11], deformable convolution [3], depthwise seperable convolution [10,27], and multiple branches [30].

ViT: Recently, ViT [5] integrated the original Transformer [32] developed for natural language processing and established new state-of-the-art performances on image classification and downstream tasks. Because ViT has a simple structure and uniform representation, there are a lot of works that improve ViT model in both learning and cost. PVT [33] builds a multi-scale vision transformer network that gradually decreases spatial dimensions across stages. On each stage of PVT, key and value matrices are down-sampled to smaller token sizes. Instead of computing attention from all tokens, Swin [19] models local attention in predefined windows and also constructs hierarchical networks inspired by CNNs-based models. With these insightful properties, Swin outperforms the strong baseline ResNet [8] and sets new records in detection, segmentation and tracking performance. MobileViTv2 [22] proposes a separable self-attention operation that reduces the cost of original self-attention from $O(N)^2$ to $O(N)$.

Compensation for weak inductive biases of self-attention operation, methods [4,18,19,23] integrates relative positional information to attention maps. CPE [2] introduces a conditional positional encoding based on local relative neighborhood of 3×3 depthwise convolution. Rather than marrying convolution operations to Transformer models, MobileViT [21] embeds Transformer blocks to stage 3, 4, 5 of MobileNetv2 [27]. Similar paradigm, NextViT [14] designs a hybrid network for embedded devices based on integration of the group convolution blocks in earlier stages and original self-attention blocks in later stages. EfficientFormer [15] adapt the idea of PoolFormer [38] and MetaFormer [39] and neural architecture search for constrained devices.

Based on the intuitive designs of Transformer and its variants, HorNet [24] extends matrix multiplication of self-attention operation to high-order interactions based on depth-wise separable convolution and recursive gates. Focal-Net [37] uses multi-scale depth-wise separable convolutions and gated aggregation at each convolution to output multiple modulations.

Fourier Transform: FFC [1] proposes fast Fourier convolution and independently applies convolution and ReLU activation functions on the real and imaginary input features. Lama [29] adapt FFC operation to image inpainting. GFNet [25] learns global features in Fourier domain based on circular convolution and ViT models. AFNO [6] separates complex tensors into real and imaginary parts and utilizes the MLP module to mix these two parts. In this paper, we extend the circular convolution in GFNet to be dynamic and efficient. In GFNet, complex features and global filters are multiplied independently on each channel. Therefore, there is a way the model can efficiently learn the feature on both the spatial and channel axes. Moreover, in our core operator, both real and imaginary parts of the complex tensors are learned together instead of separation in the AFNO network.

3   Methodology

In this section, we leverage the overall network of the ViT [5] into our DCCNet in Subsect. 3.1 and analysis the proposed dynamic circular convolution block in Subsect. 3.2.

3.1   Overall Architecture

The DCCNet follows the single-scale architecture of the original ViT [5], shown in Fig. 1. Given input image with dimension $I \in \mathbb{R}^{3 \times H \times W}$, Patch Embedding splits and flattens the image I into a sequence of tokens with size $d_P \times N$, where N is the number of the tokens[1], H and W are height and width of image. Specifically, we use patch sizes of $P \times P$ and strides with patch window value over the image to produce the total tokens $N = \frac{H*W}{P^2}$ and $d_N = 3*P^2$. Followed by non-overlap processing of the ViT implementation, 16×16 convolution with stride 16 is used in Patch Embedding as patch generation, corresponding to each token with size 16×16.

---

[1] Consistent term with original Transformer [32], also called number of patches.

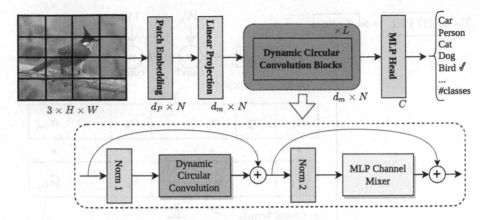

Fig. 1. The overall architecture of the DCCNet. N indicates the number of tokens with channel dimension d_m and L is the number of stacked DCC blocks. d_P, d_m are channel dimension after patch embedding, and channel dimension of the model. C is the number of predefined classes.

Linear Projection module projects a sequence of tokens with channel dimension d_P to a sequence of tokens with d_m. We use Linear layer to perform this process. The Dynamic Circular Convolution (DCC) block learns the token-token interaction that results in long-range dependencies between tokens. The DCC block includes two processes: (1) spatial mixings are performed by Dynamic Circular Convolution, and (2) MLP Channel Mixer mix token information along channel dimension. Between two processes, residual connections are used according to [38,39] and each token is normalized by Layer Normalization before forwarding to each module. The detailed analysis of the DCC block is described in Subsect. 3.2. MLP Mixer contains two linear layers with expansion rate r. During training, based on [5,25], we set $r = 4$ for all blocks.

Finally, Global Average Pooling (GAP) in MLP Head flattens a set of tokens to 1D dimension d_m and one linear layer projects flatten token d_m to number of classes C.

3.2   Dynamic Circular Convolution

The pipeline of the DCC operation is described in Fig. 2. Given the input feature $X \in \mathbb{R}^{d_m \times N}$, we reshape and permute the input X to 2D dimension $d_m \times H_P \times W_P$. Hence, the order of pixels in the input feature is still preserved. The permuted input features are processed in three steps: (1) 2D FFT (Fast Fourier Transform)transforms X in spatial domain to frequency domain by Fast Fourier Transform [1]; circular convolution is performed between transformed tensor and dynamic kernels to model global features; and 2D IFFT (Inverse Fast Fourier Transform) reserves dynamic and global tensor back to spatial domain.

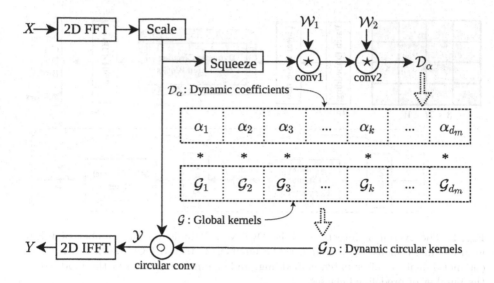

Fig. 2. The detailed architecture of the Dynamic Circular Convolution (DCC). 2D FFT and 2D IFFT denote Fast Fourier Transform and Inverse Fast Fourier Transform. $\mathcal{W}_1$, $\mathcal{W}_2$ are learnable parameters in frequency domain. Squeeze denotes mean computation along spatial dimension.

Given the permuted input with dimension $d_m \times H_P \times W_P$, complex tensor is generated by 2D FFT as follows,

$$\mathcal{X}[:, u, v] = \mathcal{F}(X) = \sum_{m}^{H_P-1} \sum_{n}^{W_P-1} X[:, m, n] e^{-j2\pi(\frac{um}{H_P} + \frac{vn}{W_P})}, \qquad (1)$$

where $\mathcal{X}[:]$ is used to get the index of the channel. u, v are the coordinate of each output complex values $\mathcal{X} \in \mathbb{C}^{d_m \times H_P \times W_P}$ and m, n are the coordinate of each input real values $X \in \mathbb{R}^{d_m \times H_P \times W_P}$. $H_P = \frac{H}{P}, W_P = \frac{W}{P}$ are the height and width of the permuted sequence of tokens. Conventionally, angular frequencies along height and width dimensions are computed as:

$$\omega_h = 2\pi f_h = 2\pi \frac{u}{H_P}, \qquad (2)$$

$$\omega_w = 2\pi f_w = 2\pi \frac{v}{W_P}. \qquad (3)$$

In Eq. 1, there is a one-to-one mapping from the real domain to the frequency domain. It means that we convert the non-periodic signal to a periodic signal based on the theorem of the Fourier transform and fully preserve all the information of the input. The image can be decomposed into a function of *sine* waves. One of the insightful property of Fourier transform is that there has a conjugate symmetry of the complex tensor $\mathcal{X}$ and leveraging such property can reduce the model complexity without losing information [1]. This view can be represented as:

$$\mathcal{X}[:,u,v] = \mathcal{X}^*[:,H_P - u, W_P - v]. \tag{4}$$

Therefore, the model complexity is $O(H_P W_P log(H_P W_P))$ with respect to the length of the input tokens. While ViT-based models have quadratic complexity with the length of the input tokens, we enjoy much lower computational costs. A half of complex tensor $\mathcal{X}_s = \mathcal{X}[:,:,0:W_P/2+1]$ need to be computed and restored. It can relax memory intensive and still extract global features. Inside the Eq. 1, since the *sum* operation is used, the *scale* step is proposed to normalize all the accumulated values. During implementation, *scale* is conducted by average operation.

The model learns global features through self-attention operations or large kernel sizes. In this paper, we employ matrix multiplication between complex tensors $\mathcal{X}$ and global kernels. These global kernels are the same size as the scaled input $\mathcal{X}_s \in \mathbb{C}^{d_m \times H_P \times W_P/2+1}$. Hence, matrix multiplication between them in the spatial domain is called circular convolution in the frequency domain. In GFNet [25], they treat global kernels independently and statically because circular convolution is separable. It leads to a way that can mix the information of the input tensor along the channel dimension. Inspired by weight generation of self-attention operation [32], we define dynamic coefficients $\mathcal{D}_\alpha \in \mathbb{C}^{d_m \times 1 \times 1}$ as follows:

$$\mathcal{D}_\alpha = \{\alpha_1, ..., \alpha_{d_m}\} = \mathcal{W}_2 \star (\mathcal{W}_1 \star f(\mathcal{X}_s)), \tag{5}$$

where $\star$ is convolution operation. $f(.)$ indicates squeeze function that converts 2D input $\mathcal{X}_s$ to 1D vector. $\mathcal{W}_1 \in \mathbb{C}^{d_m \times \frac{d_m}{r}}$ and $\mathcal{W}_2 \in \mathbb{C}^{\frac{d_m}{r} \times d_m}$ are linear transformations in the frequency domain, mixing information of the squeezed complex tensor. Then, the dynamic coefficients $\mathcal{D}_\alpha$ is used to redistribute the static global kernel $\mathcal{G} \in \mathbb{C}^{d_m \times H \times (W/2+1)}$ via element-wise matrix multiplication,

$$\mathcal{G}_D = \{\alpha_i * \mathcal{G}_i | \alpha_i \in \mathbb{C}; \mathcal{G}_i \in \mathbb{C}^{H \times (W/2+1)}\} \in \mathbb{C}^{d_m \times H \times (W/2+1)}, \tag{6}$$

The dynamic circular kernel $\mathcal{G}_D$ is convoluted with the scaled input $\mathcal{X}_s$ to output global receptive field,

$$\mathcal{Y} = \mathcal{X}_s \circ \mathcal{G}_D, \tag{7}$$

where $\mathcal{Y} \in \mathbb{C}^{d_m \times H \times (W/2+1)}$ is the output of the circular convolution and $\circ$ denotes circular convolution.

Finally, we reserve the Fourier feature back to the spatial domain using the 2D Inverse Fast Fourier Transform (IFFT) and this operation is addressed as follows:

$$Y[:,m,n] = \mathcal{F}^{-1}(\mathcal{Y}) = \frac{1}{N} \sum_u^{H-1} \sum_v^{W-1} \mathcal{Y}[:,u,v] e^{j2\pi(\frac{um}{H} + \frac{vn}{W})}, \tag{8}$$

where N is the number of tokens used for normalization.

Table 1. Comparison with state-of-the-art models on ImageNet validation set.

Method	Top-1 Acc (%)	Top-5 Acc (%)	#params	GFLOPs
T2T-ViT-7 [40]	71.7	-	4.3M	1.2
DeiT-Ti [31]	72.2	91.1	5.7M	1.3
gMLP-Ti [17]	72.3	-	7.0M	1.3
PiT-Ti [9]	73.0	-	4.9M	0.71
TNT-Ti [7]	73.9	91.9	6.1M	1.4
GFNet-Ti [25]	74.6	92.2	7.5M	1.3
LocalViT-T [16]	74.8	92.6	5.9M	1.3
ViTAE [36]	75.3	92.7	4.8M	1.5
DCCNet (our)	**75.5**	**92.7**	7.7M	1.2

4   Experiments and Results

4.1   Experiments

Datasets: The proposed DCCNet is trained and evaluated on the large-scale dataset ImageNet1k [26], and the small dataset CIFAR100 [12]. For ImageNet1k, this dataset includes 1.2M training images and 50k validation images with 1000 categories. CIFA10 contains 50k training and 10k testing images from 10 classes. Like CIFAR10, CIFAR100 contains 50k training and 10k testing images with 100 classes.

Experimental Setup: All implementations are conducted using the Pytorch framework, and the codebase is *Timm* [35] for fair comparisons with other methods. We follow the setting of methods [5, 25]. The model is trained for 300 epochs on two Tesla V100 GPUs. The batch size is 512 images per GPU, and the input images are resized to 224×224. The basic learning rate is $5 \times e^{-4}$ and learning schedule is cosine with warmup epochs of 5. The optimizer is AdamW with momentum 0.9 and weight decay 0.05. The DCCNet does not use EMA model and strong data augmentation like [19, 20].

4.2   Results

ImageNet Dataset: Table 1 shows the main results evaluated on ImageNet validation set between DCCNet and other methods. As a result, DCCNet achieves 75.5% Top-1 accuracy and 92.2% Top-5 accuracy, which surpasses state-of-the-art ViT-based models around 7M parameters and 1.2 GFLOPs, such as 71.7%

Top-1 in T2T [40], 72.2% in DeiT [31], 72.3% Top-1 in gMLP [17], 73.0% Top-1 in PiT [9], 73.9% Top-1 in TNT [7], 74.6% Top-1 in GFNet, 74.8% Top-1 in LocalViT [16], and 75.3% Top-1 in ViTAE [36]. This comparison verifies the effectiveness of the proposed DCCNet.

CIFAR 100: Table 2 describes the comparison between the DCCNet and other methods on the small dataset CIFAR100. With largely smaller parameters and GFLOPs than other methods, the DCCNet gets 84.1% Top-1 accuracy under budget 7.5M paramters and 1.2 GFLOPs.

Table 2. Results on small dataset CIFAR 100.

Method	Top-1 Acc	#params	#GFLOPs
DeiT-T [31]	67.59	5.3M	0.4
PVT-T [33]	69.62	15.8	0.6
Swin-T [19]	78.07	27.5M	1.4
DCCNet (ours)	**84.10**	**7.5**	**1.2**

Ablation Study: We investigate the effect of reduction ratio $r \in \{8, 16, 32\}$ in linear matrices of the DCC block on the model performance and cost illustrated in Table 3. When changing the reduction r, the Top-1 performances are similar. For a trade-off between accuracy and cost, we select $r = 16$ for all experiments.

Table 3. Ablation study on the reduction ratio r.

Reduction r	Top-1 Acc (%)	Top-5 (Acc%)	#params	GFLOPs
8	75.4	92.7	7.9	1.3
16	**75.5**	**92.7**	7.7	1.2
32	75.2	92.4	7.6	1.2

Amplitude and Phase Spectrum: We visualize the amplitude and phase spectrum on Fig. 3. As we can see, the detailed patterns in the amplitude spectrum are clear, and its spectrum has the symmetric property demonstrated in [1].

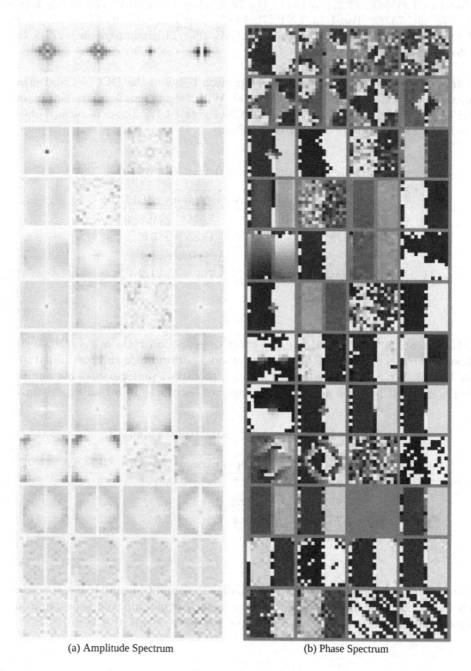

(a) Amplitude Spectrum   (b) Phase Spectrum

Fig. 3. The amplitude spectrum (a) and phase spectrum (b) of the dynamic circular convolution.

5   Conclusion

This paper presents a feature extractor based on Fast Fourier Transform and dynamic weight generations, called DCCNet. All spatial operations, especially for circular convolution, are performed in the frequency domain through the FFT. Leveraging the conjugate symmetry of FFT can result in better performance and efficient model complexity. Instead of static weight in conventional circular convolution, this work dynamically produces complex weight matrices of circular convolution conditioned on the input features. And this operator also mixes the information of a complex weight tensor along the channel dimension. This channel mixing can complement circular convolution that is separable and input-independent. Experiments are conducted on both large and small datasets, and the DCCNet achieves better performance than other methods. It verifies the effectiveness of the proposed methods and its generalization capability.

Acknowledgement. This result was supported by "Region Innovation Strategy (RIS)" through the National Research Foundation of Korea (NRF) funded by the Ministry of Education (MOE)(2021RIS-003).

References

1. Chi, L., Jiang, B., Mu, Y.: Fast Fourier convolution. In: Advances in Neural Information Processing Systems, vol. 33, pp. 4479–4488 (2020)
2. Chu, X., et al.: Conditional positional encodings for vision transformers. arXiv preprint arXiv:2102.10882 (2021)
3. Dai, J., et al.: Deformable convolutional networks. In: Proceedings of the IEEE International Conference on Computer Vision, pp. 764–773 (2017)
4. Dai, Z., Liu, H., Le, Q.V., Tan, M.: CoAtNet:: marrying convolution and attention for all data sizes. In: Advances in Neural Information Processing Systems, vol. 34, pp. 3965–3977 (2021)
5. Dosovitskiy, A., et al.: An image is worth 16 × 16 words: transformers for image recognition at scale. In: International Conference on Learning Representations (2021). https://openreview.net/forum?id=YicbFdNTTy
6. Guibas, J., Mardani, M., Li, Z., Tao, A., Anandkumar, A., Catanzaro, B.: Efficient token mixing for transformers via adaptive Fourier neural operators. In: International Conference on Learning Representations (2021)
7. Han, K., Xiao, A., Wu, E., Guo, J., Xu, C., Wang, Y.: Transformer in transformer. In: Advances in Neural Information Processing Systems, vol. 34, pp. 15908–15919 (2021)
8. He, K., Zhang, X., Ren, S., Sun, J.: Deep residual learning for image recognition. In: Proceedings of the IEEE Conference on Computer Vision and Pattern Recognition, pp. 770–778 (2016)
9. Heo, B., Yun, S., Han, D., Chun, S., Choe, J., Oh, S.J.: Rethinking spatial dimensions of vision transformers. In: Proceedings of the IEEE/CVF International Conference on Computer Vision, pp. 11936–11945 (2021)
10. Howard, A.G., et al.: MobileNets: efficient convolutional neural networks for mobile vision applications. arXiv preprint arXiv:1704.04861 (2017)

11. Huang, G., Liu, Z., Van Der Maaten, L., Weinberger, K.Q.: Densely connected convolutional networks. In: Proceedings of the IEEE Conference on Computer Vision and Pattern Recognition, pp. 4700–4708 (2017)
12. Krizhevsky, A., Hinton, G., et al.: Learning multiple layers of features from tiny images (2009)
13. Krizhevsky, A., Sutskever, I., Hinton, G.E.: ImageNet classification with deep convolutional neural networks. Commun. ACM **60**(6), 84–90 (2017)
14. Li, J., et al.: Next-ViT: next generation vision transformer for efficient deployment in realistic industrial scenarios. arXiv preprint arXiv:2207.05501 (2022)
15. Li, Y., et al.: EfficientFormer: Vision transformers at MobileNet speed. In: Oh, A.H., Agarwal, A., Belgrave, D., Cho, K. (eds.) Advances in Neural Information Processing Systems (2022). https://openreview.net/forum?id=NXHXoYMLIG
16. Li, Y., Zhang, K., Cao, J., Timofte, R., Van Gool, L.: LocalViT: bringing locality to vision transformers. arXiv preprint arXiv:2104.05707 (2021)
17. Liu, H., Dai, Z., So, D., Le, Q.V.: Pay attention to MLPs. In: Advances in Neural Information Processing Systems, vol. 34, pp. 9204–9215 (2021)
18. Liu, Z., et al.: Swin transformer V2: scaling up capacity and resolution. In: Proceedings of the IEEE/CVF Conference on Computer Vision and Pattern Recognition, pp. 12009–12019 (2022)
19. Liu, Z., et al.: Swin transformer: hierarchical vision transformer using shifted windows. In: Proceedings of the IEEE/CVF International Conference on Computer Vision, pp. 10012–10022 (2021)
20. Liu, Z., Mao, H., Wu, C.Y., Feichtenhofer, C., Darrell, T., Xie, S.: A ConvNet for the 2020s. In: Proceedings of the IEEE/CVF Conference on Computer Vision and Pattern Recognition, pp. 11976–11986 (2022)
21. Mehta, S., Rastegari, M.: MobileViT: light-weight, general-purpose, and mobile-friendly vision transformer. In: International Conference on Learning Representations (2022). https://openreview.net/forum?id=vh-0sUt8HlG
22. Mehta, S., Rastegari, M.: Separable self-attention for mobile vision transformers. arXiv preprint arXiv:2206.02680 (2022)
23. Min, J., Zhao, Y., Luo, C., Cho, M.: Peripheral vision transformer. In: Oh, A.H., Agarwal, A., Belgrave, D., Cho, K. (eds.) Advances in Neural Information Processing Systems (2022). https://openreview.net/forum?id=nE8IJLT7nW-
24. Rao, Y., et al.: HorNet: efficient high-order spatial interactions with recursive gated convolutions. In: Advances in Neural Information Processing Systems (NeurIPS) (2022)
25. Rao, Y., Zhao, W., Zhu, Z., Lu, J., Zhou, J.: Global filter networks for image classification. In: Advances in Neural Information Processing Systems, vol. 34, pp. 980–993 (2021)
26. Russakovsky, O., et al.: ImageNet large scale visual recognition challenge. Int. J. Comput. Vis. **115**(3), 211–252 (2015)
27. Sandler, M., Howard, A., Zhu, M., Zhmoginov, A., Chen, L.C.: MobileNetV2: inverted residuals and linear bottlenecks. In: Proceedings of the IEEE Conference on Computer Vision and Pattern Recognition, pp. 4510–4520 (2018)
28. Simonyan, K., Zisserman, A.: Very deep convolutional networks for large-scale image recognition. arXiv preprint arXiv:1409.1556 (2014)
29. Suvorov, R., et al.: Resolution-robust large mask inpainting with Fourier convolutions. In: Proceedings of the IEEE/CVF Winter Conference on Applications of Computer Vision, pp. 2149–2159 (2022)

30. Szegedy, C., Vanhoucke, V., Ioffe, S., Shlens, J., Wojna, Z.: Rethinking the inception architecture for computer vision. In: Proceedings of the IEEE Conference on Computer Vision and Pattern Recognition, pp. 2818–2826 (2016)
31. Touvron, H., Cord, M., Douze, M., Massa, F., Sablayrolles, A., Jégou, H.: Training data-efficient image transformers & distillation through attention. In: International Conference on Machine Learning, pp. 10347–10357. PMLR (2021)
32. Vaswani, A., et al.: Attention is all you need. In: Advances in Neural Information Processing Systems, vol. 30 (2017)
33. Wang, W., et al.: Pyramid vision transformer: a versatile backbone for dense prediction without convolutions. In: Proceedings of the IEEE/CVF International Conference on Computer Vision, pp. 568–578 (2021)
34. Wang, W., et al.: PVT v2: improved baselines with pyramid vision transformer. Comput. Vis. Media 8(3), 415–424 (2022)
35. Wightman, R.: PyTorch image models (2019). https://doi.org/10.5281/zenodo.4414861. https://github.com/rwightman/pytorch-image-models
36. Xu, Y., Zhang, Q., Zhang, J., Tao, D.: ViTAE: vision transformer advanced by exploring intrinsic inductive bias. In: Advances in Neural Information Processing Systems, vol. 34, pp. 28522–28535 (2021)
37. Yang, J., Li, C., Dai, X., Gao, J.: Focal modulation networks. In: Oh, A.H., Agarwal, A., Belgrave, D., Cho, K. (eds.) Advances in Neural Information Processing Systems (2022). https://openreview.net/forum?id=ePhEbo039l
38. Yu, W., et al.: MetaFormer is actually what you need for vision. In: Proceedings of the IEEE/CVF Conference on Computer Vision and Pattern Recognition, pp. 10819–10829 (2022)
39. Yu, W., et al.: MetaFormer baselines for vision. arXiv preprint arXiv:2210.13452 (2022)
40. Yuan, L., et al.: Tokens-to-token ViT: training vision transformers from scratch on ImageNet. In: Proceedings of the IEEE/CVF International Conference on Computer Vision, pp. 558–567 (2021)

Classification of Lung and Colon Cancer Using Deep Learning Method

Md. Al-Mamun Provath[1], Kaushik Deb[1](✉), and Kang-Hyun Jo[2]

[1] Department of Computer Science and Engineering, Chittagong University of Engineering and Technology (CUET), Chattogram 4349, Bangladesh
u1704098@student.cuet.ac.bd, debkaushik99@cuet.ac.bd
[2] Department of Electrical, Electronic and Computer Engineering, University of Ulsan, Ulsan 44610, South Korea
acejo@ulsan.ac.kr

Abstract. Cancer seems to have a significantly high mortality rate as a result of its aggressiveness, significant propensity for metastasis, and heterogeneity. One of the most common types of cancer that can affect both sexes and occur worldwide is lung and colon cancer. It is early and precise detection of these cancers which can not only improves the rate of survival but also increase the appropriate treatment characteristics. As an alternative to the current cancer detection techniques, a highly accurate and computationally efficient model for the rapid and precise identification of cancers in the lung and colon region is provided. For the training, validation and testing phases of this work, the LC25000 dataset is used. Cyclic learning rate is employed to increase the accuracy and maintain the computational efficiency of the proposed methods. This is both straightforward and effective which facilitates the model to converge faster. Several transfer learning models that have already been trained are also used, and they are compared to the proposed CNN from scratch. It is found that the proposed model provides better accuracy, reducing the impact of inter-class variations between Lung Adenocarcinoma and another class Lung Squamous Cell Carcinoma. Implementing the proposed method increased total accuracy to 97% and demonstrate computing efficiency in compare to other method.

Keywords: Convolutional Neural Network · Transfer Learning · Lung Cancer Pathology

1 Introduction

The word cancer is used to describe a large group of diseases that affect various body parts. One of the characteristics that distinguishes cancer is the unrestrained, fast proliferation of aberrant cells that cross their normal borders and have the potential to infiltrate other organs. International Agency for Research on Cancer (IARC) of the World Health Organization (WHO) [1] reports that in 2020, cancer is the greatest cause of death worldwide, accounting for 19 million

© The Author(s), under exclusive license to Springer Nature Singapore Pte Ltd. 2023
I. Na and G. Irie (Eds.): IW-FCV 2023, CCIS 1857, pp. 56–70, 2023.
https://doi.org/10.1007/978-981-99-4914-4_5

new cases and approximately 10 million deaths. The main reason for death from cancer is metastasis, which occurs when cancer spreads from its primary place to another organ of the body without the aid of adhesion chemicals. Any organ in the human body could get cancer, but the lung, colon, rectum, liver, stomach, and breast are the most frequently affected organs. The most common cancers that cause deaths in both men and women are colon and lung cancer. Globally, there were 2.21 million new cases of lung cancer in 2020, 1.93 million cases of colorectal cancer, 1.80 million lung cancer-related deaths, and approximately 1 million colorectal cancer deaths [2]. Behaviors as a high body mass index, a drinking habit, or smoking are factors in the development of cancer. Along with genetic ones, there are physical toxins like radiation and UV rays in [2]. When lung cells mutate, they grow uncontrollably and combine into a mass known as a tumor, which is when they turn malignant. The colon, the last part of our digestive system, may develop colon cancer if it has malignant cells. In the majority of cases of colon cancer, a tumor develops as normal cells that line the colon or rectum enlarge out of control.

Without a broad spectrum of diagnostic techniques, cancer detection task is difficult. Patients usually have little or no disease symptoms, but by the time they appear, it is frequently too late. Understanding metastases is a critical topic of cancer research because metastatic illness causes 90% of cancer deaths [3]. Colon cancer frequently metastasizes to the liver, lungs, and peritoneum, while lung cancer frequently metastasizes to the brain, liver, bones, and other areas of the lungs. Although symptoms are commonly linked to the presence of cancer cells in the organ where they spread, the metastatic cells would look under a microscope to be sick primary organ cells [4]. Early detection and appropriate treatment are now the main ways to reduce the frequency of cancer-related mortality [5]. If colon cancer is discovered at Stage 0, for instance, more than 92patients between the ages of 18 and 73 can live with the appropriate medication, and 83% in Stage 1, 67%, in Stage 2, 11% in Stage 3. The relative lung cancer survival rates are 69%, 50%, 29%, and 8% in [6]. The high cost of screening equipment prevents many people from using them. 70% of deaths caused by cancer in countries other than those with greater incomes [2]. The solution to this issue may lie in a field that has nothing to do with medicine. It is medical field which use deep learning for numerous purposes in [7].

In order to categorize and forecast different kinds of biological signals, machine learning methods have been utilized. Deep Learning (DL) techniques have been developed, allowing machinery that deals with data which are by nature high in dimension including images, videos. A CNN model was developed from scratch to extract features from pathological images, carry out end-to-end training, gradually and accurately categorize the Lung and Colon Cancer pathological images. The hyperparameters were tuned to ensure the best configuration and a learning process cyclical in nature was used to reduce computation and make the model faster.

The following is a list of this paper's key contributions:

1. In order to improve classification performance, a scratch CNN model is developed.

2. The inclusion of the cyclical learning rate approach in the proposed model delivers substantial performance increases and lowers the computational expense.
3. To increase the accuracy and compare accuracy with different transfer learning methods from others method.

2   Related Works

For more than 40 years, researchers have studied the automatic assistant diagnosis of cancer by classifying histopathological images into non-cancerous or malignant patterns for analysis, which is the initial aim of the image analysis system. The complexity of image analysis, however, made it difficult to deal with the complexity of histological images. Approximately 40 years ago [8], investigated the possibility of automatic image processing, but the difficulty of analyzing complex images makes it still difficult today. Back then, implementing machine learning-based computer-aided diagnosis (CAD) required feature extraction as a crucial step. Different cancer ontologies have been looked into in studies by in [9] provide a thorough overview of cancer diagnosis by carrying out tests of various deep learning methods. Additionally, it offers comparisons of the various prominent architectures. The next few paragraphs, briefly discuss the previous works by the researcher.

A representational Sparse in nature Classification (mSRC) technique of diagnosing cancer of lung was described by in [10]. The authors used samples from needle biopsies to automatically segment regions of nuclei numbered 4372 of the diagnosis of cancer in lung. This approach has average classification accuracy of 88.10%. In [11], on the basis of the examination of CT scan images, to classify cancer an approach was followed by authors and which was dealing with CAD. They took six different statistical feature and forward and its reverse propagation are the two types of networks which were used. The comprehensive analysis demonstrates that skewness, when combined with ANN with back-propagation, yields the best classification results. In [12], a classification method which is free of label for grading cancer in colon was published. Different dedifferentiation states of colon cancer and infrared spectral histopathology imaging were used in this work. Random Forest, a supervised learning technique based on Decision Trees (DT), carried out the classification (RF).

In [13], a technique was proposed which can analyze colonoscopy video to identify cancer and that can automatically identify polyps from colonoscopy video was described by Yuan et al. They employed AlexNet, a well-known CNN based architecture, for classification, which had an accuracy rate of 91.47%. In [14], a technique for cancer in lung, stage detection was proposed by Masood et al. The researchers evaluated their model using six different datasets and used CNN and DFCNet in their research. A swarm optimization- based technique for cancer in lung prediction was presented in [15] using images from various sources. A maximum accuracy of 98% was attained using their learning algorithm of choice, the Recurrent Neural Network (RNN).

In order to detect colorectal cancer from colonoscopy videos, A method which is based on neural network was and weights of binary nature was used to classify in [16]. Collected data was evaluated and achieved classification accuracy of more than 90%. In [17] an approach of automatic in nature was developed for detecting lung cancer. They used the Wolf heuristic feature selection approach and bin smoothing for the normalization mechanism. The classifier applied in this study neural network of learning of ensemble kinds was the most intriguing aspect of the study's methodology. Its accuracy was over 99%.

In [18], proposed a CNN model after extracting more than three sets of features, from histopathological images of lung and colon cancer. Authors used convolutional layers of numbered three pooling double times, single batch normalization with dropout for this classification task. Authors have also showed a comparison of related research where the proposed method of 96.33% accuracy the method can identify tissues of desired nature, performing well than other works.

As a result, it can be concluded that the classification of both lung and colon cancer has had a significant impact for a long time. Deep learning models combined with a wide range of configurations have recently exceeded current state-of-the-art methods, as well. There is a huge amount of scope for initiating innovation and development in this developing research field to overcome this.

3   Datasets

3.1   LC25000

This dataset, has images total of 25000 and which are of different types - total five in number [19]. These variations include lung adenocarcinoma, lung squamous cell cancer, benign lung tissue, benign colonic tissue, and lung adenocarcinoma. The authors principally gathered 1250 images of tissues which are of cancer types (250 images of each category). Several techniques were used to increase images of each class (5000 images in each class). Before using the augmentation techniques, to make a square of 768 × 768 pixels from their original size of 1024× 768 cropping was used. The dataset has the nature of compliance, and validation, and use of every image in the dataset is totally free. The dataset's contents are listed in Table 1, along with the class names.

Table 1. LC25000 dataset summary.

Cancer Type	Samples
Colon Adenocarcinoma	5000
Colon Benign Tissue	5000
Lung Adenocarcinoma	5000
Lung Benign Tissue	5000
Lung Squamous Cell Carcinoma	5000
Total	**25000**

4   Methods

4.1   Cyclic Learning Rate

CNNs are one of the most effective architectural designs for the issue of image classification. To extract the most unique features from an image's pixels, CNNs utilize filtering methods. The most essential hyperparameter to adjust while deep learning deep neural networks is the learning rate, that is well known.

The learning rate can cycle between acceptable boundary values using this strategy rather than monotonically decreasing. Training using learning rates of cyclical in nature rather than choosing values increases accuracy without the necessity of trial and error method and also frequently requires fewer iterations.

The fundamental idea behind cyclical method is based on the idea that speeding up learning could have both short-term detrimental effects and long-term beneficial outcomes. This discovery inspires the concept that rather of using a stepwise fixed or exponentially declining value, the learning rate should be allowed to vary within a range of values. Due to the fact that the triangle window is the most straightforward function that contains both linear rising and linear decreasing, this led to its adoption which is illustrated in Fig. 1.

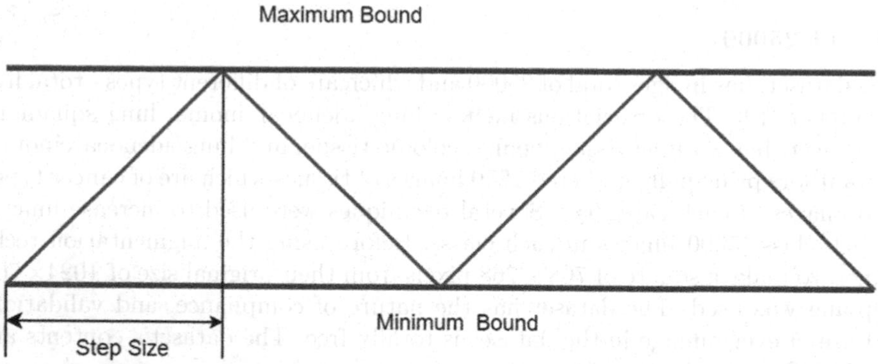

Fig. 1. Triangular learning rate policy.

The loss was estimated against the learning rate, and based on the learning rate in Fig. 2, the base lr value was adjusted to 0.003 as the loss was declining.

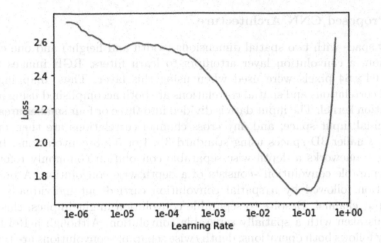

Fig. 2. Loss versus learning rate (base learning rate).

The best learning rate is determined after 8 training epochs by re-running the cyclic learning rate. The distinction of the learning rate at the onset of loss diminution and at the juncture where the loss's declination transforms into irregularity or commences to escalate constitutes optimal limits for specifying the base and maximum learning rate, respectively [20]. In conformity with this, the base learning rate is instituted at the former value, and the maximum learning rate is established at the latter value, as exemplified in Fig. 3, where the base lr was set to 0.0045 and max lr was set to 0.0301.

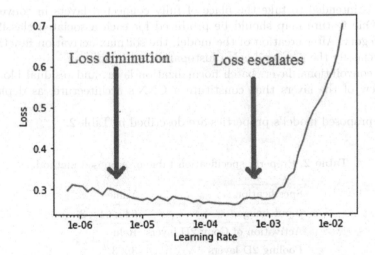

Fig. 3. Loss versus learning rate.

4.2 Proposed CNN Architecture

In a 3D space with two spatial dimensions (width and height) and one channel dimension, a convolution layer attempts to learn filters. RGB images with a size of 64×64 pixels were used when using this layer. Thus, mapping cross channel correlations and spatial correlations are both accomplished using a single convolution kernel. The input data is divided into three or four smaller areas than the original input space, and any cross channel correlations are then mapped in these smaller 3D spaces using standard 3×3 or 5×5 convolutions. In deep learning frameworks a depth wise separable convolution commonly referred to as a "separable convolution"-consists of a depth wise convolution. A pointwise convolution followed by a spatial convolution carried out individually across each input channel. Despite to separable convolution might implies, this is not to be mistaken with a spatially separable convolution. Although a ReLU non-linearity follows both operations, depths wise separable convolutions are typically performed without nonlinearities.

Each layer of the network can learn more independently due to the layer of batch normalization. It uses normalization to adjust the output of the prior layers. The input layer is scaled during normalization. When batch normalization is used, learning is more successful. To avoid overfitting the model, batch normalization was employed as a regularizer. Three Residual blocks were used in the model. Spatial convolution layers and batch normalization make up the residual block.

Dropouts are a regularization technique that prevents model overfitting. Neurons in the network are modified in some percentage randomly as dropouts are added. When neurons are turned off, the connections to their incoming and outgoing neurons are also disconnected. A pooling method called global average pooling is intended to take the place of fully connected layers in conventional CNNs. One feature map should be produced for each associated classification task category. After creation of the model, the softmax activation function was used to classify the lung and colon histopathology images.

The convolutional layer, batch normalization layer, and residual block were just a few of the layers that constitute a CNN's architecture, as depicted in Fig. 4.

Our proposed model's properties are described in Table 2.

Table 2. Property specification table of proposed method.

Specification	Value
Input image	$64 \times 64 \times 3$
Activation of Conv_2D layers	Relu
Pooling 2D layers	3×3
Output layer activation	Softmax
Optimizer for compilation	Adam

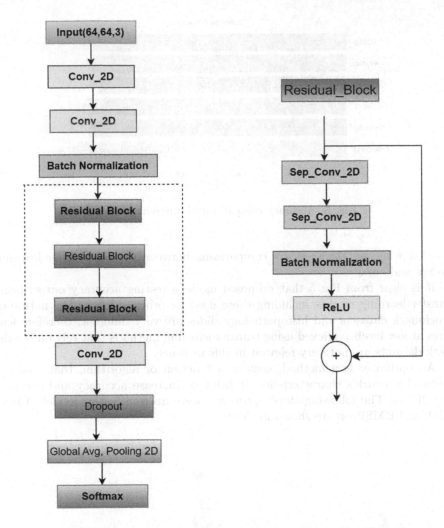

Fig. 4. The proposed method of lung and colon cancer classification.

5 Result Analysis

In this part, the system configurations have been outlined. The best model's f1-score, recall, and precision are a few of the accuracy metrics that stand out. For further study of the best model, the classification report, confusion matrix, and performance graphs are evaluated.

On LC25000, multiclass classification analyses are performed. The down sampling technique was employed to reduce the size of the image to 64 × 64. In the LC25000 dataset, various pre-trained transfer learning models were also used.

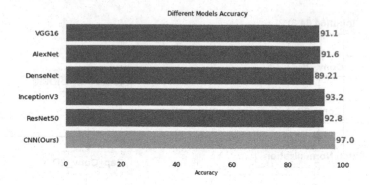

Fig. 5. Accuracy comparison of different models.

The following are the accuracy comparisons between several transfer learning models and ours:

It is clear from Fig. 5 that proposed model's testing accuracy outperforms transfer learning models including those used by other authors. The nature of benchmark datasets and histopathology slides are very different, therefore features at low levels retrieved using transfer learning methods that rely on benchmark datasets are not very relevant in this instance.

An optimizer is a method, such as a function or algorithm, that modifies a neural network's characteristics. It helps to increase accuracy and decrease overall loss. The following three optimizers were utilized in this model: Adam, SGD, and RMSProp are shown in Fig. 6.

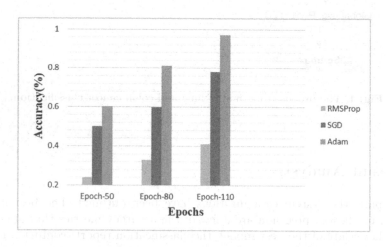

Fig. 6. Optimizer comparison curve.

Adam's accuracy in the model was the highest according to the following figure and for this Adam was chosen because its accuracy in the model was the highest, as shown by Fig. 6.

The samples numbers that are before processing the model hyper tune is the size of each batch. The batch size utilized was shown in Fig. 7, and it was determined by the number of samples before processing the model hyperparameter tune.

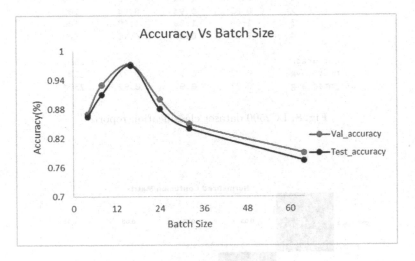

Fig. 7. Accuracy versus batch size.

Batch size 16 was chosen because it provided the highest accuracy among others, as determined by the comparison curve.

Table 3 explains how the proposed model's hyperparameters were configured.

Table 3. Hyperparameter configuration of proposed method.

Hyper Parameter	Range	Optimal Value
Batch Size	4, 8, 16, 24, 32, 64	**16**
Epoch	50, 60, 80, 90, 100, 110	**100**
Optimizer	Adam, RMSProp, SGD	**Adam**
Dropout	0.20, 0.30.0.4, 0.50	**0.4**

5.1 Proposed Model Output

A ratio of 80:10:10 for training, validation, and testing is maintained when the dataset is split in the proposed model. Several parameters are taken into account for performance analysis, as depicted in Figs. 8 and 9, to demonstrate the performance of the proposed approach. The accuracy of training and validation was included in Fig. 10.

```
               precision    recall  f1-score   support

           0        1.00      0.91      0.96       500
           1        0.97      1.00      0.98       500
           2        0.93      0.94      0.94       500
           3        1.00      1.00      1.00       500
           4        0.94      0.97      0.96       500

    accuracy                            0.97      2500
   macro avg        0.97      0.97      0.97      2500
weighted avg        0.97      0.97      0.97      2500
```

Fig. 8. LC2500 dataset classification report.

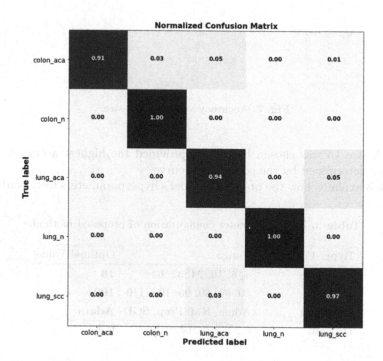

Fig. 9. LC25000 dataset normalized confusion matrix.

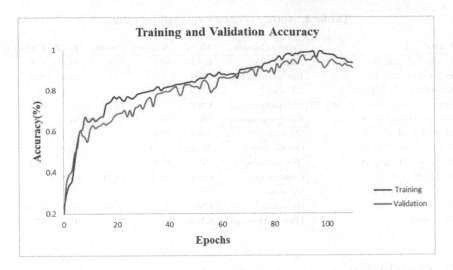

Fig. 10. Training and validation accuracy curve.

The experiment's results for multiclass classification accuracy were measured and compared to those of other authors, as shown in Table 4. Though the same dataset was not used by all of the authors, as the purpose of the task remains the same, they were compared with the proposed approach. The classification accuracy was 97% and it significantly reduces inter-class variation between two forms of cancer in Lung Adenocarcinoma and Squamous Cell Carcinoma. In prior studies [21,22] the authors neglected to integrate residual blocks, which are essential components that enable the establishment of deeper network architecture and effectively alleviate the vanishing gradient problem. Additionally, the implementation of skip connections within Residual Networks facilitates the seamless transmission of information across the network, thereby facilitating optimization. The CNN models in references [22] and [12] suffer from limited feature extraction and overfitting issues due to their shallow network architecture. The proposed model incorporates three ResNet blocks and the use of separable convolution layers within these blocks, which significantly reduces the number of parameters required and results in a compact model with expedited training times. This proposed model reduces 1.95 times training times than described in [23].

It can be concluded from Table 4 that the accuracy of the proposed method surpasses that of other authors.

Table 4. Author accuracy comparison table.

Author	Types of Images	Model	Accuracy	Precision	Recall	F Measure
Y. Shi et al., [10], 13	Biopsy Image	mSRC	88.1	84.6	91.3	86.6
Y. Xu et al., [24], 13	Histopathological	SVMs		73.7	68.2	70.8
Kuruvilla et al., [11], 14	CT scan	ANN	93.3		91.4	
Sirinukunwattana K et al., [25], 16	Histopathological	CNN		78.3	82.7	80.2
Kuepper et al., [12], 16	Histopathological	RF	95		94	
W. Shen et al., [23], 17	CT scan	CNN	87.14		93	
Z. Yuan et al., [13], 17	Colonoscopy	AlexNet	87.14		91.76	
T. Babu et al., [26], 18	Histopathological	RF	85.3			85.2
M. Akbari et al., [16], 18	Colonoscopy	CNN	90.28	74.34	68.32	71.2
Suresh et al., [21], 20	CT scan	CNN	93.9		93.4	
M. Masud et al., [22], 21	Histopathological	CNN	96.33	96.39	96.37	96.38
Proposed	**Histopathological**	**CNN**	**97**	**97**	**97**	**97**

6 Conclusion

Lung and colon cancer are attributed as mostly caused cancer types among all other types. Early identification of cancer can help patients rate of survival to increase. The prime purpose of the proposed method was to provide a more robust and reliable approach for these two forms of cancer. For this detection, transfer learning was used on a dataset of 25,000 histopathological images of colon and lung tissues. When using the suggested scratch CNN method, accuracy was greatly improved and reached 97%. The proposed methodology offers improved accuracy over current methods for detecting lung and colon cancer while also taking less time and using less computational resources. All the experiments verify the effectiveness of the proposed method regarding the task of detecting cancer. Future incorporation of attention with scratch CNN model to increase the classification accuracy and explore more details of the image.

References

1. I. A. for Research on Cancer: World Fact Sheet (2020). https://gco.iarc.fr/today/data/factsheets/populations/900-world-fact-sheets.pdf/. Accessed 26 June 2022
2. I. H. Organization: Cancer (2022). https://www.who.int/news-room/factsheets/detail/cancer/. Accessed 26 June 2022
3. Seyfried, T.N., Huysentruyt, L.C.: On the origin of cancer metastasis. Crit. Rev.^{TM} Oncog. **18**(1–2) (2013)
4. Verywellhealth: What Is Metastasis? (2022). https://www.verywellhealth.com/metastatic-cancer-2249128/. Accessed 27 June 2022
5. Sánchez-Peralta, L.F., Bote-Curiel, L., Picón, A., Sánchez-Margallo, F.M., Pagador, J.B.: Deep learning to find colorectal polyps in colonoscopy: a systematic literature review. Artif. Intell. Med. **108**, 101923 (2020)
6. C. Health: Cancer Survival Rates (2022). https://cancersurvivalrates.com/?type=colon&role=patient/. Accessed 26 June 2022

7. Das, S., Biswas, S., Paul, A., Dey, A.: AI doctor: an intelligent approach for medical diagnosis. In: Bhattacharyya, S., Sen, S., Dutta, M., Biswas, P., Chattopadhyay, H. (eds.) Industry Interactive Innovations in Science, Engineering and Technology. LNNS, vol. 11, pp. 173–183. Springer, Singapore (2018). https://doi.org/10.1007/978-981-10-3953-9_17

8. Doi, K.: Computer-aided diagnosis in medical imaging: historical review, current status and future potential. Comput. Med. Imaging Graph. **31**(4), 198–211 (2007). Computer-Aided Diagnosis (CAD) and Image-Guided Decision Support

9. te Brake, G.M., Karssemeijer, N., Hendriks, J.H.: An automatic method to discriminate malignant masses from normal tissue in digital mammograms[1]. Phys. Med. Biol. **45**(10), 2843 (2000)

10. Shi, Y., Gao, Y., Yang, Y., Zhang, Y., Wang, D.: Multimodal sparse representation-based classification for lung needle biopsy images. IEEE Trans. Biomed. Eng. **60**(10), 2675–2685 (2013)

11. Kuruvilla, J., Gunavathi, K.: Lung cancer classification using neural networks for CT images. Comput. Methods programs Biomed. **113**(1), 202–209 (2014)

12. Kuepper, C., Großerueschkamp, F., Kallenbach-Thieltges, A., Mosig, A., Tannapfel, A., Gerwert, K.: Label-free classification of colon cancer grading using infrared spectral histopathology. Faraday Discuss. **187**, 105–118 (2016)

13. Yuan, Z., et al.: Automatic polyp detection in colonoscopy videos. In: Medical Imaging, Image Processing, SPIE 2017, vol. 10133, pp. 718–727 (2017)

14. Masood, A., et al.: Computer-assisted decision support system in pulmonary cancer detection and stage classification on CT images. J. Biomed. Inform. **79**, 117–128 (2018)

15. Selvanambi, R., Natarajan, J., Karuppiah, M., Islam, S.H., Hassan, M.M., Fortino, G.: Lung cancer prediction using higher-order recurrent neural network based on glowworm swarm optimization. Neural Comput. Appl. **32**, 4373–4386 (2020)

16. Akbari, M., et al.: Classification of informative frames in colonoscopy videos using convolutional neural networks with binarized weights. In: 40th Annual International Conference of the IEEE Engineering in Medicine and Biology Society (EMBC), pp. 65–68. IEEE (2018)

17. Shakeel, P.M., Tolba, A., Al-Makhadmeh, Z., Jaber, M.M.: Automatic detection of lung cancer from biomedical data set using discrete AdaBoost optimized ensemble learning generalized neural networks. Neural Comput. Appl. **32**, 777–790 (2020)

18. Masud, M., Sikder, N., Nahid, A.-A., Bairagi, A.K., AlZain, M.A.: A machine learning approach to diagnosing lung and colon cancer using a deep learning-based classification framework. Sensors **21**(3), 748 (2021)

19. Borkowski, A.A., Bui, M.M., Thomas, L.B., Wilson, C.P., DeLand, L.A., Mastorides, S.M.: Lung and colon cancer histopathological image dataset (LC25000). arXiv preprint arXiv:1912.12142 (2019)

20. Smith, L.N.: Cyclical learning rates for training neural networks. In: IEEE Winter Conference on Applications of Computer Vision (WACV) 2017, pp. 464–472 (2017)

21. Suresh, S., Mohan, S.: ROI-based feature learning for efficient true positive prediction using convolutional neural network for lung cancer diagnosis. Neural Comput. Appl. **32**(20), 15 989–16 009 (2020)

22. Masud, M., et al.: Light deep model for pulmonary nodule detection from CT scan images for mobile devices. Wirel. Commun. Mob. Comput. **2020**, 1–8 (2020)

23. Shen, W., et al.: Multi-crop convolutional neural networks for lung nodule malignancy suspiciousness classification. Pattern Recogn. **61**, 663–673 (2017)

24. Xu, Y., et al.: Multi-label classification for colon cancer using histopathological images. Microsc. Res. Tech. **76**(12), 1266–1277 (2013)

25. Sirinukunwattana, K., Raza, S.E.A., Tsang, Y.-W., Snead, D.R., Cree, I.A., Rajpoot, N.M.: Locality sensitive deep learning for detection and classification of nuclei in routine colon cancer histology images. IEEE Trans. Med. Imaging **35**(5), 1196–1206 (2016)
26. Babu, T., Gupta, D., Singh, T., Hameed, S.: Colon cancer prediction on different magnified colon biopsy images. In: 2018 Tenth International Conference on Advanced Computing (ICoAC), pp. 277–280. IEEE (2018)

A Style-Based Caricature Generator

Lamyanba Laishram[✉][iD], Muhammad Shaheryar[iD], Jong Taek Lee[iD],
and Soon Ki Jung[iD]

School of Computer Science and Engineering, Kyungpook National University,
Daegu, Republic of Korea
{yanbalaishram,shaheryar,jongtaeklee,skjung}@knu.ac.kr

Abstract. A facial caricature is a creation of new artistic and exaggerated faces which translates into a real image to convey sarcasm or humor while keeping the identity of the subject. In this work, we proposed a new way to create caricatures by exaggerating facial features like the eyes and mouth while keeping the facial contour intact and a realistic style. Our method can be categorized into two steps. First, the facial exaggeration process transformed faces into caricature face images while maintaining facial contours. Second, the appearance style generator is trained in unpaired using the generated caricature faces to produce a facial caricature that can change to any realistic style of our preference. Experimental results show our model produces more realistic and disentangled caricature images as compared to some of the previous methods. Our method can also generate caricature images from real images.

Keywords: Caricature · Style Generator · Generative Adversarial Network

1 Introduction

In the world of comics, animation, posters, and advertising, in particular, artistic portraits are very common in our daily lives. A caricature is a representation of a person whose distinctive features are simplified or exaggerated through sketching or artistic drawings. A facial caricature is a form of art used to convey sarcasm or humor and is used commonly in entertainment.

Applications based on computer vision have a wide range and the creation of caricatures can be done without the need for an artist. Similar to the way an artist approach creating caricatures, a method based on computer vision can also be divided into two stages: (i) identifying the distinct features and exaggerating those features, and (ii) applying styles to the deformed image according to the artist's taste. The separation of these two categories provides flexibility and disentanglement which eventually results in the generation of good-quality caricatures.

Earlier approaches for creating a facial caricature require professional skills to get good results [2]. Traditional artworks tended to emphasize exaggerating facial forms by increasing the shape representation's divergence from the average,

© The Author(s), under exclusive license to Springer Nature Singapore Pte Ltd. 2023
I. Na and G. Irie (Eds.): IW-FCV 2023, CCIS 1857, pp. 71–82, 2023.
https://doi.org/10.1007/978-981-99-4914-4_6

as in the case of 2D landmarks or 3D meshes [3,14,27]. With the advancement in applications of computer vision techniques, several automated caricature generations have emerged [4,11,33]. Moreover, automatic portrait style transfer based on image style transfer [22,24,32] and image-to-image translation [21] have been extensively studied. Recently with the development in the Generative adversarial networks (GANs) [13], the state-of-the-art face generator StyleGAN [19,20] provides disentangled and high-fidelity artistic images via transfer learning.

In recent years, Deep learning techniques are very successful in performing image-to-image translation by learning from representation data examples [15,16]. Unfortunately, paired real and caricature are not commonly found. The translation process is not feasible to be trained in a supervised manner and building such a dataset is tedious. One of the readily available caricature datasets is WebCaricature [17], which consists of 6042 caricatures and 5974 photographs from 252 different identities. In our work, we created a set of 55,000 caricature images from the FFHQ dataset [19] for automatic caricature generation which we will discuss in Sect. 3.

Due to the limited data availability of paired images, most of the research on image-to-image translation in this work is starting to move towards training on unpaired images [5,16,40] and learning from unpaired portrait and caricature [4,35]. However, learning unpaired images can introduce highly varied exaggerations from different artists with divergent styles. Most images will have different poses and scales which might result in difficulty to distinguish facial features. In our method, we performed an unpaired learning approach using a specific caricature design of exaggerating face parts while still maintaining the facial contour of the real image.

We aim to create a method of generating new caricature faces from a real image with realistic details and obtain different stylization results. Our method first modifies a real face into a caricature face and then used that to train a generative model to produce different styles. A summary of our contribution is as follows:

- We proposed a method of generating facial caricature images with big eyes and big mouths using face patches. The method can generate different faces and can apply for multiple style transfers on a specific face.
- Our method is an unpaired learning process of creating a caricature face first from a real face image. A powerful style network is then trained using the generated caricature faces to synthesize different styles transfer.
- Our generated caricature is more realistic and high-quality as compared with the previous methods while still providing a completely disentangling style.

The remainder of our work is organized as follows: The related work in the creation of caricature and style transfer are discussed in Sect. 2. The methodology behind the creation of our caricature and the style transfer are discussed in Sect. 3. Experimental results are shown and analyzed in Sect. 4. We finally conclude our work in Sect. 5.

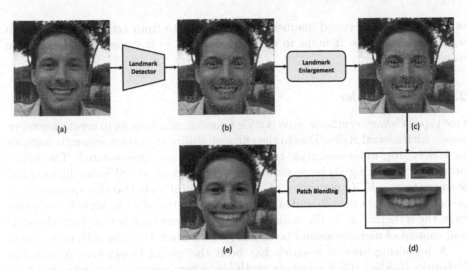

Fig. 1. Facial caricature generation pipeline: (a) input image, (b) facial landmarks using a landmark detector, (c) enlarged landmark location for eyes and mouth regions, (d) segmented and scaled eyes and mouth patches, and (d) final caricature result generated after blending the scaled face patches to the original face image.

2 Related Work

In this section, we discuss some of the works related to our paper: caricature creation and style transfer.

2.1 Caricature Creation

The generation of caricature is to identify and exaggerate distinct features of a face while still maintaining the identity of the individual. The creation of caricatures can be performed in three ways: deforming facial attributes, style transfer, or methods using both.

Traditional methods perform by magnifying the deviation from the mean, either by explicitly identifying and warping landmarks [12,25] or by utilizing data-driven approaches to estimate distinctive facial characteristics [26,38]. With the advancement in generative networks, some image-to-image translation work [23,39] has been done to apply transfer style. However, because these networks are unsuitable for techniques with large spatial variation, their outputs have low visual quality.

Cao et al. [4] use two CycleGANs which are trained on image and landmarks space for texture rending and geometry deformation. WarpGAN [33] can produce better visual quality and more shape exaggeration by providing flexible spatial variability on both image geometry and texture. CariGAN [4] is a GAN trained using unpaired images to learn the image-to-caricature translation. Shi et al. [33] proposed an end-to-end GAN framework that trains warping and style. Deformation fields are used by AutoToon [11] to apply the exaggerations. AutoToon is trained in a supervised manner using paired data from artist-warp photos to learn warping fields. It maps to only one domain, so it cannot produce diverse exaggerations.

2.2   Style Transfer

One type of image synthesis issue is style transfer, which seeks to create a content image with several styles. Due to the efficient ability to extract semantic features by CNNs [10], numerous style transfer networks are implemented. The initial process of rendering styles is performed by Gatys et al. [8] using hierarchical features from a VGG network [34]. The first neural style transfer approach was put out by Gatys et al. [9] and employs a CNN to transfer the style information from the style picture to the content image. The drawback is that both the style and content of pictures should be similar, which is not the case with caricatures.

A promising area of research has been the use of Generative Adversarial Networks (GANs) [13] for picture synthesis, where cutting-edge outcomes have been shown in applications like text-to-image translation [31] and image inpainting [37]. Using Generative Adversarial Networks (GANs) [13] for image synthesis has been a promising field of study, where state-of-the-art results have been demonstrated in applications ranging from text to image translation [31], image inpainting [37] and many more. Unpaired image translation is accomplished by CycleGAN [40] using a cycle consistency loss. StarGAN [5,6] uses a single generator to learn mappings between various picture domains. To capture the geometric transformation, it is challenging to learn photo-to-caricature mapping directly in an image-to-image translation approach.

StyleGAN [18–20] generates high-fidelity face images with hierarchical channel style control. StyleGAN was refined by Pinkney and Adler [30] using sparse cartoon data, and they discovered that approach was effective in producing realistic cartoon faces. DualStyleGAN [36] offers customizable management of dual styles transfer for both the expanded artistic portrait domain and the original face domain.

3   Methodology

The goal of our method is to generate a caricature face that looks realistic and train a state-of-the-art style generator with our newly generated caricature face. Our method provides completely disentangling styles for the generated caricature faces. Our whole method is sectioned into two steps: face caricature creation and face style generation. Face caricature creation focuses on the creation of exaggerated faces with enlarged eyes and mouths from real faces. Face style generation focuses on the generation of caricature faces with realistic and distinct styles.

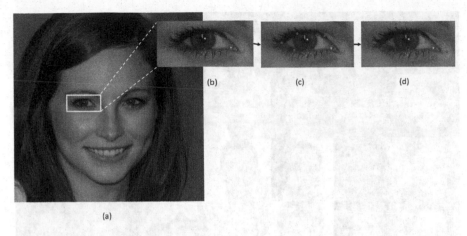

Fig. 2. Generated facial patches: (a) image from the FFHQ dataset [19], (b) visualizing the left eye from our point of view, (c) the landmark positions of the left eye, and (d) increasing the landmark indexes for improving blending results.

3.1 Face Caricature Creation

Real-face images are used for the creation of a caricature face. The face images are randomly sampled from the FFHQ dataset [19] which covers diverse gender, races, ages, expressions, poses and etc. The first process is to find the facial landmark points as shown in Fig. 1. The pre-trained facial landmark detector inside the dlib library [1] is used to estimate the location map of facial structures on the face. Dlib is a commonly used open-source library that can recognize 68 (x, y) coordinates of the structure of a face image. These 68 landmarks are specifically assigned for each part of the face like eyes, eyebrows, nose, mouth, and face contour.

Our implementation specifically focuses on the enlargement of the eyes and mouth region of the face. The indexes of the landmarks of the eyes can be categorized into two groups, such as the left eye and the right eye. The left eye is represented by indexes 37 to 42 whereas the right eye is by indexes 43 to 48. The mouth area consists of the upper lips and the lower lips. When we consider the mouth as a whole, we take only the top landmarks indexes of the upper lip and the bottom indexes of the bottom lips. Indexes 49 to 60 represent the mouth region. All these landmark positions are shown in Fig. 1.

Using the eyes and mouth landmarks indexes, we segmented two eye regions and a mouth region patch. Before creating these patches, the corresponding landmarks are increased to make the interested area of the patches bigger as shown in Fig. 2. The patches are then scaled first to a factor of 1.5 and then blend

Fig. 3. Our generated caricature images from real images.

back to the original center location of the eyes and mouth part respectively. The scaled patches regions are patched back to the original image using the Poisson image editing technique [29] which blends in seamlessly. The blending technique affects the image illumination and the texture. The Poisson seamless editing can be represented as follows:

$$v = argmin_v \sum_{i \in S, j \in N_i \cap S} ((v_i - v_j) - (s_i - s_j))^2 + \sum_{i \in S, j \in N_i \cap \neg S} ((v_i - t_j) - (s_i - t_j))^2$$

where v is the pixel values of the new image, s is the pixel values of the source image, t is the pixel values of the target image, S is the destination domain, and N_i a set of neighboring pixels of i.

Our final caricature faces are realistic as it is produced from real images. We illustrate some of our caricature datasets in Fig. 3.

3.2 Style Transfer Generator

For the style transfer process, we trained a powerful style-based generator called StyleGAN [19, 20]. We trained the generator only using our newly produced face caricature images which have enlarged eye and mouth regions. The architecture of StyleGAN consists of two networks: a mapping network and a synthesis network as shown in Fig. 4. A mapping network f is an 8-layer MLP that maps a given latent code $z \in Z$ to produce $w \in W$, defined as $f : Z \rightarrow W$. The synthesis network g are 18 convolutional layers that are controlled through adaptive instance normalization (AdaIN) [7] at each layer with the learned affine transformation "A" of latent code w. A scalable Gaussian noise input "B" is also fed in each layer of the synthesis network g.

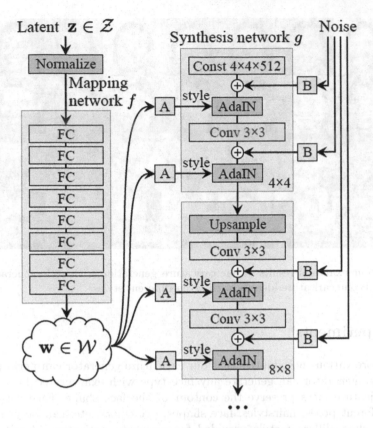

Fig. 4. StyleGAN Architecture [19,20].

The architecture is designed in a way that each style controls only one convolution. Random latent codes can be used to control the styles of the generated images. After we train our new caricature images, the generator can produce caricature images with different styles of facial attributes like skin tone, hair color, shapes, etc. Note that, unlike previous caricature generation, we trained our generator using only our generated caricature faces and no paired data.

3.3   Implementation

Our experiment is implemented with the diverse set of face FFHQ dataset [19]. We collected 55,000 FFHQ images for the face caricature generation and the style transfer training. The image resolution we worked on is 256×256. The style generator is trained with the same network architecture and other hyperparameters as the original Stylegan-ADA generator [18]. Our core algorithm is developed using PyTorch 1.7.1 [28] and CUDA 11.3. The experiment is performed using four NVIDIA TITAN Xp GPUs and a batch size of 16.

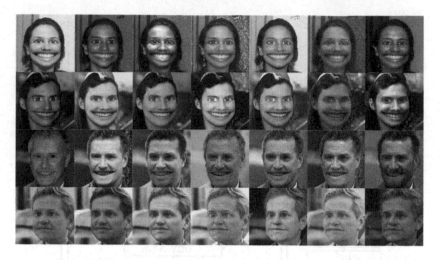

Fig. 5. Four examples results of our caricature generation with style generator and each row is one caricature identity with seven different styles.

4   Experiments

We explore various possibilities that our caricature generator can perform. Our caricature generator can generate any face type with exaggerated facial parts. Our caricature faces preserve the contour of the face shape. Face caricatures with different poses, hairstyles, face shapes, eye colors, etc. can be generated. Figure 5 show different style provided for a specific caricature identity. Each row represents one identity and numerous style techniques can be applied to the generated caricature. This is possible because of the disentanglement nature of the StyleGAN generator. The latent space of StyleGAN is disentangled and we used it to our benefit. The generated images have a realistic style as we produced the caricature faces from the real images. Our caricature generator can also generate a caricature image from a real image. We demonstrate the effectiveness of our method by applying it to a different range of images gathered from publicly available content. These include images characterized by different facial expressions, poses, and illumination.

We qualitatively compare our caricature generation method with the previous caricature creation methods like AutoToon [11] and WrapGAN [33] as shown in Fig. 6. We find that all three methods produced very different results. The style of WarpGAN is tightly linked to its warping, which results in irregularities or deformation of facial features, and the quality of the caricature is degraded considerably. On the other hand, AutoToon exaggerates facial characteristics while maintaining their general quality and consistency in a way that is true to the original image, particularly with regard to specifics like the eyes, ears,

Fig. 6. Comparing our method with WarpGAN [33] and AutoToon [11].

and teeth. AutoToon needs paired learning method to generate these results. Our method doesn't change the face contours and exaggerates only the specific face region. The identity information and facial expression are also preserved. Our result looks more realistic as compared to other techniques, yet shows facial deformation. Since our generator is trained only on our caricature faces and not paired images, it is difficult to obtain our generator result directly from real images. We believe that we can improve our results by introducing an encoder to guide the latent space of the generator. This will be our future work.

5 Conclusion

In this paper, we proposed a framework for generating realistic unpaired caricature images. We proposed a new approach to keep the facial contours intact while exaggerating the facial parts like the eyes and mouth regions. We used a powerful style-based architecture to produce a realistic caricature from real face images. Our approach supports flexible controls to change the style of the generated caricature faces. Experimental results demonstrate that the proposed method creates caricatures that are more realistic than other state-of-the-art caricature generation methods. Although our model achieved superior results, there still exist problems that need to be tackled in caricature generation. The caricature generation is limited to all the drawbacks of the StyleGAN architecture. We will further improvements in the caricature generation process in the future.

Acknowledgment. This work was supported by the Institute of Information & Communications Technology Planning & Evaluation (IITP) grant funded by the Korean government (MSIT) (No. 2019-0-00203, Development of 5G-based Predictive Visual Security Technology for Preemptive Threat Response) and also by the MSIT(Ministry of Science and ICT), Korea, under the Innovative Human Resource Development for Local Intellectualization support program (IITP-2022-RS-2022-00156389) supervised by the IITP (Institute for Information & communications Technology Planning & Evaluation).

References

1. dlib c++ library. http://dlib.net
2. Akleman, E., Palmer, J., Logan, R.: Making extreme caricatures with a new interactive 2D deformation technique with simplicial complexes. In: Proceedings of Visual, vol. 1, p. 2000. Citeseer (2000)
3. Brennan, S.E.: Caricature generator: the dynamic exaggeration of faces by computer. Leonardo **18**(3), 170–178 (1985)
4. Cao, K., Liao, J., Yuan, L.: Carigans: unpaired photo-to-caricature translation. arXiv preprint arXiv:1811.00222 (2018)
5. Choi, Y., Choi, M., Kim, M., Ha, J.W., Kim, S., Choo, J.: Stargan: unified generative adversarial networks for multi-domain image-to-image translation. In: Proceedings of the IEEE Conference on Computer Vision and Pattern Recognition, pp. 8789–8797 (2018)
6. Choi, Y., Uh, Y., Yoo, J., Ha, J.W.: Stargan v2: diverse image synthesis for multiple domains. In: Proceedings of the IEEE/CVF Conference on Computer Vision and Pattern Recognition, pp. 8188–8197 (2020)
7. Deng, Y., Tang, F., Dong, W., Sun, W., Huang, F., Xu, C.: Arbitrary style transfer via multi-adaptation network. In: Proceedings of the 28th ACM International Conference on Multimedia, MM 2020, pp. 2719–2727. Association for Computing Machinery, New York (2020)
8. Gatys, L., Ecker, A.S., Bethge, M.: Texture synthesis using convolutional neural networks. Adv. Neural Inf. Process. Syst. **28** (2015)
9. Gatys, L.A., Ecker, A.S., Bethge, M.: Image style transfer using convolutional neural networks. In: Proceedings of the IEEE Conference on Computer Vision and Pattern Recognition, pp. 2414–2423 (2016)
10. Gatys, L.A., Ecker, A.S., Bethge, M., Hertzmann, A., Shechtman, E.: Controlling perceptual factors in neural style transfer. In: Proceedings of the IEEE Conference on Computer Vision and Pattern Recognition, pp. 3985–3993 (2017)
11. Gong, J., Hold-Geoffroy, Y., Lu, J.: Autotoon: automatic geometric warping for face cartoon generation. In: Proceedings of the IEEE/CVF Winter Conference on Applications of Computer Vision, pp. 360–369 (2020)
12. Gooch, B., Reinhard, E., Gooch, A.: Human facial illustrations: creation and psychophysical evaluation. ACM Trans. Graph. (TOG) **23**(1), 27–44 (2004)
13. Goodfellow, I., et al.: Generative adversarial networks. Commun. ACM **63**(11), 139–144 (2020)

14. Han, X., et al.: Caricatureshop: personalized and photorealistic caricature sketching. IEEE Trans. Visualization Comput. Graph. **26**(7), 2349–2361 (2018)
15. Hinton, G.E., Salakhutdinov, R.R.: Reducing the dimensionality of data with neural networks. Science **313**(5786), 504–507 (2006)
16. Huang, X., Liu, M.Y., Belongie, S., Kautz, J.: Multimodal unsupervised image-to-image translation. In: Proceedings of the European Conference on Computer Vision (ECCV), pp. 172–189 (2018)
17. Huo, J., Li, W., Shi, Y., Gao, Y., Yin, H.: Webcaricature: a benchmark for caricature recognition. arXiv preprint arXiv:1703.03230 (2017)
18. Karras, T., Aittala, M., Hellsten, J., Laine, S., Lehtinen, J., Aila, T.: Training generative adversarial networks with limited data. Adv. Neural Inf. Process. Syst. **33**, 12104–12114 (2020)
19. Karras, T., Laine, S., Aila, T.: A style-based generator architecture for generative adversarial networks. In: Proceedings of the IEEE/CVF Conference on Computer Vision and Pattern Recognition, pp. 4401–4410 (2019)
20. Karras, T., Laine, S., Aittala, M., Hellsten, J., Lehtinen, J., Aila, T.: Analyzing and improving the image quality of stylegan. In: Proceedings of the IEEE/CVF Conference on Computer Vision and Pattern Recognition (CVPR) (2020)
21. Kim, J., Kim, M., Kang, H., Lee, K.: U-gat-it: unsupervised generative attentional networks with adaptive layer-instance normalization for image-to-image translation. arXiv preprint arXiv:1907.10830 (2019)
22. Li, C., Wand, M.: Combining markov random fields and convolutional neural networks for image synthesis. In: Proceedings of the IEEE Conference on Computer Vision and Pattern Recognition, pp. 2479–2486 (2016)
23. Li, W., Xiong, W., Liao, H., Huo, J., Gao, Y., Luo, J.: Carigan: caricature generation through weakly paired adversarial learning. Neural Netw. **132**, 66–74 (2020)
24. Liao, J., Yao, Y., Yuan, L., Hua, G., Kang, S.B.: Visual attribute transfer through deep image analogy. arXiv preprint arXiv:1705.01088 (2017)
25. Liao, P.Y.C.W.H., Li, T.Y.: Automatic caricature generation by analyzing facial features. In: Proceeding of 2004 Asia Conference on Computer Vision (ACCV2004), Korea, vol. 2 (2004)
26. Liu, J., Chen, Y., Gao, W.: Mapping learning in eigenspace for harmonious caricature generation. In: Proceedings of the 14th ACM International Conference on Multimedia, pp. 683–686 (2006)
27. Mo, Z., Lewis, J.P., Neumann, U.: Improved automatic caricature by feature normalization and exaggeration. In: ACM SIGGRAPH 2004 Sketches, p. 57 (2004)
28. Paszke, A., et al.: Pytorch: an imperative style, high-performance deep learning library. Adv. Neural Inf. Process. Syst. **32** (2019)
29. Pérez, P., Gangnet, M., Blake, A.: Poisson image editing. In: ACM SIGGRAPH 2003 Papers, pp. 313–318 (2003)
30. Pinkney, J.N., Adler, D.: Resolution dependent gan interpolation for controllable image synthesis between domains. arXiv preprint arXiv:2010.05334 (2020)
31. Reed, S., Akata, Z., Yan, X., Logeswaran, L., Schiele, B., Lee, H.: Generative adversarial text to image synthesis. In: International Conference on Machine Learning, pp. 1060–1069. PMLR (2016)
32. Selim, A., Elgharib, M., Doyle, L.: Painting style transfer for head portraits using convolutional neural networks. ACM Trans. Graph. (ToG) **35**(4), 1–18 (2016)
33. Shi, Y., Deb, D., Jain, A.K.: Warpgan: automatic caricature generation. In: Proceedings of the IEEE/CVF Conference on Computer Vision and Pattern Recognition, pp. 10762–10771 (2019)

34. Simonyan, K., Zisserman, A.: Very deep convolutional networks for large-scale image recognition. arXiv preprint arXiv:1409.1556 (2014)
35. Wu, R., Tao, X., Gu, X., Shen, X., Jia, J.: Attribute-driven spontaneous motion in unpaired image translation. In: Proceedings of the IEEE/CVF International Conference on Computer Vision, pp. 5923–5932 (2019)
36. Yang, S., Jiang, L., Liu, Z., Loy, C.C.: Pastiche master: exemplar-based high-resolution portrait style transfer. In: Proceedings of the IEEE/CVF Conference on Computer Vision and Pattern Recognition, pp. 7693–7702 (2022)
37. Yeh, R., Chen, C., Lim, T.Y., Hasegawa-Johnson, M., Do, M.N.: Semantic image inpainting with perceptual and contextual losses. arXiv preprint arXiv:1607.07539 2(3) (2016)
38. Zhang, Y., et al.: Data-driven synthesis of cartoon faces using different styles. IEEE Trans. Image Process. 26(1), 464–478 (2016)
39. Zheng, Z., Wang, C., Yu, Z., Wang, N., Zheng, H., Zheng, B.: Unpaired photo-to-caricature translation on faces in the wild. Neurocomputing 355, 71–81 (2019)
40. Zhu, J.Y., Park, T., Isola, P., Efros, A.A.: Unpaired image-to-image translation using cycle-consistent adversarial networks. In: Proceedings of the IEEE International Conference on Computer Vision, pp. 2223–2232 (2017)

Attribute Auxiliary Clustering for Person Re-Identification

Ge Cao and Kang-Hyun Jo[✉]

Department of Electrical, Electronic and Computer Engineering, University of Ulsan,
Ulsan 44610, Korea
{caoge,acejo}@ulsan.ac.kr

Abstract. The main objective of the person re-identification task is
to retrieve the specific identity under multiple non-overlapping camera
scenarios. Though unsupervised person re-ID has already achieved great
performance and even surpasses some classic supervised re-ID methods,
the existing methods pay much attention to training the neural networks
with the memory-based idea which ignore the quality of the generated
pseudo label. The quality of the clustering process does not only depend
on the intra-cluster similarity but also on the number of clusters. In this
paper, our approach employs an attribute auxiliary clustering method
for person re-ID task. The proposed method could divide the generated
cluster by the leveraged attribute label. Employed the attribute auxiliary
clustering, the task changed from unsupervised case to weakly supervised
case. The method is compared with state-of-the-art and analyzes the
effectiveness caused by the variation of the cluster number. The proposed
approach achieves great performance on the public Market-1501 datasets.

Keywords: Weakly supervised person re-identification · Attribute
auxiliary clustering · Cluster number variation

1 Introduction

The main objective of the person re-identification task is to retrieve the specific identity under multiple non-overlapping camera scenarios [1]. With the
increasing requirements for video surveillance and the urge for lower label anno-
tating costs, unsupervised person re-ID got more attention in the past few
years. For dealing with the unsupervised person re-ID task, purely unsupervised
re-ID [3,11,12,16,20] and the unsupervised domain adaptation are the widely
applied method [2,12,22,23].

In this paper, we focus on the purely unsupervised person re-ID task. The
state-of-the-art methods [3] extracted feature embedding through neural network [13] and then employed the clustering algorithms, DBSCAN [4] commonly
to generate the pseudo label for training samples. With the generated pseudo
label, we can train as a supervised case. Finally, a contrastive loss [27] is employed
for training. Though the existing method has already achieved great performance, it still didn't reach the upper bound of the baseline, where the upper

© The Author(s), under exclusive license to Springer Nature Singapore Pte Ltd. 2023
I. Na and G. Irie (Eds.): IW-FCV 2023, CCIS 1857, pp. 83–94, 2023.
https://doi.org/10.1007/978-981-99-4914-4_7

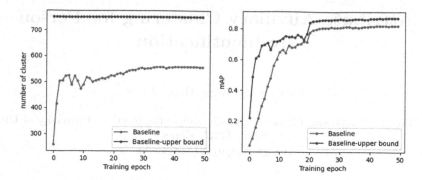

Fig. 1. The left and right subfigure shows the comparison of the number of clusters and performance between baseline and its upper bound (supervised), respectively.

bound means the performance when the clustering process gains the ideal results (Assuming the clustering results are completely correct). In Fig. 1, we show the comparison of the number of clusters and performance between the baseline ClusterContrast [3] and its upper bound (supervised). The left subfigure shows that even after the training finished, the clustering process could only divide the training samples into around 500 clusters which is much less than the ideal number of clusters. Correspondingly, when we can get the ideal clustering results the upper bound obviously surpasses the baseline by a large margin.

Fig. 2. Parts of clustering results selected from the final epoch's clustering results, where the samples of the same row are selected from the same cluster. Among them, the samples in the blue box and green box are captured from different identities. (Color figure online)

The result demonstrates that the unsupervised method has not achieved the ideal performance and the key reason lies in the low quality of clustering quality. Figure 2 displays parts of clustering results selected from the final epoch's clustering results, where the samples of the same row are selected from the same cluster. Among them, the samples in the blue box and green box are captured from different identities. The results show that the clustering could not recognize the highly similar vision features. But for human beings, we can easily find that the first four samples of the first row are captured from a male but the last four samples of the first row are captured from a female and in the same condition as the second row. In this paper, we generate the clustering results both in feature space and attribute space. The attributes of the identity annotate the sample at the semantic level. Our contribution could be summarized in three-fold:

- We leverage the attribute label and propose the attribute auxiliary clustering (AAC) method to explore the attribute auxiliary weakly supervised person re-ID task.
- The analysis of performance caused by cluster number variation is indicated in this paper.
- We comprehensively evaluate and compare the performance of AAC with state-of-the-art, which surpasses other weakly supervised person re-ID works.

2 Related Work

2.1 Unsupervised Person Re-ID Works

Despite the classic algorithm computing without deep learning, unsupervised person re-ID can be categorized into two situations. With the annotated label in the source domain, unsupervised domain adaptation (UDA) [2,12,22,23] methods are the first category. Among them, ECN [22] firstly applied the memory bank idea [19] to store the features and update with the training process. SpCL [12] proposed a novel self-paced contrastive learning framework that gradually creates a more reliable cluster, which to refine the memory dictionary features. The second category is purely unsupervised person re-ID (USL) [3,11,12,16,20] which only focuses on the target dataset and does not leverage any labeled data. MMCL [11] employed the memory bank in the USL field and calculated the pseudo label with similarity. CAP [16] applied the cluster method DBSCAN to generate the pseudo label and construct the memory bank at cluster-level and proxy-level (detailed in camera id). ClusterContrast [3] summarized the mainstream contrastive learning-based USL method and mainly focused on controlling the cluster size for consistency in the training process. The proposed AAC is based on the ClusterContrast framework, and due to the leveraging of the attribute label, AAC is exploring the re-ID field under the weakly supervised case.

2.2 Attribute Auxiliary Person Re-ID

Thanks to the work and attribute annotation by Lin et al. [25], researchers are easier to train and learn the identity embedding with auxiliary attributes.

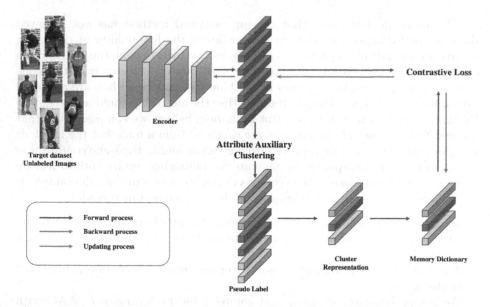

Fig. 3. The overview pipeline of the proposed method. The proposed attribute auxiliary clustering (AAC) method is applied for generating the pseudo label for the training samples. The ClusterNCE loss which is introduced in Eq. 1 is applied for the contrastive loss.

GPS [24] constructs the relationship graph for identity attribute and human body part, which could represent the unique signature of the identity. The graph-based signature can also be employed in unsupervised cases [18]. TJ-AIDL [17] simultaneously trains with attribute level and feature level to transfer attribute and identity label information to the target domain. The proposed AAC re-allocated the clustering results rather than applying the attribute for training in the attribute-semantic space.

3 Methodology

The pipeline for purely unsupervised person re-ID is described in Sect. 3.1, which includes the re-ID problem formulation and training strategy followed [3]. The proposed attribute auxiliary clustering method is demonstrated in Sect. 3.2.

3.1 USL Person Re-ID Pipeline

For the training process, given target dataset $X = \{x_1, x_2, ..., x_{N_t}\}$, we can extract discriminative feature embeddings $F = \{f_1, f_2, ..., f_{N_t}\}$ by the encoder network [13], where N_t denotes the number of training samples. The follow-up series of works employed for USL training is shown in Fig. 3. For the testing process, given query sample q and gallery samples $G = \{g_1, g_2, ..., g_{N_g}\}$, get the

Fig. 4. Parts of clustering results selected from the final epoch's clustering results, where the samples of the same row are selected from the same cluster. Among them, the samples in the blue box and red box are captured from different identities. (Color figure online)

feature embedding f_q and $\{f_{g_1}, f_{g_2}, ..., f_{g_2}\}$ from the trained encoder network, then calculate the similarity between f_q and f_g, and finally rank the list.

In the training process, after extracting feature embedding from the encoder network, we employ the classic clustering algorithm DBSCAN [4] for generating the pseudo labels for training samples, which are denoted as $\{y_1, y_2, ..., y_{N_t}\}$. This work applies the ClusterNCE loss followed ClusterContrast [3] as the contrastive loss:

$$L = -log \frac{exp(f_q \cdot \phi_+/\tau)}{\sum_{k=0}^{K} exp(f_q \cdot \phi_k/\tau)} \quad (1)$$

where ϕ_+ is the positive cluster representation vector of q, and ϕ_k is negative unique representation vector of the k-th cluster. The cluster representation ϕ_k is initialized by Eq. 2:

$$\phi_k = \frac{1}{|N_k|} \sum_{f_i \in N_k} f_i \quad (2)$$

where N_k is the set of samples in the k-th cluster, and it is verified as the encoder network trains in the process. During the training process, we select K samples in P clusters and construct the training minibatch. The cluster representation vectors are updated by:

$$\phi_k \leftarrow m\phi_k + (1 - m)q \quad (3)$$

where m is the momentum updating rate. And the above process followed [3] is framed as the baseline in this paper.

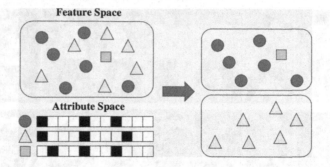

Fig. 5. Illustration of the proposed attribute auxiliary clustering (AAC) method. The samples in different shapes denote the sample captured from different identities. The samples are classified as the same cluster initially and re-clustered into the different clusters by applying AAC.

3.2 Attribute Auxiliary Clustering

Though baseline [3] has already gained state-of-the-art performance in the USL field, it still has plenty of space for improvement as shown in Fig. 1.

The Upper Bound of Baseline: The upper bound means that we get the completely correct clustering results in every epoch. Obviously, the existing technology cannot reach that case, so the upper bound would happen when we directly apply the ground truth of the training label. For the baseline-upper-bound, we divide the training samples into N_t clusters directly applying the GT, so it is under the supervised case. The results are shown in Fig. 1 and Table. 1, which surpasses the baseline by a large margin. Due to the great potential for improving the clustering quality, we leverage the attribute label $A = \{a_1, a_2, ..., a_{N_t}\}$ for fine-tuning the clustering results. Operating with the clustering results of the final epoch of the baseline, there are mainly two cases. The first case is shown in Fig. 2, where a cluster contains samples captured from two or more identities and the samples from each identity could be separately clustered. And another case is shown in Fig. 4, where a cluster contains many clusters but the samples from some identities are just one or two, which cannot be individually clustered.

The process of AAC is shown in Fig. 5, where the samples in different shapes denote the sample captured from different identities. The samples are classified as the same cluster initially and re-clustered into the different clusters by applying AAC.

In the training process, given the training samples $\{x_1, x_2, ..., x_{N_t}\}$ and corresponding attribute label $\{a_1, a_2, ..., a_{N_t}\}$, we extract the feature embedding $\{f_{g_1}, f_{g_2}, ..., f_{g_{N_t}}\}$ from the encoder network. Then DBSCAN [4] is employed for generating the pseudo labels $\{y_1, y_2, ..., y_{N_t}\}$. The samples which have the same pseudo labels y_i are classified as the same cluster and some clusters contain different attribute labels a_i. For the samples which are in the same cluster and the number of the samples with the same attribute label more than a threshold δ, we document their attribute label as $t_1, t_2, ..., t_K$, where K means the number of different attribute label in one cluster. The signal δ is set for avoiding generating some bad clusters with only a few samples which would be unbalanced distributed. So in the AAC algorithm, we will ignore the second case above.

We use the $y_i \rightarrow y_i'$ to denote the process that the training sample x_i should be re-clustered with new pseudo labels y_i':

$$y_i \rightarrow y_i'$$

$$s.t. \sum_{i=0, i \neq k}^{N_t} a_i \bigoplus t_k = 0 \tag{4}$$

The discussions of the threshold δ and the start epoch for applying the AAC method are introduced in the ablation study.

4 Experiments

4.1 Datsets and Implementation

Datasets. *Market-1501* [14] is a widely used public person re-ID dataset, which captured 12,936 samples with 751 identities in the training set, 3,368 and 15,913 samples captured from 750 identities for query and gallery set. The attribute label is provided by [25], which has 27 attributes for each training sample.

Implementation. The ResNet50 [13] pre-trained on ImageNet [21] is employed for the encoder network. Followed [3], the feature embedding is 2048-d extracted by a global average pooling, batch normalization, and the L2-normalization layer.

The input of the samples is resized to 128×256 and processed by random horizontal flipping, padding, random cropping, and random erasing. The batch size is equal to 256 (16 samples from each identity). Adam is applied for the optimizer with 5e–4 of the weight decay. The initial learning rate is 5.5e–4 and reduced to ten times smaller every 20 epochs in a total of 60 epochs.

The maximum distance is set to 0.6 and the minimal number of clusters is set to 4 for the DBSCAN setting. The threshold δ is set to 5. and from the first epoch, we start to apply the AAC method.

4.2 Comparison with State-of-the-Arts

We compare the proposed method with stat-of-the-arts. The method with attributes weakly supervised is few so we compare it with some SOTA USL papers. For Table 1, the 'Setting' means the training case they applied and 'Auxiliary' means whether any auxiliary information is leveraged. And the mAp, rank-1 score, rank-5 score, and rank-10 score of the proposed AAC method surpasses the baseline [3] by 3.9%, 2.0%, 0.4%, and 0.6%, respectively.

Table 1. Comparison results with the state-of-the-arts on Market-1501 [14] dataset. In the table, AAC denotes the proposed attribute auxiliary clustering algorithm by this paper, GT denotes the ground truth, and the signal † denotes the results are tested under the same implementation with the proposed idea. The best results are bold in this table. Additionally, the upper bound of the baseline is shown as the maximum limit of unsupervised work.

Method	Reference	Setting	Auxiliary	Market1501			
				mAP	rank-1	rank-5	rank-10
LOMO [5]	CVPR15	USL	None	8.0	27.2	41.6	49.1
BOW [6]	ICCV15	USL	None	14.8	35.8	52.4	60.3
UDML [7]	CVPR16	USL	None	12.4	34.5	52.6	59.6
DECAMEL [8]	TPAMI18	USL	None	32.4	60.2	76.0	81.1
TJ-AIDL [17]	CVPR18	Weakly	Attribute	26.5	58.2	74.8	81.1
DBC [10]	BMVC19	USL	None	41.3	69.2	83.0	87.8
BUC [9]	AAAI19	USL	None	38.3	66.2	79.6	84.5
MMCL [11]	CVPR20	USL	None	45.5	80.3	89.4	92.3
SpCL [12]	NeurIPS20	USL	None	73.1	88.1	95.1	97.0
GCL [20]	CVPR21	USL	None	66.8	87.3	93.5	95.5
CAP [16]	AAAI21	USL	Camera ID	79.2	91.4	96.3	97.7
A2G [15]	Access21	Weakly	Attribute	71.6	87.4	95.2	97.2
ClusterContrast† [3]	ACCV22	USL	None	82.1	92.3	96.9	97.6
AAC	This paper	Weakly	Attribute	**86.0**	**94.3**	**97.9**	**98.5**
Baseline-upper	This paper	Supervised	GT	87.2	95.0	98.3	99.1

Figure 6 shows the performance comparison and cluster number comparison among the baseline [3] (USL), AAC (weakly supervised), and baseline upper bound (supervised). The right subfigure shows that the performance of the proposed AAC surpasses the baseline a lot and is already close to the supervised upper bound. For the left subfigure which shows the cluster number variation with the training epoch, the cluster number increases very rapidly after applying AAC in some of the first epochs. It is caused by the poor clustering quality, as shown in Fig. 7, the clustering results of some of the first epochs are very bad for training, most clusters contain many samples captured from many identities. So when we apply the AAC idea with a small threshold δ, the cluster number would increase a lot and then decrease to the stable situation with the training.

4.3 Ablation Studies

In this section, we introduce the extended experiments about the starting epoch for applying the AAC method and the effectiveness contributed by a changed number of clusters. As shown in Fig. 7, the samples are mostly clustered into wrong pseudo labels, so it is necessary for exploring whether the AAC should be applied in the initial epoch. Table 2 demonstrates the performance when applying AAC in different start epochs with threshold $\delta = 10$, and Fig. 8 shows the

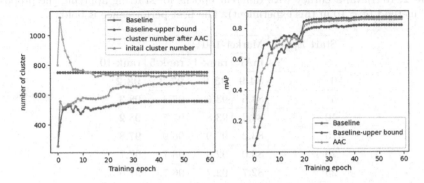

Fig. 6. The left subfigure shows the comparison of the number of clusters among the baseline, baseline upper bound (supervised), initial cluster number (before applying AAC), and cluster number after AAC (after applying AAC). The right subfigure shows the comparison of the mAP performance among the baseline, baseline upper bound, and the proposed AAC. The value of AAC is tested under the best performance.

Fig. 7. Parts of clustering results selected from the first epoch's clustering results, where the samples of the same row are selected from the same cluster. Among them, the samples are mostly clustered into the wrong pseudo-label.

Table 2. Retrieval accuracy with different epochs for starting applying the proposed AAC method ($\delta = 10$ in this experiment). The best performance is bold.

Start Epoch	Market-1501			
	mAP	rank-1	rank-5	rank-10
0	**84.9**	**93.6**	**97.3**	**98.2**
5	84.6	93.6	97.4	98.3
10	84.2	93.8	97.5	98.2
15	83.2	92.9	96.9	97.8
20	83.0	92.6	96.7	97.7
25	82.7	92.7	96.7	97.6
30	82.6	92.4	96.6	97.7
35	82.2	92.3	96.5	97.5
40	82.0	92.3	96.5	97.6

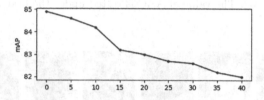

Fig. 8. The performance when applying AAC in different epochs.

performance when applying AAC with the different epochs. The results indicate that applying AAC during the training process achieves the best performance.

About the ablation study for the threshold δ, we test the performance from 4–10 for the Market-1501 dataset. The results do not have a linear pattern and we achieve the best performance with $\delta = 5$.

Discussions: The effectiveness of applying AAC from the first epoch is best because of the low inter-class variations which caused a low initial cluster number in the Market-1501 dataset (the cluster numbers of some of the first epochs are much smaller than the total identity number) (Table 3).

Table 3. Retrieval accuracy with different epochs for starting applying the proposed AAC method. The best performance is bold.

δ	Market-1501			
	mAP	rank-1	rank-5	rank-10
3	85.8	94.3	97.8	98.8
4	85.9	94.3	97.9	98.5
5	**86.0**	**94.2**	**97.6**	**98.4**
6	85.5	94.1	97.6	98.5
7	85.4	93.7	97.3	98.3
8	85.4	93.6	97.3	98.1
9	85.7	93.8	97.8	98.7
10	83.0	92.6	96.7	97.7

5 Conclusions

This paper proposes the attribute auxiliary clustering method for weakly supervised person re-identification work. It re-allocates the pseudo label for training samples and effectively improves the performance and convergence speed compared with the baseline. The experiments show that the proposed idea achieves state-of-the-art.

Acknowledgements. This result was supported by "Regional Innovation Strategy (RIS)" through the National Research Foundation of Korea(NRF) funded by the Ministry of Education(MOE)(2021RIS-003).

References

1. Ye, M., Shen, J., Lin, G., Xiang, T., Shao, L., Hoi, S.C.H.: Deep learning for person re-identification: a survey and outlook. arXiv e-prints (2020)
2. Song, L., et al.: Unsupervised domain adaptive re-identification: theory and practice. PR 1, 2 (2020)
3. Dai, Z., Wang, G., Yuan, W., Liu, X., Zhu, S., Tan, P.: Cluster contrast for unsupervised person re-identification. arXiv e-prints (2021)
4. Ester, M., Kriegel, H.-P., Sander, J., Xu, X., et al.: A density-based algorithm for discovering clusters in large spatial databases with noise. In: KDD (1996)
5. Liao, S., Hu, Y., Zhu, X., Li, S.Z.: Person re-identification by local maximal occurrence representation and metric learning, arXiv e-prints arXiv:1406.4216 (2014)
6. Zheng, L., Shen, L., Tian, L., Wang, S., Wang, J., Tian, Q.: Scalable person re-identification: a benchmark, pp. 1116–1124 (2015)
7. Peng, P., et al.: Unsupervised cross-dataset transfer learning for person reidentification. In: IEEE Conference on Computer Vision and Pattern Recognition (CVPR) 2016, pp. 1306–1315 (2016)
8. Yu, H., Wu, A., Zheng, W.: Unsupervised person re-identification by deep asymmetric metric embedding. IEEE Trans. Pattern Anal. Mach. Intell. **42**(4), 956–973 (2020)

9. Lin, Y., Dong, X., Zheng, L., Yan, Y., Yang, Y.: A bottom-up clustering approach to unsupervised person re-identification. In: Proceedings of the AAAI Conference on Artificial Intelligence, vol. 33, pp. 8738–8745 (2019)
10. Ding, G., Khan, S.H., Tang, Z.: Dispersion based clustering for unsupervised person re-identification. In: BMVC (2019)
11. Wang, D., Zhang, S.: Unsupervised person re-identification via multi-label classification. arXiv e-prints, arXiv:2004.09228 (2020)
12. Ge, Y., Zhu, F., Chen, D., Zhao, R., Li, H.: Self-paced contrastive learning with hybrid memory for domain adaptive object re-id. In: NeurIPS (2020)
13. He, K., Zhang, X., Ren, S., Sun, J.: Deep residual learning for image recognition. In: CVPR (2016)
14. Zheng, L., Shen, L., Tian, L., Wang, S., Wang, J., Tian, Q.: Scalable person re-identification: a benchmark. In: ICCV (2015)
15. Tang, G., Gao, X., Chen, Z., Zhong, H.: Graph neural network based attribute auxiliary structured grouping for person re-identification. IEEE Access (2021). https://doi.org/10.1109/ACCESS.2021.3069915
16. Wang, M., Lai, B., Huang, J., Gong, X., Hua, X.S.: Camera-aware proxies for unsupervised person re-identification. In: AAAI (2021)
17. Wang, J., Zhu, X., Gong, S., Li, W.: Transferable joint attribute-identity deep learning for unsupervised person re-identification. In: Proceedings of the IEEE Conference on Computer Vision and Pattern Recognition, pp. 2275–2284 (2018)
18. Cao, G., Tang, Q., Jo, K.: Graph-based attribute-aware unsupervised person re-identification with contrastive learning. In: International Workshop on Intelligent Systems (IWIS), Ulsan, Korea, Republic of 2022, pp. 1–6 (2022). https://doi.org/10.1109/IWIS56333.2022.9920894
19. Wu, Z., Xiong, Y., Yu, S., Lin, D.: Unsupervised feature learning via non-parametric instance-level discrimination. arXiv e-prints (2018)
20. Chen, H., Wang, Y., Lagadec, B., Dantcheva, A., Bremond, F.: Joint generative and contrastive learning for unsupervised person re-identification. arXiv e-prints (2020)
21. Deng, J., Dong, W., Socher, R., Li, L., Li, K., Li, F.-F.: Imagenet: a large-scale hierarchical image database. In: IEEE Conference on Computer Vision and Pattern Recognition 2009, pp. 248–255 (2009)
22. Zhong, Z., Zheng, L., Luo, Z., Li, S., Yang, Y.: Invariance matters: exemplar memory for domain adaptive person re-identification. arXiv e-prints, arXiv:1904.01990 (2019)
23. Fu, Y., Wei, Y., Wang, G., Zhou, Y., Shi, H., Huang, T.: Self-similarity grouping: a simple unsupervised cross domain adaptation approach for person re-identification. arXiv e-prints, arXiv:1811.10144 (2018)
24. Nguyen, B.X., Nguyen, B.D., Do, T., Tjiputra, E., Tran, Q.D., Nguyen, A.: Graph-based person signature for person re-identifications. In: IEEE/CVF Conference on Computer Vision and Pattern Recognition Workshops (CVPRW) 2021, pp. 3487–3496 (2021). https://doi.org/10.1109/CVPRW53098.2021.00388
25. Lin, Y., Zheng, L., Zhedong Zheng, Y.W., Zhilan, H., Yan, C., Yang, Y.: Improving person re-identification by attribute and identity learning. Pattern Recogn. **95**, 151–161 (2019)
26. Yu, H.-X., Zheng, W.-S., Wu, A., Guo, X., Gong, S., Lai, J.-H.: Unsupervised person re-identification by soft multilabel learning. arXiv e-prints arXiv:1903.06325 (2019)
27. van den Oord, A., Li, Y., Vinyals, O.: Representation learning with contrastive predictive coding. arXiv preprint arXiv:1807.03748 (2018)

YOLO5PKLot: A Parking Lot Detection Network Based on Improved YOLOv5 for Smart Parking Management System

Duy-Linh Nguyen⑩, Xuan-Thuy Vo⑩, Adri Priadana⑩,
and Kang-Hyun Jo⁽✉⁾⑩

Department of Electrical, Electronic and Computer Engineering, University of Ulsan,
Ulsan 44610, South Korea
{ndlinh301,priadana}@mail.ulsan.ac.kr, xthuy@islab.ulsan.ac.kr,
acejo@ulsan.ac.kr

Abstract. In recent years, the YOLOv5 network architecture has demonstrated excellence in real-time object detection. For the purpose of applying in the smart parking management system, this paper proposes a network based on the improved YOLOv5, named YOLO5PKLot. This network focus on redesigning the backbone network with a combination of the lightweight Ghost Bottleneck and Spatial Pyramid Pooling architectures. In addition, this work also resizes the anchors and adds a detection head to optimize parking detection. The proposed network is trained and evaluated on the Parking Lot dataset. As a result, YOLO5PKLot achieved 99.6% mAP on the valuation set with only fewer network parameters and computational complexity than others.

Keywords: Convolutional neural network (CNN) · Ghost Bottleneck · Smart parking management system · Parking lo detection · Parking lot dataset · YOLOv5

1 Introduction

Currently, there are about 1.45 billion cars in the world and it is increasing every year. The report in [18] predicts that in 2023 the number of vehicles sold is about 71 million units. The rapid increase both in the number and type of vehicles has led to the expansion of parking lots in supermarkets, shopping malls, city offices, etc. Automated operations to manage and distribute parking spaces are essential. For a long time ago, researchers and engineers have been designing automated parking management systems. These techniques are mainly based on various types of sensors to determine the status of parking spaces such as ultrasonic [19], infrared [5], geomagnetic [21], and wireless [20]. This type of parking usually requires the installation and maintenance of each sensor per parking space. Therefore, these methods increase the cost quite a lot when deployed in large-scale parking lots. In general, the sensing methods achieve high prediction but have a large cost. From the above analysis along with

© The Author(s), under exclusive license to Springer Nature Singapore Pte Ltd. 2023
I. Na and G. Irie (Eds.): IW-FCV 2023, CCIS 1857, pp. 95–106, 2023.
https://doi.org/10.1007/978-981-99-4914-4_8

the development of the computer vision field, this paper proposes a vision-based parking lot detection network. This work improves the famous object detection network YOLOv5 by focusing on redesigning the backbone network and adding a new detection head to increase the object detection ability. This network uses lightweight architectures in Ghost Bottleneck (Ghost) to greatly reduce network parameters and computational complexity, serving real-time applications on low-computing devices. The paper provides several main contributions as follows:

1 - A modified Ghost Bottleneck block is proposed to apply to the backbone of YOLOv5.

2 - Redesigns YOLOv5 backbone network with a combination of lightweight Ghost Bottleneck and Spatial Pyramid Pooling (SPP) architectures.

3 - Adds a detection head with new anchor sets to improve the prediction task.

The remainder of the paper is distributed as follows: Section 2 introduces the techniques related to parking lot detection. Section 3 details the proposed techniques. Section 4 presents and analyzes the experimental results. Section 5 concludes the issue and future development orientation.

2   Related Work

2.1   Traditional-Based Method

These methods are implemented through two main steps, feature extraction, and parking classification. The feature extraction process generates one or more feature vectors using traditional techniques. Specifically, [1,8] used Local Phase Quantization (LPQ) and Local Binary Patterns (LBP) as feature extractors and classifiers using Support Vector Machine (SVM). Later, the authors developed new methods based on the change of camera and parking areas [2,3]. [4] applies Quaternionic Local Ranking Binary Pattern (QLRBP) for feature extraction, Support Vector Machine (SVM), and k-nearest neighbors (k-NN) are used for classification. In [10] the LBP and the Histogram of Oriented Gradients (HOG) were used as feature extractors for the SVM classifier. The advantage of the above methods is that it is easy to implement, but the accuracy is not high.

2.2   Machine Learning-Based Method

With the remarkable development of object detection networks in the computer vision field, smart parking management systems are also developed based on popular networks. [9] refines the YOLOv3 architecture by adding residual blocks to the original network to improve feature extraction for parking classification. [6] designs a lightweight version of YOLOv3 with MobileNetV2 architecture to improve parking classification. A faster R-CNN two-stage detection network was applied in [15] with different camera angles and parking changes. [16,17] exploit the power of the Mask R-CNN network to extract individual cars and then classify parking conditions. Generative Adversarial Networks (GANs) are also used to directly detect occupancy and vacancies using drone imagery [14]. The advantage of machine learning methods is high detection and classification accuracy but requires networks to reach a certain depth and complexity to ensure operation in real parking conditions.

3   Methodology

Figure 1 details the proposed parking lot detection network. This network is refined based on the original YOLOv5 architecture [13] with three main modules: backbone, neck, and head.

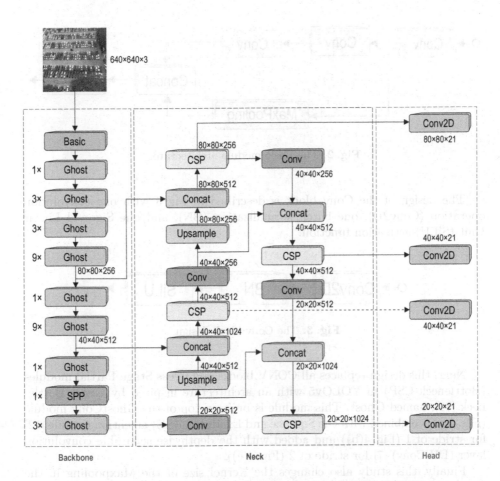

Fig. 1. The proposed parking lot detection network (YOLO5PKLot).

3.1 Proposed Network Architecture

The backbone module follows the design of the backbone in the YOLOv5 architecture, but this work changes a few essential modules. The techniques are applied to reduce a lot of the network parameters and computational complexity but still ensure good feature extraction. Specifically, the Focus module in YOLOv5 is replaced by the Basic module shown in Fig. 2. This module is designed with two main branches. One branch consists of 3 Conv blocks contiguously, the another branch is a Max pooling layer that is attached after the first Conv block in the first branch. The output feature maps from these two branches are concatenated and followed by another Conv block.

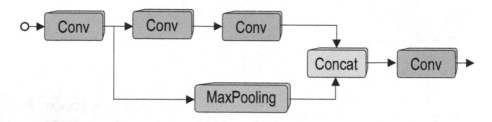

Fig. 2. The Basic module architecture.

The design of the Conv block is described in Fig. 3 with one convolution operation (Conv2D), one batch normalization (BN), and one Sigmoid Linear Unit (SiLU) activation function.

Fig. 3. The Conv block design.

Next, this design replaces all CONV blocks and Cross Stage Partial modules (Bottleneck CSP) in YOLOv5 with an architecture inspired by Ghost Bottleneck [11], named Ghost. This module is built on top of the GhostConv module (Fig. 4(a)) combined with the Squeeze and Excitation (SE) attention module [12] for stride of 1 (Fig. 4(b)) and added with the depthwise separable convolution layer (DWConv) [7] for stride of 2 (Fig. 4(c)).

Finally, this study also changes the Kernel size of the Maxpooling in the Spatial Pyramid Pooling (SPP) module from 5×5, 9×9, and 13×13 to 3×3, 5×5, and 7×7. The changed SPP module is shown as in Fig. 5.

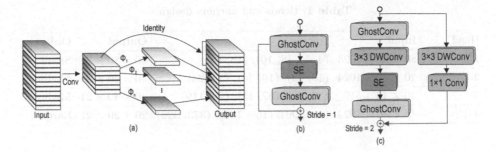

Fig. 4. (a) Ghost convolution, (b) Ghost Bottleneck module with the stride of 1, and (c) Ghost Bottleneck module with the stride of 2.

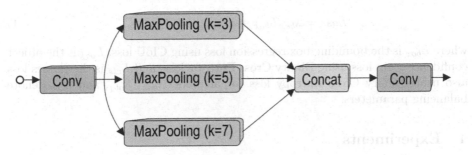

Fig. 5. The Spatial Pyramid Pooling (SPP) module.

The neck module still reuses YOLOv5's Path Aggregation Network (PAN) architecture to combine the current feature maps with previous feature maps in the first stage. Multi-scale feature maps are generated with enriched information. These are the input of the detection heads. The CONV block in this module is replaced by the new Conv described above.

The detection head module utilizes three heads from the YOLOv5 architecture with feature maps from PAN neck including $80 \times 80 \times 256$, $40 \times 40 \times 512$, and $20 \times 20 \times 1024$. To increase detection ability, this work adds a detection head at a feature map of size $40 \times 40 \times 1024$ in the early stage of the PAN module. The study also resizes all anchor sizes to be suitable for the size of the objects in the PKLot dataset. The details of the detection heads and the anchor's designs are shown in Table 1.

Table 1. Heads and anchors design.

Head	Input	Anchors	Output	Object
1	$80 \times 80 \times 1024$	(4, 5), (8, 10), (13, 16)	$80 \times 80 \times 21$	Small
2 (Added)	$40 \times 40 \times 1024$	(10, 13), (16, 30), (33, 23)	$40 \times 40 \times 21$	Medium
3	$40 \times 40 \times 512$	(30, 61), (62, 45), (59, 119)	$40 \times 40 \times 21$	Medium
4	$40 \times 40 \times 1024$	(116, 90), (156, 198), (373, 326)	$20 \times 20 \times 21$	Large

3.2 Loss Function

The loss function used in this paper is defined as follows:

$$Loss = \lambda_{box}L_{box} + \lambda_{obj}L_{obj} + \lambda_{cls}L_{cls} \tag{1}$$

where L_{box} is the bounding box regression loss using CIoU loss, L_{obj} is the object confidence score loss using Binary Cross Entropy loss, and L_{cls} is the classes loss also using Binary Cross Entropy loss to calculate. λ_{box}, λ_{obj}, and λ_{cls} denote balancing parameters.

4 Experiments

4.1 Dataset

This experiment uses the Parking Lot Dataset [8] to train and evaluate the performance of the proposed network. This dataset is proposed by authors from the Federal University of Parana. The PKLot dataset contains 12,416 high-resolution images (1280×720 px) extracted from cameras of three different parking lots. The images were taken in sunny, cloudy, and rainy day conditions. Parking spaces are labeled as occupied and empty classes. To perform the experiment, this dataset was split into three subsets: training (8,691 images), evaluation (2,483 images), and testing (1,242 images). To be adaptive to the training process, this work reduces the image size to 640×640 px and converts the standard PKLot dataset format to YOLOv5 format.

4.2 Experimental Setup

This study uses the original code of YOLOv5 [13] to generate modifications based on the Python programming language and the Pytorch framework. The proposed network is trained and evaluated on a GeForce GTX 1080Ti GPU. The Adam optimization is used. The learning rate is initially set to 10^2 and the final by 10^5. The momentum start at 0.8 and then increased to 0.937. The training process goes through 300 epochs with a batch size of 32. The balancing parameters $\lambda_{cls} = 0.5$, $\lambda_{box} = 0.05$, and $\lambda_{obj} = 1$, respectively. Several data augmentation methods are applied such as flip up-down, flip left-right, mixup, and mosaic.

4.3   Experimental Result

To evaluate the performance, this experiment performs training and evaluation from scratch YOLOv5 (n, s, m, l, x) versions and the proposed network. Besides, this work also compares with other previous networks that have been conducted on the PKLot dataset. As a result, the proposed network achieves 99.6% mean Average Precision (mAP) on IoU = 0.5 and 87.0 mAP on IoU = 0.5:0.95. The results shown in Table 2 demonstrate that the network outperforms previous networks with 4.9% mAP when compared to the best competitor (GAN in [14]). When compared with tiny versions of YOLOv5, the proposed network achieves comparable performance to YOLOv5s and YOLOv5n while the network parameter (4,155,700 parameters) is only half that of YOLOv5s and more than two times that of YOLOv5n. In terms of computational complexity, the YOLO5PKLot network is only 2.8 GFLOPs, the smallest of all the comparison networks. The qualitative results of the proposed network on the PKLot dataset are shown in Fig. 6.

Table 2. Comparison result of proposed detection network with retrained YOLOv5 and other networks on PKLot dataset.

Model	Parameter	Weight	GFLOPs	mAP@0.5	mAP@0.5:0.95	Inference
YOLOv5x	86,224,543	169.3 MB	204.2	99.7	99.3	203 ms
YOLOv5l	46,636,735	91 MB	114.3	99.7	99.1	159 ms
YOLOv5m	21,060,447	42.5 MB	50.4	99.7	98.0	125 ms
YOLOv5s	7,050,367	14.4 MB	15.3	99.6	97.0	114 ms
YOLOv5n	1,766,623	3.8 MB	4.2	99.6	93.8	?
YOLOv3 [9]	N/A	N/A	N/A	93.3	N/A	N/A
Faster R-CNN [15]	N/A	N/A	N/A	91.9	N/A	N/A
Mask R-CNN [16]	N/A	N/A	N/A	92.0	N/A	N/A
GAN [14]	N/A	N/A	N/A	94.7	N/A	N/A
YOLO5PKLot	4,155,700	8.6	2.8	99.6	87.0	3 ms

With the outstanding ability in calculation and parking detection as above mentioned, YOLO5PKLot can be applied in parking lot management systems with available low computing devices such as CPU and edge devices. However, during the testing, the YOLO5PKLot also revealed several weaknesses that made the accuracy decrease when detecting objects in bad weather conditions, the parking lot was obscured, the parking lot was far away from the camera, and different camera angles. Several detection mistakes are shown in Fig. 7.

Fig. 6. The qualitative results of the proposed network on the test set of PKLot dataset with IoU threshold = 0.5. The numbers denote the classes: 0 is space-empty, and 1 is space-occupied.

4.4   Ablation Study

Ablation study 1 conducted training and evaluation of proposed networks with backbone using the Ghost module combined with the SPP module as standard. Then replace the SPP with the Spatial Pyramid Pooling - Fast (SPPF) module and completely remove the SPP architectures for comparisons. The results in

Fig. 7. Several detection mistakes in parking lot detection. (a) The parking lots are at a far distance, (b) The parking lots are obscured from each other, and (c) The parking lots are obscured by other objects (trees).

Table 3 show that when only using the Ghost module, the network performance decreases by 0.2% mAP on IoU = 0.5. When using SPP and SPPF modules, the efficiency is similar at 99.6% mAP on IoU = 0.5 but SPPF is less than 0.05% mAP on IoU = 0.5:0.95.

Table 3. Ablation studies with different backbone designs on the PKLot dataset.

Module	Proposed network		
Ghost	✓	✓	✓
SPPF		✓	
SPP			✓
Parameter	3,635,615	4,155,700	4,155,70
Weight (MB)	7.6	8.6	8.6
GFLOPs	2.8	2.8	2.8
mAP@0.5	99.4	99.6	99.6
mAP@0.5:0.95	87.4	86.5	87.0

In another ablation study, this work compared the performance of three and four detection heads. From the results in Table 4, it can be seen that adding a detection head increases the detection ability by 0.1% mAP on IoU = 0.5. The network parameter increased slightly and the computational complexity remained the same at 2.8 GFLOPs.

Table 4. Ablation studies with different head numbers on the PKLot dataset.

Head	Parameter	Weight (MB)	GFLOPs	mAP@0.5
3	4,150,303	7.6	2.8	99.5
4	4,155,700	8.6	2.8	99.6

5 Conclusion

This paper presents a method to improve the YOLOv5 architecture for parking lot detection in smart parking management systems. The proposed network consists of three main parts: backbone, neck, and head modules. The backbone is redesigned using lightweight architectures to reduce network parameters and computational complexity. The neck is optimized with the addition of activation functions behind convolution operation and BN. The head module added a new detection head and resized the anchors to increase the detection performance of the network. In the future, this network will be further developed with attention modules to address the network's weaknesses when detecting far-distant parking spaces and adapting to different camera angles.

Acknowledgement. This result was supported by "Regional Innovation Strategy (RIS)" through the National Research Foundation of Korea (NRF) funded by the Ministry of Education (MOE) (2021RIS-003).

References

1. Almeida, P., Oliveira, L.S., Silva, E., Britto, A., Koerich, A.: Parking space detection using textural descriptors. In: 2013 IEEE International Conference on Systems, Man, and Cybernetics, pp. 3603–3608 (2013). https://doi.org/10.1109/SMC.2013.614

2. Lisboa de Almeida, P.R., Oliveira, L.S., de Souza Britto, A., Paul Barddal, J.: Naïve approaches to deal with concept drifts. In: 2020 IEEE International Conference on Systems, Man, and Cybernetics (SMC), pp. 1052–1059 (2020). https://doi.org/10.1109/SMC42975.2020.9283360

3. Almeida, P.R., Oliveira, L.S., Britto, A.S., Sabourin, R.: Adapting dynamic classifier selection for concept drift. Exp. Syst. Appl. **104**, 67–85 (2018). https://doi.org/10.1016/j.eswa.2018.03.021. https://www.sciencedirect.com/science/article/pii/S0957417418301611

4. Antoni Suwignyo, M., Setyawan, I., Wirawan Yohanes, B.: Parking space detection using quaternionic local ranking binary pattern. In: 2018 International Seminar on Application for Technology of Information and Communication, pp. 351–355 (2018). https://doi.org/10.1109/ISEMANTIC.2018.8549756

5. Chen, H.C., Huang, C.J., Lu, K.H.: Design of a non-processor OBU device for parking system based on infrared communication. In: 2017 IEEE International Conference on Consumer Electronics, ICCE-TW, Taiwan, pp. 297–298 (2017). https://doi.org/10.1109/ICCE-China.2017.7991113

6. Chen, L.-C., Sheu, R.-K., Peng, W.-Y., Wu, J.-H., Tseng, C.-H.: Video-based parking occupancy detection for smart control system. Appl. Sci. **10**, 1079 (2020). https://doi.org/10.3390/app10031079

7. Chollet, F.: Xception: deep learning with depthwise separable convolutions. In: Proceedings of the IEEE Conference on Computer Vision and Pattern Recognition (CVPR), July 2017

8. de Almeida, P.R., Oliveira, L.S., Britto, A.S., Silva, E.J., Koerich, A.L.: PKLot - a robust dataset for parking lot classification. Exp. Syst. Appl. **42**(11), 4937–4949 (2015). https://doi.org/10.1016/j.eswa.2015.02.009. https://www.sciencedirect.com/science/article/pii/S0957417415001086

9. Ding, X., Yang, R.: Vehicle and parking space detection based on improved yolo network model. J. Phys. Conf. Ser. **1325**, 012084 (2019). https://doi.org/10.1088/1742-6596/1325/1/012084

10. Dizon, C.C., Magpayo, L.C., Uy, A.C., Tiglao, N.M.C.: Development of an open-space visual smart parking system. In: 2017 International Conference on Advanced Computing and Applications (ACOMP), pp. 77–82 (2017). https://doi.org/10.1109/ACOMP.2017.29

11. Han, K., Wang, Y., Tian, Q., Guo, J., Xu, C., Xu, C.: GhostNet: more features from cheap operations. CoRR abs/1911.11907 (2019). arXiv:1911.11907

12. Hu, J., Shen, L., Sun, G.: Squeeze-and-excitation networks. CoRR abs/1709.01507 (2017), arXiv:1709.01507

13. Jocher, G., et al.: ultralytics/yolov5: v7.0 - YOLOv5 SOTA Realtime Instance Segmentation, November 2022. https://doi.org/10.5281/zenodo.7347926

14. Li, X., Chuah, M.C., Bhattacharya, S.: UAV assisted smart parking solution. In: 2017 International Conference on Unmanned Aircraft Systems (ICUAS), pp. 1006–1013 (2017). https://doi.org/10.1109/ICUAS.2017.7991353

15. Martín Nieto, R., García-Martín, Hauptmann, A.G., Martínez, J.M.: Automatic vacant parking places management system using multicamera vehicle detection. IEEE Trans. Intell. Transp. Syst. **20**(3), 1069–1080 (2019). https://doi.org/10. 1109/TITS.2018.2838128
16. Mettupally, S.N.R., Menon, V.: A smart eco-system for parking detection using deep learning and big data analytics. In: 2019 SoutheastCon, pp. 1–4 (2019). https://doi.org/10.1109/SoutheastCon42311.2019.9020502
17. Sairam, B., Agrawal, A., Krishna, G., Sahu, S.P.: Automated vehicle parking slot detection system using deep learning. In: 2020 4th International Conference on Computing Methodologies and Communication (ICCMC). pp. 750–755 (2020). https://doi.org/10.1109/ICCMC48092.2020.ICCMC-000140
18. Scotiabank: number of cars sold worldwide from 2010 to 2022, with a 2023 forecast (in million units). https://www.statista.com/statistics/200002/international-car-sales-since-1990/. Accessed 01 January 2023
19. Shao, Y., Chen, P., Cao, T.: A grid projection method based on ultrasonic sensor for parking space detection, pp. 3378–3381, July 2018. https://doi.org/10.1109/ IGARSS.2018.8519022
20. Yuan, C., Qian, L.: Design of intelligent parking lot system based on wireless network. In: 2017 29th Chinese Control And Decision Conference (CCDC), pp. 3596–3601 (2017). https://doi.org/10.1109/CCDC.2017.7979129
21. Zhou, F., Li, Q.: Parking guidance system based on ZigBee and geomagnetic sensor technology. In: 2014 13th International Symposium on Distributed Computing and Applications to Business, Engineering and Science, pp. 268–271 (2014). https:// doi.org/10.1109/DCABES.2014.58

Texture Synthesis Based on Aesthetic Texture Perception Using CNN Style and Content Features

Yukine Sugiyama[1]([⊠]), Natsuki Sunda[1], Kensuke Tobitani[1,2] (iD), and Noriko Nagata[1] (iD)

[1] Kwansei Gakuin University, Sanda, Hyogo 669-1337, Japan
{ggs53875,nagata}@kwansei.ac.jp, tobitani@sun.ac.jp
[2] University of Nagasaki, Nishi-Sonogi, Nagasaki 851-2195, Japan

Abstract. We propose a texture synthesis method that controls the desired visual impressions using CNN style features and content features. Diversifying user needs has led to the personalization of products according to individual needs. In the custom made garment service, users can select and combine fabrics, patterns, and shapes of garments prepared in advance to design garments that meet their tastes and preferences. Furthermore, controlling the visual impressions will enable the service to provide designs that better match the user's preferences. In image synthesis, controllable texture synthesis have been performed with style and content, however, few previous studies have controlled images based on impressions (including aesthetics). In this study, we aim to synthesize textures with desired visual impressions by using style and content features. For this purpose, we first (1) quantify the affective texture by subjective evaluation experiments and (2) extract style features and content features using VGG-19 from pattern images for which evaluation scores are assigned. The explanatory variables are style and content features, and the objective variables are evaluation scores. We construct an impression estimation model using Lasso regression for each of them. Next, (3) based on impression estimation models, we control the visual impressions and synthesize textures. In (2), we constructed highly accurate visual impression estimation models using style and content features. In (3), we obtained synthesis results that match human intuition.

Keywords: Impression · Style · Content · Lasso Regression

1 Introduction

In product design, there is a growing interest in visual impressions. Visual impressions refer to the impression evoked by the surface properties of materials and are considered important in evaluating the quality and desirability of a product. In addition, the customization and personalization of products are becoming more common as the Internet spreads and users need to diversify. One example is a custom made clothing service. In this service, users can design clothes according to their tastes by selecting and combining fabrics, patterns, and shapes of clothes prepared in advance. However, developing

© The Author(s), under exclusive license to Springer Nature Singapore Pte Ltd. 2023
I. Na and G. Irie (Eds.): IW-FCV 2023, CCIS 1857, pp. 107–121, 2023.
https://doi.org/10.1007/978-981-99-4914-4_9

a system that supports users in creating their original designs is necessary to promote further personalization. Yet, creating original designs is difficult for users who do not know design. This study proposes a method to automatically synthesize texture images based on the user's desired visual impressions information. These techniques will enable design support based on human preferences, satisfaction, and other emotional values.

2 Previous Research

Research on texture analysis and synthesis has been conducted for many years, and various texture features have been proposed [1–3]. Gatys et al. proposed an image transformation algorithm focusing on style features and content features extracted from VGG-19 [4], a convolutional neural network used for object recognition. The proposed method produces images in which the style image's style is transferred to the shape and structure of the objects depicted in the content image and shows highly accurate results. This study suggests that style features retain more color and pattern information in the image, while content features retain more shape information [5, 6].

In addition, although there are many studies that control for the aesthetics of texture such as preference and emotion [7–11], there are few studies that control for impressions (aesthetic concepts) such as "flashy" and "slim."

3 Proposed Method

In this study, we construct a model for estimating visual impressions using style and content features and synthesizing textures with the desired visual impressions' control. An overview of the proposed method is shown in Fig. 1. The first step is to extract style and content features from the pretrained middle layer of VGG-19. Next, we construct a visual impression evaluation model by formulating the relationship between the evaluation points assigned to the pattern image and the extracted style features and content features, respectively, using Lasso regression. Finally, based on the constructed model, style and content features are calculated and textures synthesized, which control visual impressions.

This enabled us to construct the model while suppressing overlearning, and to formulate the relationship between texture and impression. Textures were generated based on this relationship.

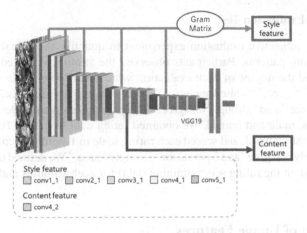

(a) Overview of feature extraction.

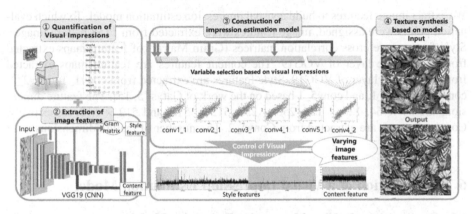

(b) Overall overview of the proposed method.

Fig. 1. Overview of the proposed method.

4 Quantification of Visual Impressions

4.1 Collection and Selection of Evaluation Terms

We collected and selected evaluation words related to the visual impressions evoked by the patterns. For the experimental method, we conducted free description and goodness of fit experiments based on the method of Tobitani [12]. Finally, a total of 10 evaluation words were selected for the subjective evaluation experiment: "cheerful," "bright," "colorful," "complex," "multilayered," "cool-looking," "free," "cute," "elegant," and "sophisticated" [13].

4.2 Subjective Evaluation Test

We conducted a subjective evaluation experiment to quantify the visual impressions evoked by clothing patterns. Participants observed the stimuli presented on an LCD monitor and rated the degree of each evaluation word on a 7point scale consisting of "strongly agree," "agree," "somewhat agree," "neither agree nor disagree," "somewhat disagree," "disagree," and "strongly disagree." The participants were undergraduate and graduate students, male and female. We obtained rating data from 5 to 10 persons per stimulus and per rating word, and scored each rating scale in 1-point increments, with -3 points for "strongly disagree" and 3 points for "strongly agree." We defined the calculated mean value based on the rating score (training data) for each stimulus and rating word [14].

5 Extraction of Image Features

We extract image features to build a visual impression estimation model. To which evaluation points were assigned, image features were extracted from 1158 pattern images. Style features are cross correlation matrices (Gram Matrix) of feature maps extracted from the middle layer of VGG19. The content features are feature maps extracted from the middle layer of VGG19. Style features are extracted from conv1_1, conv2_1, conv3_1, conv4_1, and conv5_1 based on the work of Gatys [5, 15]. The feature dimensions are 64×64, 128×128, 256×256, 512×512, and 512×512, respectively. Content features are extracted from Conv4_2. The number of feature dimensions is $28 \times 28 \times 512$.

6 Construction of a Visual Impression Estimation Model

6.1 Construction of a Visual Impression Estimation Model

We formulate the relationship between visual impressions and style and content features. Lasso regression is used in the formulation. Lasso regression is a penalized regression model in which the L1 regularization term is used to construct a regression model while preventing overlearning by setting the unselected variables to 0. Lasso regression is chosen (or used) because the explanatory variables are high dimensional, and excessive learning is expected. The penalty parameter of Lasso regression is the value obtained when K-split cross validation minimizes the mean squared error. K = 11 by Sturges' rule. Objective variables are the evaluation points, explanatory variables are style features and content features, and Lasso regression is used to construct visual impressions' evaluation models.

6.2 Results and Discussion

The determination coefficients for each model are shown in Tables 1 and 2. In the model using style features, the average coefficient of determination of the five models was more than 0.5 for seven out of ten words, confirming that a highly accurate visual impressions evaluation model could be constructed. In Table 2, the coefficient of determination was 0.5 or higher for 9 out of the 10 words. For the words with low coefficients of determination, "free," "elegant," and "refined," the variation of evaluation scores is slight (Fig. 2). This means that the relationship between visual impressions and image characteristics cannot be modeled precisely. Therefore, in the following texture synthesis, we will perform texture synthesis for the seven words, excluding these evaluation words.

Table 1. Coefficients of determination for impression estimation models.

(a) Coefficients of determination for impression estimation models constructed using style features.

evaluation term	conv1_1	conv2_1	conv3_1	conv4_1	conv5_1	average
cheerful	0.582	0.699	0.628	0.694	0.648	0.650
bright	0.711	0.784	0.760	0.801	0.695	0.750
colorful	0.330	0.565	0.608	0.695	0.603	0.560
complex	0.229	0.530	0.543	0.623	0.642	0.513
multilayered	0.167	0.488	0.570	0.673	0.661	0.512
cool-looking	0.699	0.775	0.776	0.809	0.716	0.755
free	0.172	0.386	0.408	0.487	0.332	0.357
cute	0.372	0.550	0.501	0.568	0.549	0.508
elegant	0.229	0.317	0.393	0.460	0.411	0.362
sophisticated	0.138	0.198	0.212	0.305	0.393	0.249

(b) Coefficients of determination for impression estimation models constructed using content features.

evaluation term	conv4_2
cheerful	0.713
bright	0.803
colorful	0.728
complex	0.800
multilayered	0.832
cool-looking	0.887
free	0.616
cute	0.692
elegant	0.554
sophisticated	0.371

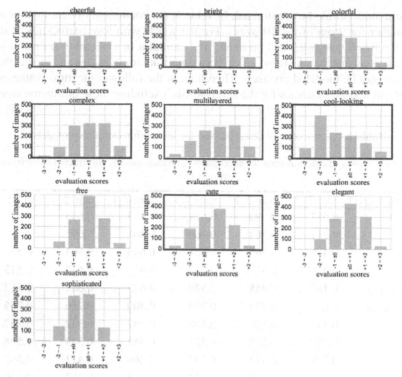

Fig. 2. Distribution of evaluation points (vertical axis: number of images, horizontal axis: evaluation points).

7 Texture Synthesis

7.1 Method

Based on the model constructed in Sect. 6, style features and content features with controlled visual impressions are calculated, and textures are synthesized. The texture synthesis process is completed in five different steps. (i) Extract style features and content features from the input image. (ii) Exaggerate the extracted image features. Equation 1. Does the control The extracted image features are denoted as $P\_original$, the regression coefficients obtained by building the model are transformed to fit the shape of the image features as $\hat{\omega}lasso$ and the weights are denoted as S. (iii) Style and content features are extracted from the output images. (iv) Calculate the errors of style features and content features from the features of input and output images. Hereafter, the error of the style feature is denoted as style loss (L_style) and that of the content feature as content loss ($L\_content$). (v) The sum of style loss plus weight α and content loss plus weight β is denoted as L_total. Update the output image to minimize Eq. (2) L_total. Iterate (iii) to (v) up to 300 times.

The image features are controlled by Eq. 1. By applying the weight parameter S to the regression coefficients of the Lasso regression, the part of the image for which no variable is selected is kept at 0, and only the values for the part of the image strongly related to the affective texture are changed.

$$P\_controlled = P\_original \times (1 + \hat{\omega} lasso \times S) \tag{1}$$

$$L\_total = \alpha \times L\_style + \beta \times L\_content \tag{2}$$

As for the content features, since the total number of variables selected by this method was small, we added variables by entering values 0.8 times the selected coefficient of determination for variables with a high correlation (correlation coefficient of 0.8 or higher) with the selected variables.

7.2 Results

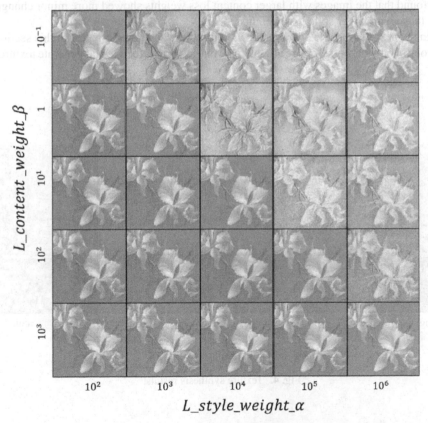

Fig. 3. Synthesized results with varying weights α and β for the evaluation word "cheerful."

The results of synthesized images by varying weights α and β are shown in Fig. 3. The input image size was set to 224×224, and $S = 10$ for the control of style features and $S = 10^4$ for the control of content features. These images are shown to change in accordance with changes in the α and β weights.

Next, we observe the changes in the image when one of the values of α and β is fixed. First, Fig. 4(a) shows the case where $\alpha = 10^6$ and $\beta = 1$, and the style loss weights increase. In the case of "cheerful," the entire image is yellowish (Fig. 4(b)). In the case of "bright," the brightness seems to have increased, and in the case of "colorful," the saturation seems to have increased, respectively, as appropriate. The image in the "cool-looking" group was tinted a bluish hue (Fig. 4(c)). In addition, "complex" emphasized the veins of leaves (Fig. 4(d)), and "multilayered" emphasized shadows and other elements to give a visual impression of depth (Fig. 4(e)). In the "Cute" group, the brightness was increased while the saturation was decreased, giving the image a pastel tone.

On the other hand, Fig. 4(d) shows the case where the content loss weights are increased to $\alpha = 1$ and $\beta = 10^6$. Changes in texture were observed in the "complex" and "multilayered" cases. In both cases, shading is emphasized, and light areas are especially emphasized in the "multilayered" case. However, for the evaluation terms in general, it was found that the images with larger content loss weights showed more minor changes than those with larger style loss weights.

In the next section, we examine the validity of the generated images. In this section, we control only the style features found to be particularly effective and generate textures.

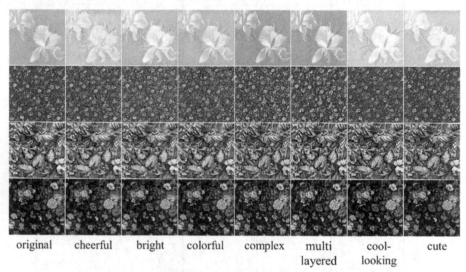

| original | cheerful | bright | colorful | complex | multi layered | cool- looking | cute |

(a) Synthesized results for a=10⁶, ß=1.

Fig. 4. Texture synthesis results.

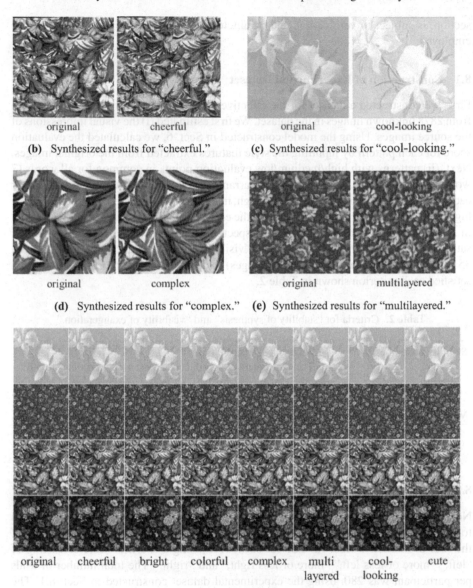

(b) Synthesized results for "cheerful."   (c) Synthesized results for "cool-looking."

(d) Synthesized results for "complex."   (e) Synthesized results for "multilayered."

(f) Synthesized results for a=1, ß=10⁶.

Fig. 4. (*continued*)

8   Verification

This section quantitatively verifies whether the emotional quality evoked by the synthesized images is significantly improved compared to the original images. In this section, only the control of style features, which showed appropriate changes in the previous section, is subject to verification, and parameters of $\alpha = 10^6$, $\beta = 1$, and $S = 10$ are employed.

8.1 Construction of Experimental Dataset

First, we constructed a dataset for the effectiveness experiment. Stimuli were selected from 2878 unknown images in the dataset. We first estimated (i) the visual impressions of the source images. Using the model constructed in Sect. 6, we calculated the evaluation score for each pattern by inputting the style features extracted from the original images. Next, (ii) patterns with high/medium/low evaluation points in common for all words (7 words) were extracted. The patterns were arranged in the order of the highest score for each word and divided into three groups: high, medium, and low. Then, the patterns in the high, medium, and low rank groups for all the evaluation terms were extracted, resulting in 51, 7, and 14 patterns in this order, respectively. Finally, we selected patterns that satisfied (iii) "stability of synthesis" and "visibility of exaggeration." We synthesized 35 images (5 times for 7 words = 35 images) and selected 10 patterns as stimuli that satisfied each criterion shown in Table 2.

Table 2. Criteria for "stability of synthesis" and "visibility of exaggeration."

Stability of synthesis	· No image is blacked out · The same quality is produced at least 4 out of 5 times for all words · The structure of the pattern is established
Visibility of exaggeration	· The change is easy to see compared to the original image

8.2 Effectiveness Verification Experiment

Next, we conducted an effect verification experiment. Participant participants were asked to observe the stimulus pairs presented on an LCD monitor and to answer which of the four evaluation words was true for each word using a fourtrial scale consisting of "left," "more or less left," "more or less right," and "right." The total number of trials per participant was 280, using the experimental dataset constructed in Sect. 8.1. The participants were 10 undergraduate and graduate students (5 males and 5 females, aged 23.3 ± 1.19 years). To eliminate the influence of the order effect, the order in which the stimulus pairs were presented was randomized for each participant, and the order of the evaluation words was randomized for each trial.

8.3 Results and Discussion

The validity of this method was verified by conducting a statistical analysis of the data obtained in Sect. 8.2 and obtaining the psychological scale values. Multiple comparisons were conducted using the yardstick method to evaluate whether there was a statistically significant difference between each stimulus. As a result, we confirmed that the psycho-metric values of the synthesized images with exaggerated visual impressions qualities were significantly higher than those of the original images in the proportions shown in Table 3. The changes in the psychological scale values are shown in Fig. 5.

Table 3. Percentage of patterns with significantly increased psychological scale values.

Exaggerated visual impressions	$p <. 01(**)$	$p <. 05(*)$
cheerful	0. 7	0. 8
bright	0. 7	0. 8
colorful	0. 1	0. 1
complex	0. 3	0. 4
multilayered	0. 3	0. 4
cool-looking	0. 9	0. 9
cute	0. 0	0. 0

The three words "cheerful," "bright," and "cool-looking" significantly increased the psychometric scale values for most patterns. Since these are low order visual impressions qualities perceived from color information, they varied regardless of the pattern's taste. The psychometric values of "complex" and "multilayered" patterns increased significantly in about half of the patterns. The patterns that showed a significant increase were those with delicate patterns, and the lines became thicker and more three dimensional according to the patterns. On the other hand, the patterns with larger scales did not show such changes, which may explain the non-significance of the results.

Next, the psychological scale value of "colorful" increased for most patterns but was non-significant for all of them. One of the reasons for this is that the degree of change was smaller than the other words. At the present stage, the weight parameter in Eq. 7.4 is unified as $S = 10$ for all words, but for "colorful," we confirmed that the degree of change approaches the other words by setting a more significant value of S (Fig. 6). Therefore, further study is needed to adjust the parameters.

Additionally, none of the patterns significantly increased in the "cute" category, and half of the patterns significantly decreased in the "cute" category. One of the possible reasons for this is the influence of the original images. It is assumed that patterns with low saturation in the original images are faced with a decrease in saturation, and the balance of the color scheme perceived as "cute" is lost. Furthermore, since "cute" is a higher order sensory quality consisting of various elements, it is also considered affected by individual differences. Therefore, we conducted a factor analysis of each participant's psychological scale of "cute" for each image. Due to the factor analysis, three factors were extracted, with a cumulative contribution rate of 60.2%. Table 4 shows the factor loadings matrix after rotation, and Table 5 shows the factor correlation matrix.

118   Y. Sugiyama et al.

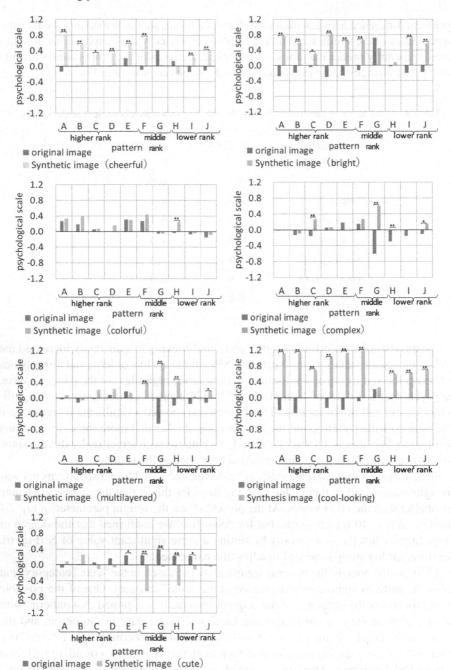

Fig. 5. Change in psychological scale values.

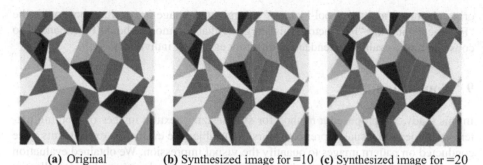

(a) Original   (b) Synthesized image for =10   (c) Synthesized image for =20

Fig. 6. Comparison of different values of the magnification parameter in "Colorful."

Table 4. Factor loadings matrix after rotation.

participant	factor		
	F1	F2	F3
No. 1	1.178	−0.322	0.013
No. 9	0.704	0.240	−0.168
No. 7	0.550	0.285	0.031
No. 8	0.502	0.326	0.022
No. 10	0.462	0.061	0.403
No. 5	0.034	0.784	0.075
No. 6	0.175	0.655	−0.086
No. 2	−0.159	0.536	0.073
No. 4	−0.062	−0.036	0.853
No. 3	−0.013	0.155	0.542

Table 5. Factor correlation matrix.

factor	F1	F2	F3
F1	1	0. 665	0. 494
F2	0. 665	1	0. 466
F3	0. 494	0. 466	1

Comparing the factor scores for each image revealed that participants had different evaluation tendencies with each factor. Participants with the "F2" factor tended to rate "cute" highly for the synthesized images with "cheerful" and "bright" exaggerated. Participants with the "F3" factor tended to rate the original and synthesized images with the exaggerated "colorful" highly. Participants with the "F1" factor tended to rate the original image, and the "cool-looking" exaggerated image lower than those with the "F2" factor and the "F3" factor. This suggests that the model should be expanded to consider future evaluation tendencies differences among individuals.

9 Conclusion

In this study, we proposed a method for synthesizing texture images of clothing patterns with desired visual impressions. First, (1) subjective evaluation experiments were conducted on pattern images to quantify the visual impression. We obtained evaluation scores for 10 words that express the visual impressions for the image dataset collected from floral patterns. Next, (2) style and content features were extracted from the pattern images used in the subjective evaluation experiment using the pretrained VGG19. Then, we constructed a visual impressions evaluation model by formulating the relationship between the quantified visual impressions, the extracted style features, and the content features using regression. As a result, we could model visual impressions with high accuracy while selecting features that are mainly strongly related to visual impressions. Finally, (3) based on the obtained model, we calculated the image features when the desired visual impressions quality is exaggerated and synthesized images by optimizing the model to minimize the error between the features and the original images. (4) To verify the validity of the proposed method, we synthesized unknown images with the desired exaggerated visual impressions. It was found that the changes in the images synthesized using the content features were smaller than those synthesized using the style features. In addition, the experiment demonstrated the method's effectiveness in which the emotional quality evoked by the synthesized images was significantly improved compared to the original images.

As future research topics, we will extend the model to a higher order visual impression consisting of various elements, such as "cute," to consider individual differences. In addition, we will quantitatively verify the degree to which the degree of exaggeration of the visual impressions quality changes by adjusting the weight parameters set when changing the style features according to the taste of the words and patterns.

References

1. Julesz, B.: Textons, the elements of texture perception, and their interactions. Nature **290**(5802), 91–97 (1981)
2. Portilla, J., Simoncelli, E.P.: A parametric texture model based on joint statistics of complex wavelet coefficients. Int. J. Comput. Vision **40**(1), 49–70 (2000)
3. Tobitani, K., Shiraiwa, A., Katahira, K., Nagata, N., Nikata, K., Arakawa, K.: Modeling of "high-class feeling" on a cosmetic package design. J. Jpn. Soc. Precis. Eng. **87**(1), 134–139 (2021)
4. Simonyan, K., Zisserman, A.: Very deep convolutional networks for large-scale image recognition (2014). arXiv preprint arXiv:1409.1556
5. Gatys, L.A., Ecker, A.S., Bethge, M.: Image style transfer using convolutional neural networks. In: Proceedings of the IEEE Conference on Computer Vision and Pattern Recognition (CVPR), pp. 2414–2423 (2016)

6. Wang, P., Li, Y., Vasconcelos, N.: Rethinking and improving the robustness of image style transfer. In: Proceedings of the 2021 IEEE/CVF Conference on Computer Vision and Pattern Recognition (CVPR), pp. 124–133. IEEE, Nashville (2021)
7. Yu, N., Barnes, C., Shechtman, E., Amirghodsi, S., Lukac, M.: Texture mixer: a network for controllable synthesis and interpolation of texture. In: Proceedings of the IEEE/CVF Conference on Computer Vision and Pattern Recognition (CVPR), pp. 12164–12173 (2019)
8. Li, Y., Fang, C., Yang, J., Wang, Z., Lu, X., Yang, M.: Diversified texture synthesis with feed-forward networks. In: Proceedings of the IEEE Conference on Computer Vision and Pattern Recognition (CVPR), pp. 3920–3928 (2017)
9. Yang, S., Wang, Z., Wang, Z., Xu, N., Liu, J., Guo, Z.: Controllable artistic text style transfer via shape-matching GAN. In: Proceedings of the IEEE/CVF International Conference on Computer Vision (ICCV), pp. 4442–4451 (2019)
10. Chen, H., et al.: DualAST: dual style-learning networks for artistic style transfer. In: Proceedings of the IEEE/CVF Conference on Computer Vision and Pattern Recognition (CVPR), pp. 872–881 (2021)
11. Rombach, R., Blattmann, A., Lorenz, D., Esser, P., Ommer, B.: High-resolution image synthesis with latent diffusion models. In: Proceedings of the IEEE/CVF Conference on Computer Vision and Pattern Recognition (CVPR), pp. 10684–10695 (2022)
12. Tobitani, K., Matsumoto, T., Tani, Y., Fujii, H., Nagata, N.: Modeling of the relation between impression and physical characteristics on representation of skin surface quality. J. Inst. Image Inf. Telev. Eng. 71(11), 259–268 (2017)
13. Mori, T., Uchida, Y., Komiyama, J.: Relationship between visual impressions and image information parameters of color textures. J. Jpn. Res. Assoc. Text. End-uses 51(5), 433–440 (2010)
14. Sunda, N., Tobitani, K., Tani, I., Tani, Y., Nagata, N., Morita, N.: Impression estimation model for clothing patterns using neural style features. In: Proceedings of the Springer International Conference on Human-Computer Interaction, pp. 689–697 (2020)
15. Takemoto, A., Tobitani, K., Tani, Y., Fujiwara, T., Yamazaki, Y., Nagata, N.: Texture synthesis with desired visual impressions using deep correlation feature. In: 2019 IEEE International Conference on Consumer Electronics (ICCE), pp. 1–2. IEEE, Las Vegas (2019)

Robust Scene Text Detection Under Occlusion via Multi-scale Adaptive Deep Network

My-Tham Dinh, Minh-Trieu Tran, Quang-Vinh Dang, and Guee-Sang Lee(✉) ⓘ

Department of Artificial Intelligence Convergence, Chonnam National University, Gwangju, South Korea
gslee@jnu.ac.kr

Abstract. Detecting text under occlusion in natural images is a challenge in scene text detection, which is severely sensitive and dramatically affects the performance of this field. Despite several research papers discussing the issue of occluded text in natural images, they still struggle to accurately identify word regions that are split by occlusion phenomena. In this paper, we first exploit the salient attention maps from Gradient Class Activation Maps Plus Plus (Grad-CAM++) to obtain knowledge of the important regions in the images. Furthermore, to effectively capture the different scales of text instances and enhance feature representations, we create a MulTi-scale adaptive Deep network (MTD). In addition, from ICDAR 2015 benchmark, we build occluded text, namely Realistic Occluded Text Detection dataset (ROTD), and then combine a part of ROTD dataset with the ICDAR 2015 dataset for the training stage to gain occluded text perception. Throughout these works, our model significantly improves the accuracy of text detection containing partially occluded text in natural scenes. Our proposed method achieves state-of-the-art results on partial occlusion text detection with F1-score of 69.6% on ISTD-OC, 78.7% on our ROTD, and validates competitive performance F1-score of 82.4% on ICDAR 2015 benchmark.

Keywords: Scene Text Detection · Occluded Text · Deep Learning

1 Introduction

With the development of deep learning, scene text detection [1–6], scene text segmentation [27, 29, 32], scene text recognition [31], and text spotting [30] have many achievements in scene text reading. As a key prior component of this field, text detection in natural scenes has played an essential role in computer vision, signal, and image processing. However, due to the variety of orientations, shapes, or sizes, it is still a challenging task, although many existing methods have achieved noticeable breakthroughs [1–6, 9, 11–15, 17–19]. For example, DBNet++ [2] achieves consistently state-of-the-art accuracy and speed on five benchmarks of scene text detection. Furthermore, TextPMs [3] obtains state-of-the-art performance in terms of detection accuracy both on polygonal and on quadrilateral datasets.

Unlike the previous prevalent problems in scene text detection, few researchers work on addressing partially occluded text problems [7, 8, 10], which can significantly

© The Author(s), under exclusive license to Springer Nature Singapore Pte Ltd. 2023
I. Na and G. Irie (Eds.): IW-FCV 2023, CCIS 1857, pp. 122–134, 2023.
https://doi.org/10.1007/978-981-99-4914-4_10

affect detection performance. For instance, [7] is detection and recognition task that can also achieve effective detection by restoring missing text. However, this method only assumes to detect text with few character-based distortion. Besides, in [8], the main task is to create ISTD-OC text occlusion dataset, involving different occlusion levels (from 0% to 100%), and evaluates the efficiency of state-of-the-art deep learning frameworks on ISTD-OC. Nevertheless, these frameworks are sensitive to occlusions and fail on text regions detection with text bounding boxes splitting by the occlusion phenomena, as in Fig. 1.

a) Failure examples text instances detection
by previous method

b) Solved failure cases by our proposed method

Fig. 1. Several examples of failure text detection with text bounding boxes splitting by the occlusion phenomena of previous deep network architectures (a), and solved by our method (b) on ISTD-OC dataset.

In this paper, we design an approach to address this problem more efficiently. We apply a transfer learning Guided Grad-CAM++ Attention maps relying on Grad-CAM++ pre-trained on ImageNet [15] to obtain salient text regions. In addition, we give more robust feature representations with various sizes by exploring MTD. Our core contributions are as follows:

- We take advantage of the pre-trained from Grad-CAM++ from ImageNet [15] to gain the Guided Attention salient maps as one kind of specific information for training process, after that, we transfer the attention knowledge to our text detection under occluded text task.
- Our model MTD enhances both receptive fields by obtaining diverse scales and feature representation capability by learning multi-level information of features. Additionally, we adopt CBAM attention to improve the channel and spatial awareness abilities. Hence, our method is able to get richer feature representations.
- We also build our own occluded dataset ROTD based on ICDAR 2015 benchmark and combine only 10% as experimental results in Fig. 6 with the original one during training phase to learn more efficiently and accurately about occluded text awareness.

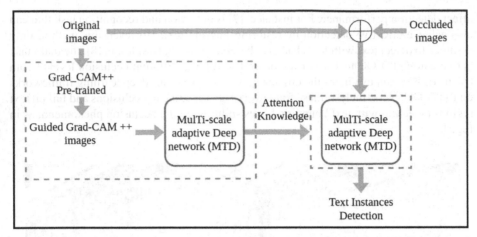

Fig. 2. This figure illustrates the overall architecture of the proposed method. Our approach includes three steps: Firstly, applying Guided Grad-CAM++ Attention maps for training process, next, transferring the learning knowledge to the main task, and finally, predicting text instances detection under occlusion.

2 Related Work

2.1 Scene Text Detection

Text detectors in natural images have achieved many remarkable results by many methods. Most of them are roughly divided into two phases, regression-based, and segmentation-based.

In the first category, several impressed research employed regression-based method [3, 13, 17, 18, 20] that regresses directly bounding boxes of the text instances. EAST [13] could predict score maps from the fully convolutional network and multi-oriented text instances. Similarly, Deep-Reg [18] designed a per pixel-regression approach to detect multi-oriented tasks. However, it can be noted that these models are inadequate to cope with the occluded text challenge.

Additionally, another attractive method is segmentation-based [1–6, 11, 12, 14, 19] that usually locates text regions following pixel-level prediction with post-processing algorithms. A progressive scale expansion algorithm is exploited in PSENet [11] to expand the detection areas with whole text instances. PAN [1] detected scene text instances and tackled overlap problem by clustering and aggregating text pixels by predicted similarity vectors.

2.2 Occluded Text Detection

Partially occluded text in scene images, which may threaten prediction accuracy, is still a difficult challenge in scene text detection. [8] proved that several models from PAN [1], PSENet [11], CRAFT [12], and EAST [13] are still ineffective in detecting occluded text instances. In the same way, [7] handled the missing text issue by inheriting the strength of the characteristic Discrete Cosine Transform. Nevertheless, these methods have still failed significantly on text instances with text bounding boxes splitting by the occlusion phenomena. Therefore, this paper refines the capability of occlusion perception for scene text detection.

Fig. 3. Visualization of attention maps: Grad-CAM++ and Guided Grad-CAM++ from ICDAR 2015 images.

3   Methodology

Our overall architecture is illustrated in Fig. 2. Firstly, we create Guided Grad-CAM++ maps from pre-trained of Grad-CAM++ [15] on ImageNet [26] as in Fig. 3, which focus on attention information and mitigate complex backgrounds. By learning attention information in scene images, our approach can capture the spatial context of text instances. And then, passing them over MTD as shown in Fig. 4, including a ResNet18 [22] backbone, CBAM attention [16], a Multi-scale FEN (MFEN) [14], and features fusion. Due to the robustness of learning both extracted features with different scales and multi-level information features with less computation, our model enlarges the receptive fields and enhances the feature representation capabilities. After that, we follow as a PAN postprocessing [1] of prediction network to detect bounding boxes of text instances as in Fig. 4. Finally, transferring the learning attention knowledge of Guided Grad-CAM++ maps to the main task: Text detection containing occluded text. To help our model understand apparently occlusion knowledge from occluded images, we also employ a novel realistic occluded dataset (ROTD) by the OpenCV tool in Algorithm 1 and fuse a few ROTD images combined with the original ICDAR 2015 benchmark for training in the main phase.

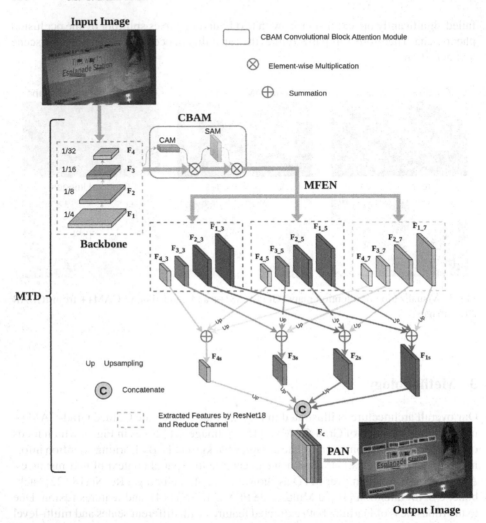

Fig. 4. Illustration of our proposed MTD network for occluded scene text detection.

3.1 Transfer Learning Knowledge from Guided Grad-CAM++ Attention

Gradient Class Activation Maps Plus Plus (Grad-CAM++) [15] improves the localization of both single, multiple instances, and produced perfect results for object classification and localization in the current state-of-the-art methods. Guided Grad-CAM++ Attention is carried out pointwise multiplication by salient maps of Grad-CAM++ with pixel-space visualization by Guided Backpropagation. Therefore, to learn the important context in features, we apply pre-trained Grad-CAM++ on ImageNet [26] to obtain those salient maps containing the attention knowledge, then through them to MTD to get the valuable knowledge on ICDAR 2015. After that, transfer these weights to our main task: scene text detection under occlusion in scene images.

3.2 Multi-scale Adaptive Deep Network

As illustrated in Fig. 4, the input image (736x736) is fed into the feature extraction by ResNet18 [22] with pixel ratios $\frac{1}{4}, \frac{1}{8}, \frac{1}{16}, \frac{1}{32}$ corresponding to F_1, F_2, F_3, and F_4. To reduce the time-consuming while keeping the general feature information, as PAN [1], we reduce the number of channels of each feature map to 128 by convolutional kernel 1x1. However, due to a lightweight backbone, features are often weak representation capabilities, so we apply CBAM attention [16], which perfectly illustrates the effectiveness of capturing spatial attention (SAM) along with channel attention (CAM). Thus, we can obtain richer feature representations. Then, MFEN is capable of the receptive field enhancement and different resolutions of text regions perception due to simultaneously progress with three different scales convolution kernels $3 \times 3, 5 \times 5$, and 7×7. In the details, the structure of each MFEN is based on MobileNetv2 [23], which uses depthwise separable convolution (depth-wise convolution 3×3 and pointwise convolution 1×1). Thus, the spatial information on features $F_{1\_n}, F_{2\_n}, F_{3\_n}, F_{4\_n}$ (n is kernel size) are captured more adequately. Afterward, to prepare for predicting task, features of different depths are integrated into an enriched feature F_c by upsampling and concatenating extracted features. Finally, we inherit the post-processing of PAN [1] that detects text instances followed by pixel aggregation algorithms. This method clusters the neighbor pixels and merges them in the iterating process; consequently, text kernel is gradually expanded to text region.

$$F_{2\_n} = Upsample(F_{2\_n}|F_{1\_n}) \tag{1}$$

$$F_{3\_n} = Upsample(F_{3\_n}|F_{1\_n}) \tag{2}$$

$$F_{4\_n} = Upsample(F_{4\_n}|F_{1\_n}) \tag{3}$$

$$F_c = Concatenate\big((F_{1_n}, F_{2_n}, F_{3_n}, F_{4_n})|1\big) \tag{4}$$

3.3 Loss Function

Our loss function L can be formulated as a weighted sum of the loss for text region, text kernel and sum of loss for similarity vector by segmentation network:

$$L = L\_reg + \alpha L\_ker + \beta(L\_agg + L\_disc) \tag{5}$$

where L_{reg}, and L_{ker} define loss of text regions and text kernels as (6), (7), respectively. L_{agg} and L_{disc} are aggregation loss and discrimination loss of post-processing stage as in PAN in (8), (9). According to the numeric values of the losses, $\alpha = 0.5, \beta = 0.25$ are two constants selecting to keep the balance among these losses.

In more details, prediction of text regions and text kernels are basically a pixel-wise classification text or non-text problem, so we apply dice loss [24] to handle these works.

$$L_{reg} = \sum_i Dice(P_{reg}, G_{reg}) \tag{6}$$

$$L_{ker} = \sum_i Dice(P_{ker}, G_{ker}) \tag{7}$$

where P_{reg}, G_{reg} are the prediction and ground truth of text region, respectively. P_{ker}, G_{ker} are the prediction and ground truth of text kernel.

$$L_{agg} = \frac{1}{N} \sum_j^N \frac{1}{|T_j|} \sum_{pix \in T_j} \ln(D(pix, T_{kerj}) + 1) \tag{8}$$

where N, T_j define the number and jth of text instances. The distance between text pixel pix and text kernel jth T_{kerj} of the same instance should be small, which is denoted by $D(pix, T_{kerj})$. This function is calculated by maximum of similarity vector between pix and T_{kerj} This function is set with a constant 0.5 as PAN experimentally.

$$L_{disc} = \frac{1}{N_j N_k} \sum_{j,k=1}^N \ln(D(T_{kerj}, T_{kerk}) + 1) \tag{9}$$

Similar to aggregation loss, where N, $(D(T_{kerj}, T_{kerk})$ define the number of text instances, the distance between the text kernel T_{kerj} and the text kernel T_{kerk}, respectively, corresponding ith, kth.

4 Experimental Results

4.1 Dataset

ICDAR 2015 [25] is the incidental scene text of challenge four on the website https:// rrc.cvc.uab.es/?ch=4. It consists of 1000 incidental natural images for training process and 500 images for testing set. ICDAR 2015 dataset is one of the popular datasets for scene text detection, including word-level text instances with multi-oriented texts.

ISTD-OC [8], named Incidental Scene Text Dataset - Occlusion, was conducted for occluded text detection and recognition task in workshop CBDAR 2021. ISTD-OC contains the rectangle shape for ICDAR 2015 benchmark with different levels of occlusions from zero to a hundred percent. The number of images is 1500 occluded images for detection, but only 500 evaluation images are published.

We create a novel Realistic Occluded Text Detection (ROTD) dataset in Algorithm 1 with two steps: The first, find the color of a random pixel inside the box, providing localization in Ground Truth of ICDAR 2015. In the second step, draw the arbitrary shape inside the bounding box with the color value obtained above. The arbitrary shape is initialized with the number of possibly sharp edges n = 7, the magnitude of the perturbation from unit circle r = 0.7, and the number of points in the path N = n*3 + 1, experimentally. The difference between our proposed dataset and ISTD-OC is incidental shape and color, making the part of missing texts look real as in Fig. 5. Our ROTD dataset includes 1000 training and 500 testing images.

Algorithm 1 Realistic Occluded Text Detection (ROTD) dataset

Input: ICDAR 2015 images
Method: OpenCV
Output: Occluded text images

1: **while** Bounding box (bbox) has described-text: **do**
2:      Find location of bbox with described-text (x_a, y_a).
3:      Get color value $(0 - 255)$ of a random pixel inside the bounding box above.
4:      **if** pixel=255 **then**
5:          pixel=0
6:      **else**
7:          pixel=pixel/255
8:      **end if**
9:      Initial: Set n, r, N
10:     Draw shape with initial parameters and the color value got from Step 1.
11:     Save occluded images.
12: **end while**

Fig. 5. ICDAR 2015 is represented for normal scene texts, ISTD-OC is occluded text images with rectangle shape, our ROTD is occluded text images with arbitrary shape.

In this work, to help model understand deeply context of normal texts and occluded texts, we choose random only 10% training images following our experimental results (the highest F1-score performance 67.21%) in Fig. 6 and associate with original ICDAR 2015 training set during training stage, totally 1100 images (1000 original ICDAR 2015 images and 100 occluded text ROTD images). Additionally, to compare fairly with

ISTD-OC, as proved in paper [8], we selected 70% occlusion on ISTD-OC as a standard testing set for our evaluation.

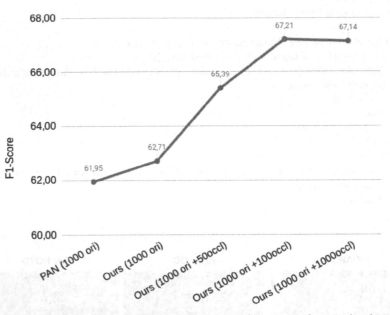

Fig. 6. This graph shows the comparison of F1-score performances of proportional scene text occlusion images.

4.2 Implementation

The whole training phase involves two steps: training with Guided Grad-CAM++ maps from pre-trained Grad-CAM++ on ICDAR 2015 benchmark, and transferring these weights for predicting occluded text detection in main task.

We utilize a Multi-scale Adaptive Deep network (MTD) for both training processes with a lightweight backbone ResNet18 [22] pre-trained on ImageNet [26]. Besides, we apply stochastic gradient descent (SGD) for optimization of all networks, and the initial learning rate of 1×10^{-3}. In the first stage, our proposed method is trained with a batch size of 8 for 600 epochs. In another one, we train batch size 8 in original images combining with 10% occluded images (1100 training images) for only 400 epochs. Furthermore, we follow PAN to make data augmentation: random scale, random horizontal flip, random rotation, and random crop. To implement our tasks, we use a GTX 2080Ti GPU for training and testing process. Several visualization examples are shown in Fig. 7.

4.3 Comparison Results

The comparison results with previous methods on occluded text ISTD-OC, ICDAR 2015 benchmark, and our own ROTD dataset are demonstrated in Table 1, Table 2 and

a) ISTD-OC testing images

b) ICDAR 2015 testing images

c) Our ROTD testing images

Fig. 7. Illustration of bounding box representations for text detection on three testing sets: ISTD-OC, ICDAR 2015 and our ROTD.

Table 3, respectively. As shown, our method is superior for 70% occluded text detection on ISTD-OC by 69.6%, 78.7% on ROTD dataset, and performs better in detecting the text instances on ICDAR 2015 by 82.4%.

Table 1. Comparison of Occluded Text Detection on ISTD-OC. "P", "R", and "F" represent Precision, Recall, and F1-score, respectively. $*\approx$ is represented the results from the mentioned graph performances in [8].

Method	P	R	F
PAN [1]	≈ 64	≈ 44	≈ 61
PSENet [11]	≈ 58	≈ 52	≈ 62
EAST [13]	≈ 43	≈ 51	≈ 60
PAN(1100 training images)	78.5	57.7	66.5
Ours	77.7	63.0	69.6

To further verify the effectiveness of our proposed method for text detection with missing texts, we conduct elaborate ablation studies on the influence of utilizing CBAM attention. From Table, we can realize that the F1-score on two test sets keep increasing (Table 4).

Table 2. Comparison of state-of-the-art scene text detection on ICDAR 2015 without external data.

Method	P	R	F
PAN [1]	82.9	77.8	80.3
PSENet [11]	81.5	79.7	80.6
EAST [13]	83.6	73.5	78.2
MFEN[14]	84.5	79.7	82.0
Ours	85.8	79.3	82.4

Table 3. Comparison of our model with validation on ROTD dataset.

Method	P	R	F
PAN [1]	70.1	50.2	58.5
Ours (1000 training images)	72.2	55.0	62.4
Ours (1100 training images)	82.1	75.6	78.7

Table 4. Quantitative results of applying CBAM attention on ICDAR 2015 and ISTD-OC. "P", "R", and "F" represent Precision, Recall, and F1-sore, respectively.

Method	ICDAR 2015			ISTD-OC		
	P	R	F	P	R	F
Ours w/o CBAM	83.9	79.6	81.7	74.5	53.6	62.4
Ours w/i CBAM	85.8	79.3	82.4	73.3	54.5	62.7

5 Conclusion

In this paper, we have presented a method for addressing text bounding boxes splitting by the occlusion phenomena problem with three stages: We first focus on perceiving attention information from Guided Grad-CAM++ maps to prepare knowledge for the main task. Next, we employ a novel MTD network, which is capable of enlarging the receptive fields and enriching feature representations while bringing minor extra computation. Finally, to aware text occlusion knowledge, we conduct a new dataset ROTD, and combine a part of them with original images (ICDAR 2015) for training process. Therefore, the proposed method outperforms the state-of-the-art on ISTD-OC dataset. Extensive experiment on ICDAR 2015 shows the competitive result compare to other recent methods.

Limitation: The algorithm might produce inaccurate predictions for text instances that are oriented vertically, and miss the "text inside text" cases.

Acknowledgement. This research was supported by Basic Science Research Program through the National Research Foundation of Korea (NRF) funded by the Ministry of Education (NRF-2018R1D1A3B05049058).

References

1. Wang, W., et al.: Efficient and accurate arbitrary-shaped text detection with pixel aggregation network. In: Proceedings of the IEEE/CVF International Conference on Computer Vision, pp. 8440–8449 (2019)
2. Liao, M., Zou, Z., Wan, Z., Yao, C., Bai, X.: Real-time scene text detection with differentiable binarization and adaptive scale fusion. IEEE Trans. Pattern Anal. Mach. Intell. **45**, 919–931 (2022)
3. Zhang, S., Zhu, X., Chen, L., Hou, J., Yin, X.: Arbitrary shape text detection via segmentation with probability map. IEEE Trans. Pattern Anal. Mach. Intell. (2022)
4. Tang, J., et al.: Few could be better than all: feature sampling and grouping for scene text detection. In: Proceedings of the IEEE/CVF Conference on Computer Vision and Pattern Recognition, pp. 4563–4572 (2022)
5. Yin, X., Yin, X., Huang, K., Hao, H.: Robust text detection in natural scene images. IEEE Trans. Pattern Anal. Mach. Intell. **36**, 970–983 (2013)
6. Chen, Z., Wang, W., Xie, E., Yang, Z., Lu, T., Luo, P.: FAST: searching for a faster arbitrarily-shaped text detector with minimalist kernel representation. in arXiv preprint arXiv:2111. 02394 (2021)
7. Ayush, M., Palaiahnakote, S., Umapada, P., Tong, L., Michael, B.: A new method for detection and prediction of occluded text in natural scene images. In: Signal Processing: Image Communication, p. 116512 (2022)
8. Aline, G.S., Byron, L.D.B., Estanislau, B.L.: How far deep learning systems for text detection and recognition in natural scenes are affected by occlusion?. In: International Conference on Document Analysis and Recognition, pp. 198–212 (2021)
9. Bolei, Z., Aditya, K., Agata, L., Aude, O., Antonio, T.: Learning deep features for discriminative localization. In: Proceedings of the IEEE Conference on Computer Vision and Pattern Recognition, pp. 2921–2929 (2016)
10. Ayush, M., Palaiahnakote, S., Umapada, P., Tong, L., Michael, B., Daniel, L.: A new context-based method for restoring occluded text in natural scene images. In: International Workshop on Document Analysis Systems, pp. 466–480 (2020)
11. Wang, W., Xie, E., Li, X., Hou, W., Lu, T., Yu, G., Shao, S.: Shape robust text detection with progressive scale expansion network. In: Proceedings of the IEEE/CVF Conference on Computer Vision and Pattern Recognition, pp. 9336–9345 (2019)
12. Baek, Y., Lee, B., Han, D., Yun, S., Lee, H.: Character region awareness for text detection. In: Proceedings of the IEEE/CVF Conference on Computer Vision and Pattern Recognition, pp. 9365–9374 (2019)
13. Zhou, X., et al.: East: an efficient and accurate scene text detector. In: Proceedings of the IEEE Conference on Computer Vision and Pattern Recognition, pp. 5551–5560 (2017)
14. Dinh, M., Lee, G.: Arbitrary-shaped scene text detection based on multi-scale feature enhancement network. In: Korea Computer Congress, pp. 669–671 (2022)
15. Aditya, C., Anirban, S., Prantik, H., Balasubramanian, V.N.: Grad-cam++: generalized gradient-based visual explanations for deep convolutional networks. In: 2018 IEEE Winter Conference on Applications of Computer Vision (WACV), pp. 839–847 (2018)

16. Woo, S., Park, J., Lee, J.-Y., Kweon, I.S.: CBAM: convolutional block attention module. In: Ferrari, V., Hebert, M., Sminchisescu, C., Weiss, Y. (eds.) Computer Vision – ECCV 2018. LNCS, vol. 11211, pp. 3–19. Springer, Cham (2018). https://doi.org/10.1007/978-3-030-012 34-2_1

17. Dai, P., Zhang, S., Zhang, H., Cao, X.: Progressive contour regression for arbitrary-shape scene text detection. In: Proceedings of the IEEE/CVF Conference on Computer Vision and Pattern Recognition, pp. 7393–7402 (2021)

18. He, W., Zhang, X., Yin, F., Liu, C.: Deep direct regression for multi-oriented scene text detection. In: Proceedings of the IEEE International Conference on Computer Vision, pp. 745–753 (2017)

19. Sheng, T., Chen, J., Lian, Z.: Centripetaltext: an efficient text instance representation for scene text detection. In: Advances in Neural Information Processing Systems, pp. 335–346 (2021)

20. Tian, Z., et al.: Learning shape-aware embedding for scene text detection. In: Proceedings of the IEEE/CVF Conference on Computer Vision and Pattern Recognition, pp. 4234–4243 (2019)

21. Ramprasaath, R.S., Michael, C., Abhishek, D., Ramakrishna, V., Devi, P., Dhruv, B.: Gradcam: visual explanations from deep networks via gradient-based localization. In: Proceedings of the IEEE International Conference on Computer Vision, pp. 618–626 (2017)

22. He, K., Zhang, X., Ren, S., Sun, J.: Deep residual learning for image recognition. In: Proceedings of the IEEE Conference on Computer Vision and Pattern Recognition, pp. 770–778 (2016)

23. Andrew, G.h., et al.: Mobilenets: efficient convolutional neural networks for mobile vision applications, pp. 770–778. arXiv preprint arXiv:1704.04861 (2017)

24. Carole, H.S., Li, W., Tom, V., Sebastien, O., Cardoso, M.J.: Generalised dice overlap as a deep learning loss function for highly unbalanced segmentations. In: Deep Learning in Medical Image Analysis and Multimodal Learning for Clinical Decision Support, pp. 240–248 (2017)

25. Dimosthenis, K., et al.: ICDAR 2015 competition on robust reading. In: 2015 13th International Conference on Document Analysis and Recognition (ICDAR), pp. 1156–1160 (2015)

26. Jia, D., Wei, D., Richard, S., Li, L., Li, K., Li, F.F.: Imagenet: a large-scale hierarchical image database. In: 2009 IEEE Conference on Computer Vision and Pattern Recognition, pp. 248–255 (2009)

27. Dang, Q.V., Lee, G.-S.: Document image binarization with stroke boundary feature guided network. IEEE Access 9, 36924–36936 (2021)

28. Wu, Y., et al.: Google's neural machine translation system: bridging the gap between human and machine translation (2016). arXiv preprint arXiv:1609.08144

29. Dang, Q.-V., Lee, G.-S.: Document image binarization by GAN with unpaired data training. Int. J. Contents, 8–18 (2020)

30. Wang, W., et al.: Pan++: towards efficient and accurate end-to-end spotting of arbitrarily-shaped text. IEEE Trans. Pattern Anal. Mach. Intell. 44, 5349–5367 (2021)

31. Aviad, A., et al.: Sequence-to-sequence contrastive learning for text recognition. In: Proceedings of the IEEE/CVF Conference on Computer Vision and Pattern Recognition, pp. 15302–15312 (2021)

32. Xu, X., Zhang, Z., Wang, Z., Price, B., Wang, Z., Shi, H.: Rethinking text segmentation: A novel dataset and a text-specific refinement approach. In: Proceedings of the IEEE/CVF Conference on Computer Vision and Pattern Recognition, pp. 12045–12055 (2021)

33. Dan, D., Liu, H., Li, X., Cai, D.: Pixellink: detecting scene text via instance segmentation. In: Proceedings of the AAAI Conference on Artificial Intelligence (2018)

Classifying Breast Cancer Using Deep Convolutional Neural Network Method

Musfequa Rahman[1], Kaushik Deb[1(✉)], and Kang-Hyun Jo[2]

[1] Department of Computer Science and Engineering, Chittagong University of
Engineering and Technology (CUET), Chattogram 4349, Bangladesh
u1704050@student.cuet.ac.bd, debkaushik99@cuet.ac.bd
[2] Department of Electrical, Electronic and Computer Engineering, University of
Ulsan, Ulsan 44610, South Korea
acejo@ulsan.ac.kr

Abstract. The efficacy of conventional classification systems is contingent upon the accurate representation of data and a substantial portion of the effort invested in feature engineering, which is a laborious and time-consuming process requiring expert domain knowledge. In contrast, deep learning has the capacity to automatically identify and extract discriminative information from data without the need for manual feature creation by a domain expert. In particular, Convolutional Neural Networks (CNNs), a type of deep feedforward network, have garnered attention from researchers. This study conducts several preliminary experiments to classify breast cancer histopathology images using deep learning, given the small number and high resolution of training samples. The proposed approach is evaluated on the publicly available BreaKHis dataset, utilizing both a scratch model and transfer learning pre trained models. A comparison of the proposed scratch method to alternative techniques was carried out using a suite of performance evaluation metrics. The results indicate that the scratch model, with its independent magnification factor, achieved greater accuracy, with a binary classification accuracy of 99.5% and a multiclass classification accuracy of 96.1%.

Keywords: Transfer Learning · Convolutional Neural Network ·
Magnification Factor · Breast Cancer Classification

1 Introduction

Currently, one of the leading causes of human death is cancer which is cell growth of type abnormal that the invading body parts have high potential. Precancerous lesions give way to malignant tumors as part of the multi phase process by which cancer cells are transformed. Alcohol and cigarette use, physical inactivity, old age, pollution, and a few additional disorders like Hepatitis C, Hepatitis B and HIV are all risk factors for the development of cancer. World Health Organization (WHO) sates that according to their estimation, here will be 10.6 million cancer related deaths and 19.3 million new cases worldwide in 2020 [1].

Any part of the human body can be affected by cancer cells including liver, lungs, breast etc. Among other types of cancer, breast cancer is one of the most

© The Author(s), under exclusive license to Springer Nature Singapore Pte Ltd. 2023
I. Na and G. Irie (Eds.): IW-FCV 2023, CCIS 1857, pp. 135–148, 2023.
https://doi.org/10.1007/978-981-99-4914-4_11

common for women and the mortality of breast cancer is also very high, accounting for 1 in 4 new cases and 1 in 6 cancer related deaths worldwide in [1]. Breast cancer, which accounted for 35.3% of all fresh tumors of female and contributes 20.8% to cancer deaths in total in 2012, had the highest age standardized incidence of any female cancer, according to data from the International Agency for Research on Cancer (IARC) of the WHO states [1]. In 2020, study shows of 27 million fresh cases of cancer occurred [2]. Breast tissue cells proliferate out of control and infiltrate adjacent tissues via blood and lymphatic vessels to cause breast cancer. Breast cancer can also occur in fatty tissue. Breast discomfort, skin that is pitted and red or discolored on the breast, lumps or tissue thickening that feels different from surrounding tissue, and breasts that enlarge entirely or partially are typical symptoms of breast cancer. Breast tissue, which is detected by a breast lump, develops into breast cancer, along with other modifications to the usual environment [3]. Mammography, breast cancer screening and other clinical Ultrasound, biopsies and other techniques. Only a biopsy [4] can definitively verify whether the suspicious region is malignant in terms of diagnosis. The pathologists make their diagnoses by looking at histology slides, which is regarded as the definitive gold standards. However, the traditional method requires a heavy burden from qualified experts. Pathologists who lack sufficient diagnostic experience are more likely to make errors in diagnosis.

Deep learning algorithms have obtained results on image classification and object detection tests that are on par with those of human experts [5]. The most popular deep learning framework for learning complicated discriminative characteristics between image classes is the convolutional neural network. Over the years, many CNN architectures have delivered outstanding results on the enormous ImageNet dataset. On medical images, CNNs are being used to produce state-of-the-art results. Patch wise classification is one of the existing deep learning methods for the task of classifying breast cancer (BC) histology images [6]. By doing this, CNN typically ignores the general properties of the entire tissue and only extracts local features near the nucleus. In addition to the drawback of patching, CNN's shallow architecture does not allow for the extraction of finer and more abstract features from patient breast histopathology images.

In order to gradually and reliably categorize the Breast Cancer pathological images, we developed a CNN model from scratch to extract characteristics from images and carry out the training which is end to end in nature. Hence, the following is a list of this paper's key contributions:

1. To increase classification performance, we developed a scratch CNN model.
2. Because of the independence of our developed model's accuracy against magnification factors, it can be used with different magnification factors.
3. To improve the quality of the breast histopathology images, we developed a histopathological image enhancement method.

2   Related Works

The original goal of the image analysis system was to categorize pathological images. For more than 40 years, this concept has been investigated in the context of automatic assistance cancer detection. The complexity of image analysis, however, made it difficult to deal with the inherent complexity of histological images [7]. The workload of pathologists can be reduced by modern deep learning method [8]. The absence of extensive datasets and class disparity are the key challenges in the field of breast cancer classification research. Since images have intrinsic problems including inadequate contrast, noise, and lack of visual acuity, models have been developed to build and improve image processing.

For the recognition of breast cancer histopathology images, several researchers apply customized features. BreaKHis, dataset of breast available to public, was proposed by [9]. Six different features utilized the dataset's classification and accuracy ranged from percentage of 80 to 85. Phylogenetic diversity indexes were employed by Carvalho et al. In [10], to categorize the different forms of breast cancer. Three different features were combined by [11] for binary and eight class categorization of breast cancer histopathology images. Several researchers, notably CNNs, have become interested in deep learning as a result of its remarkable performance in image recognition in recent years.

Researchers created CNNs based CAD models based on these models and used them to diagnose cancers. There are two general categories of CNNs as pre trained CNNs [12] and CNNs which have been made from begin called scratch [13]. Additionally, deep networks can be created using transfer learning with samples which are few in number. Many researchers additionally employ CNN an extractor of features, which performs the task of extraction of features using various techniques.

For instance, in [14] employed 3-norm for feature fusion, ResNet50 for feature extraction from image patches of various sizes, and SVM for classification. On the basis of images produced from Haar wavelet decomposition, in [15] retrieved features using VGG16 and merged various properties of the next level layers for breast cancer identification. To assess the histopathology images and resolve the class imbalance issue. In [16], used ResNet50 and weighted learning machine. Using DenseNet121 [17] to extract overall features from slides. In order to diagnose breast and prostate cancer automatically, in [18] developed a 5-layered multi input CNN that took into account both RGB pictures and phase shearlet coefficients. This CNN achieved an amazing accuracy rate of 88% for a different dataset. In [19], a thorough analysis of the architecture and functioning of each network is performed and the performance of each network is then evaluated based on how accurately it diagnoses and classifies cancer causes in breast. CNN provide a little bit better precision than layer perceptron for the detection.

As a result, it can be concluded that the classification of cancer in breast has had a significant impact for a long time. Deep learning models combined with a wide range of configurations have recently exceeded current state-of-the-art methods as well. There is a huge amount of scope for initiating innovation and development in this developing research field to overcome this.

3 Datasets

3.1 BreakHis

The images found from biopsy cancers in breast were gathered from January 2014 to December 2014 through clinical investigations and were included in the BreaKHis dataset [9]. All patients with breast cancer clinical symptoms to take part in the trial over the time period. Hematoxylin and eosin staining was used after surgical open biopsy (SOB) sample collection. Pathologists working in the P&D laboratory can mark these images and use them for histological investigations. Four sub classes are further separated into each kind. Adenosis (A), Fibroadenoma (F), Phyllodes Tumor (PT) and Tubular Adenoma (TA) are examples of Benign lesions, while Ductal Carcinoma (DC), Lobular Carcinoma (LC), Mucinous Carcinoma (MC) and Papillary Carcinoma (PC) are examples of Malignant lesions. The images are 700 × 460 pixels in size and were created in a three channel RGB (red, green, and blue) true color space with magnifications of 40X, 100X, 200X and 400X. The distribution of images is summarized in Table 1.

Table 1. BreaKHis dataset summary.

Magnification Factor	Benign	Malignant	Total
40X	625	1370	1995
100X	644	1437	2081
200X	623	1390	2013
400X	588	1232	1820
Total	2480	5429	7909

4 Methods

4.1 Preprocessing

Preprocessing is a necessary step in order to improve the performance for any type of breast cancer histopathological image classification model. In this work, a method was developed for improving histopathological images in low light.

Histopathological Image Enhancement Method. Due to their poor visibility, low light images are not suitable for computer vision algorithms or human inspection. Image enhancement is the process of focusing attention to details that are obscured in an image or enhancing contrast in low contrast images. To provide an accurate contrast enhancement, we developed an image contrast enhancement algorithm. To synthesize multi exposure images and determine the best exposure ratio, a weight matrix for image fusion using illumination estimation techniques is used first, followed by a response model and help to ensure that the synthetic image is properly exposed in the areas where the original image was underexposed. To produce the enhancement result, both types of images are finally fused in accordance with the weight matrix. The preprocessing method for enhancing the histopathological images are shown in Fig. 1. Illumination estimation techniques to obtain the weight matrix for image fusion. Exposure ratio is used so that the synthetic image is well exposed in the regions where the original image is under exposed. The output for enhancing the histopathological images is shown in Fig. 2. So, the it can be,

$$E = I \times W + I' \times (1 - W) \tag{1}$$

where W indicates the weight matrix and I indicates real image and E indicates the enhanced image and then I' indicates the exposure image. For breast histopathology slides, MIRNet [20] was compared with our approach of histopathological image enhancement. Using the metrics for measuring the quality of an image. Image enhancement metrics are utilized as objective measures to evaluate the effectiveness of image enhancement techniques in ameliorating the quality and visual appearance of an image. These metrics furnish quantitative assessments of the degree of improvement accomplished by the enhancement process, thereby enabling a rigorous analysis of the efficacy of the applied enhancement techniques.

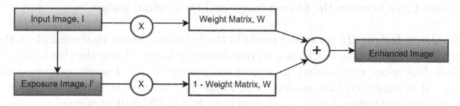

Fig. 1. Histopathological image enhancement method.

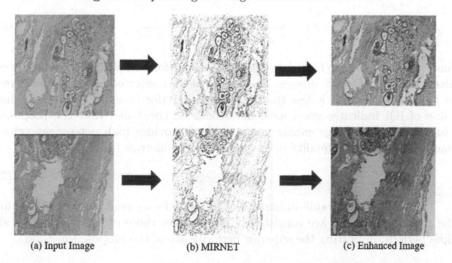

(a) Input Image   (b) MIRNET   (c) Enhanced Image

Fig. 2. Histopathological image enhancement method output from: (a) Input image. (b) MIRNET. (c) Enhanced image.

Entropy measures an image's content and indicates how much uncertainty or randomness it has. Higher value of entropy indicates an image with higher details.

$$E(I) = -\sum_{k=0}^{L-1} p(k) \log_2(p(k)) \tag{2}$$

Peak Signal Noise Ratio (PSNR) affects how an image is represented, is the ratio between the maximum power and corrupting noise. The PSNR is frequently used to evaluate how well an image may be reconstructed. The original data in this case is the signal, while the introduced error is the noise.

$$PSNR = 10 \log_{10} \frac{MAX_i^2}{MSE} \tag{3}$$

$$PSNR = 20 \log_{10} \frac{MAX_i}{MSE} \tag{4}$$

$$PSNR = 20 \log_{10} MAX_i - 10 \log_{10} MSE \tag{5}$$

Where, MAXi is the maximum possible pixel value of the image. MSE is Mean Square Error between the filtered image and the original image.

Similarity Index (SI) is ratio of pixels in the enhanced image that coincide with pixels in original image is known as the similarity index. When the this is larger than 40% when represented in percent or greater than 0.4 when expressed in ones, it is suggested that an improved image be regarded as being comparable to the original image. Lower value (less than 40%) of SI indicates good measure. It's measurement is given by-

$$SI = \frac{m_{ab}2xy2m_am_b}{m_am_bx^2 + y^2\,m_a{}^2 + m_b^2} \tag{6}$$

Image Quality Index (IQI) is a common metric for comparing the number of pixels that separate two images. The quality of the converted image is considered to be good if the IQI is less than but close to 1 (for example 0.8704). Higher value of IQI indicates good measure. It can be concluded that the proposed histopathological image enhancement method provides high percentage values than MIRNet for the quality image measurement metrics (Table 2).

$$IQI = 1 - SI \tag{7}$$

The comparative table illustrates that the enhancement metrics values for the proposed method are consistently higher than those of MIRNet across all time periods, indicating the superior performance of the proposed method.

Table 2. Enhancement comparison between MIRNet and proposed method.

Performance Metrics	Input Image	MIRNet	Ours
Entropy	6.004	4.0417	**6.7127**
PSNR		14.1574	**14.6509**
SI		67.3573	**29.7719**
IQI		95.3723	**96.7513**

4.2 Proposed CNN Architecture

One of the most effective architectures for the problem of image classification is CNNs. CNNs use filtering techniques to extract the most innovative features from an image's pixels. Deep neural networks are used in images as they extract characteristics features from images, as opposed to classic ML algorithms that pick up engineered features for detection of cancer in breast. Machine learning neural networks (ML-NNs) are a type of learning and they typically require a training stage to determine the optimal weights.

CNNs are used to analyze patterns in an image. In the few early layers of CNNs, the network can identify lines and corners. However, as go deeper, these patterns may transfer via neural network and start to recognize more complicated features. CNNs are exceptionally good at identifying objects in images because of this feature. The suggested approach analyzes histopathologic images using CNNs for classification of breast cancer. The convolutional layer, pooling layer, batch normalization layer, and fully connected layer were just a few of the layers that constitute a CNN's architecture, as depicted in Fig. 3.

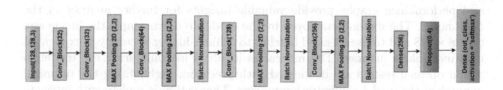

Fig. 3. The proposed method of breast cancer classification.

The convolution layer utilizes filters that carry out convolution operations while dimensionally scanning the input image. Convolution is a linear procedure where a set of weights are multiplied and the input images are represented by metrics resembling those of conventional neural networks. All of the features were computed using the input layers and filters and are included in the output, which is known as the feature map or activation map. Here, used RGB images with a size of 128×128 pixels when using this layer. 3×3 kernel size convolutional layers with successive use of 32, 32, 64, 128 and 256 filters. As the activation function, ReLU was employed. The rectifier function was being used to increase the non linearity of the images.

The convoluted feature's spatial size is decreased by the Pooling layer. By lowering the dimensions, this will decrease the total power required to process the slides. Max Pooling determines a pixel's maximum value from a portion of the image that the kernel has processed. By choosing the maximum value for each input channel over a pool size (2, 2) input window, down sampled the input along its spatial dimensions are performed.

In Normalization, the input layers are scaled. Learning becomes more effective when batch normalization is utilized. Thus, batch normalization as regularization to prevent model overfitting is used here. A layer that is densely connected to the layer above it means that every neuron in the layer is attached to every neuron in the layer above it. A typical layer having many connections called dense layer after performing the operation on input returns the result. To do the activation (dot (input, kernel) + bias) operation, this formula is applied in it.

The regularization method used to avoid model overfitting is called dropouts. Dropouts are added to the network's neurons, which are changed at random in some proportion. The connections to the neurons' incoming and outgoing neurons are likewise broken off when they are turned off. To improve the model's learning, this is done. After that, turned off 40% of the neurons and utilized dropouts after the network's dense layers. After building the model, classification of the breast histopathology images using the Softmax activation function.

5   Result Analysis

The dedicated section pertaining to the model configuration entails a comprehensive overview of the key accuracy metrics such as precision, recall, and f1-score, which are pivotal in assessing the efficacy of the proposed model vis-à-vis the state-of-the-art models. In addition, the classification report, confusion matrix, and performance graphs provide valuable insights for further analysis of the best model. The method employed by the model to downsample the image size to 128×128 and to use 24-sized batches to achieve higher accuracy is explicated in a meticulous manner. The intricacies involved in configuring the model to attain optimal results are delineated with precision, highlighting the technical nuances of the model configuration process. The section is replete with intricate technical details, which render it an indispensable resource for researchers and practitioners seeking to replicate or build upon the proposed model.

However, applied different pretrained transfer learning model in the dataset. However, to further test the effectiveness of the proposed model, several different pre-trained transfer learning models were applied to the dataset and their accuracy was compared to that of the proposed model. The accuracy comparison chart clearly illustrates that all the transfer learning methods utilized resulted in lower accuracies than the proposed model, as depicted in Fig. 4. This finding reinforces the notion that the proposed model is superior in terms of its ability to classify histopathology images accurately. Additionally, the comprehensive analysis of the various transfer learning models used provides valuable insights into the performance of each method and their limitations in comparison to the proposed model.

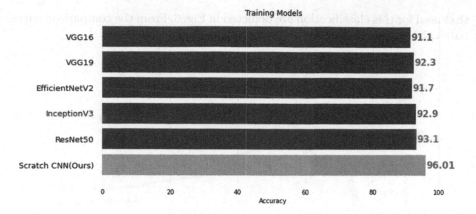

Fig. 4. Accuracy comparison of different models.

An optimizer is a technique that modifies the properties of a neural network, such as a function or algorithm. Accuracy is improved and there is decreased overall loss. Thus, utilizing the following three optimizers in Fig. 5, Adam, SGD and RMSProp are illustrated. Adam's accuracy in the proposed model was the highest according to the following figure.

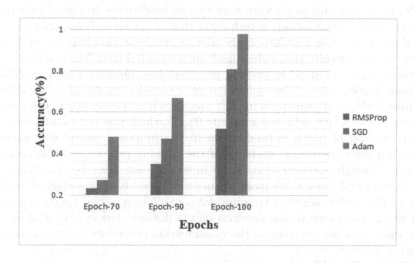

Fig. 5. Optimizer's accuracy comparison.

The batch size is the quantity of samples processed before to a model modification. The number of epochs is the total number of complete iterations through the training dataset. The minimum and maximum sizes of a batch must be one and the number of samples in the training dataset, respectively. The batch sizes that used for this classification are depicted in Fig. 6. From the comparison curve, batch size 24 provide highest accuracy among others.

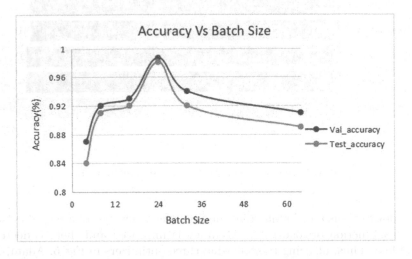

Fig. 6. Accuracy versus batch size.

Prior research endeavors were found to be inadequate in their implementation of batch normalization, a technique that accelerates the learning rate of neural networks while simultaneously offering regularization benefits to counteract overfitting. Despite this, subsequent authors opted to utilize hashing in [21], a decision that was made to prevent precision loss, however this approach has not been implemented. The utilization of a model comprising EfficientNetB2 and RestNet50, as documented in [22], was already implemented in our research however the accuracy achieved was only 93.1% which was not satisfactory. The implementation of batch normalization in the proposed model was aimed at optimizing the velocity and stability of the training process of artificial neural networks through normalization of the inputs at each layer by rescaling them. Hence, developed a new CNN model from scratch, resulting in a marked improvement in the performance of training data, exhibiting a two times increase in efficiency as compared to the previous efforts documented in [23]. The comparative analysis of the outcome of the classification procedure is presented in the following manner.

For Binary Classification

The experiment's accuracy for binary classification was tested by comparing it to the findings of other authors, which are displayed in Table 3. The classification accuracy is 99.10%, 99.15%, 99.22%, and 98.99% respectively for the independence of a very crucial factor called magnification of images by 40, 100, 200 and 400 respectively. The classification result, independent of the magnification factor achieved accuracy of 99.5%.

Table 3. Classification accuracy comparison for binary class.

Author	Model	40X	100X	200X	400X
Pratiher et al., [21]	L-Isomap and SSAEm	96.8	98.1	98.2	97
Bardou et al., [23]	CNN	94.65	98.33	94.07	97.12
	Ensemble CNN model	94.54	97.85	93.77	96.15
Yun Jianget al., [13]	BHCNet-3 + Exp	98.12	98.80	98.88	98.21
	BHCNet-3 + Cos	98.75	98.88	99.17	98.76
Proposed Method	**CNN (Scratch)**	**99.10**	**99.15**	**99.22**	**98.99**

For Multiclass Classification

The experiment's results for multiclass classification accuracy were measured and compared to those of other authors, as shown in Table 4.

Table 4. Classification accuracy comparison for multi class.

Author	Model	40X	100X	200X	400X
Bardou et al., [23]	CNN	86.34	84.00	79.93	79.74
	Ensemble CNN model	88.23	84.64	83.31	83.98
Yun Jianget al., [13]	BHCNet-3 + Exp	94.43	94.45	92.27	91.15
Abhijeet Patil et al., [24]	A-MIL	82.95	86.45	86.56	84.43
Richa Upadhyay et al., [22]	MPCS-OP (RN-50)	93.00	93.26	92.28	88.74
Proposed Method	**CNN (Scratch)**	**96.36**	**96.43**	**96.12**	**95.91**

As seen in the table, the proposed model's accuracy variance for various magnification factors is significantly less than that of other authors and also outperformed them in terms of accuracy. The experiment's results for the independent magnification factor are represented by the classification report in table 5 and confusion matrix and accuracy curve in Figs. 7 and 8.

Table 5. Classification report for multi class.

Author	Precision	Recall	F1-score	Support
adenosis	0.94	0.94	0.94	18
ductal carcinoma	0.85	1.00	0.92	22
fibroadenoma	1.00	0.93	0.96	28
lobular carcinoma	1.00	0.90	0.95	20
mucinous carcinoma	0.92	1.00	0.96	24
papillary carcinoma	1.00	0.93	0.97	15
phyllodes tumor	1.00	0.95	0.98	22
tubular adenoma	1.00	1.00	1.00	19

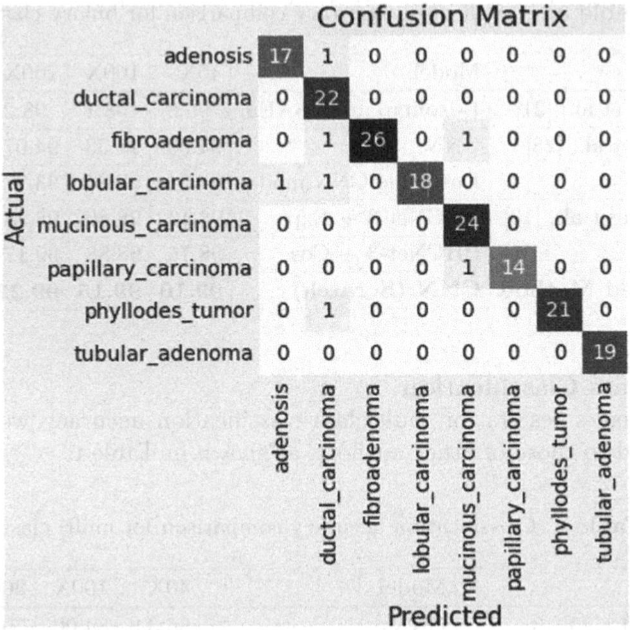

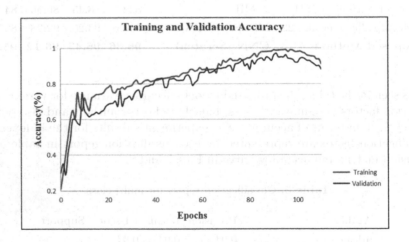

Fig. 7. Confusion matrix of multi class classification.

Fig. 8. Accuracy curve of multi class classification.

The approach suggested in this work is reliable to the problems of classification, according to experimental outcomes. The comparison findings with various baseline models identifies that the strategy proposed in the model performs better.

6   Conclusion

This study posits the deployment of a deep learning based network, constructed entirely from scratch, that boasts dense layers in higher level representation, resulting in a marked improvement over conventional classification systems. The proposed scratch method has been subjected to numerous performance evaluations, comparing it with existing technique. It has been found that the model enhance the generalizability and robustness of classification in dealing with imbalanced dataset of breast cancer histopathology images. The deep scratch network exhibits higher accuracy 96.1% compared to transfer learning models and has the potential to effectively classify both majority and minority classes. Despite the challenges posed by the BreakHis dataset, including low light images and varying magnification factors, there is a need for continuous improvement of histopathology images for better accuracy. The proposed future implementation of attention in the scratch model is aimed at further increasing classification precision and providing a more nuanced classification of histopathology images.

References

1. International Agency for Research on Cancer: "World Fact Sheet" (2020). https://gco.iarc.fr/today/data/factsheets/populations/900-world-fact-sheets.pdf/. Accessed 26 June 2022
2. World Health Organization (WHO): "20-Breast-fact-sheet" (2020). https://gco.iarc.fr/404. Accessed 26 June 2022
3. Karthiga, R., Narasimhan, K.: Automated diagnosis of breast cancer using wavelet based entropy features. In: 2018 2nd International Conference on Electronics, Communication and Aerospace Technology (ICECA), pp. 274–279. IEEE (2018)
4. Horvat, J.V., Keating, D.M., Rodrigues-Duarte, H., Morris, E.A., Mango, V.L.: Calcifications at digital breast tomosynthesis: imaging features and biopsy techniques. Radiographics 39(2), 307–318 (2019)
5. Yamashita, R., Nishio, M., Do, R.K.G., Togashi, K.: Convolutional neural networks: an overview and application in radiology. Insights Imaging 9, 611–629 (2018). https://doi.org/10.1007/s13244-018-0639-9
6. Spanhol, F.A., Oliveira, L.S., Cavalin, P.R., Petitjean, C., Heutte, L.: Deep features for breast cancer histopathological image classification. In: 2017 IEEE International Conference on Systems, Man, and Cybernetics (SMC), pp. 1868–1873. IEEE (2017)
7. Mitra, S., Shankar, B.U.: Medical image analysis for cancer management in natural computing framework. Inf. Sci. 306, 111–131 (2015)
8. Filipczuk, P., Fevens, T., Krzyżak, A., Monczak, R.: Computer-aided breast cancer diagnosis based on the analysis of cytological images of fine needle biopsies. IEEE Trans. Med. Imaging 32(12), 2169–2178 (2013)
9. Spanhol, F.A., Oliveira, L.S., Petitjean, C., Heutte, L.: A dataset for breast cancer histopathological image classification. IEEE Trans. Biomed. Eng. 63(7), 1455–1462 (2015)
10. Carvalho, E.D., et al.: Breast cancer diagnosis from histopathological images using textural features and CBIR. Artif. Intell. Med. 105, 101845 (2020)
11. Boumaraf, S., et al.: Conventional machine learning versus deep learning for magnification dependent histopathological breast cancer image classification: a comparative study with visual explanation. Diagnostics 11(3), 528 (2021)

12. Saxena, S., Shukla, S., Gyanchandani, M.: Pre-trained convolutional neural networks as feature extractors for diagnosis of breast cancer using histopathology. Int. J. Imaging Syst. Technol. **30**(3), 577–591 (2020)
13. Jiang, Y., Chen, L., Zhang, H., Xiao, X.: Breast cancer histopathological image classification using convolutional neural networks with small SE-ResNet module. PLoS ONE **14**(3), e0214587 (2019)
14. He, K., Zhang, X., Ren, S., Sun, J.: Deep residual learning for image recognition. In: Proceedings of the IEEE Conference on Computer Vision and Pattern Recognition, pp. 770–778 (2016)
15. Kausar, T., Wang, M., Idrees, M., Lu, Y.: HWDCNN: multi-class recognition in breast histopathology with Haar wavelet decomposed image based convolution neural network. Biocybern. Biomed. Eng. **39**(4), 967–982 (2019)
16. Saxena, S., Shukla, S., Gyanchandani, M.: Breast cancer histopathology image classification using kernelized weighted extreme learning machine. Int. J. Imaging Syst. Technol. **31**(1), 168–179 (2021)
17. Huang, G., Liu, Z., van der Maaten, L., Weinberger, K.Q.: Densely connected convolutional networks. In: Proceedings of the IEEE Conference on Computer Vision and Pattern Recognition, pp. 4700–4708 (2017)
18. Rezaeilouyeh, H., Mollahosseini, A., Mahoor, M.H.: Microscopic medical image classification framework via deep learning and shearlet transform. J. Med. Imaging **3**(4), 044501 (2016)
19. Desai, M., Shah, M.: An anatomization on breast cancer detection and diagnosis employing multi-layer perceptron neural network (MLP) and convolutional neural network (CNN). Clin. eHealth **4**, 1–11 (2021)
20. Chang, L., Zhou, G., Soufan, O., Xia, J.: miRNet 2.0: network-based visual analytics for miRNA functional analysis and systems biology. Nucleic Acids Res. **48**(W1), W244–W251 (2020)
21. Pratiher, S., Chattoraj, S.: Manifold learning & stacked sparse autoencoder for robust breast cancer classification from histopathological images. arXiv preprint arXiv:1806.06876 (2018)
22. Patil, A., Tamboli, D., Meena, S., Anand, D., Sethi, A.: Breast cancer histopathology image classification and localization using multiple instance learning. In: 2019 IEEE International WIE Conference on Electrical and Computer Engineering (WIECON-ECE), pp. 1–4. IEEE (2019)
23. Chhipa, P.C., Upadhyay, R., Pihlgren, G.G., Saini, R., Uchida, S., Liwicki, M.: Magnification prior: a self-supervised method for learning representations on breast cancer histopathological images. In: Proceedings of the IEEE/CVF Winter Conference on Applications of Computer Vision, pp. 2717–2727 (2023)
24. Bardou, D., Zhang, K., Ahmad, S.M.: Classification of breast cancer based on histology images using convolutional neural networks. IEEE Access **6**, 24680–24693 (2018)

Front Cover Image Database of Japanese Manga and Typeface Estimation of Their Title

Shota Ishiyama, Kosuke Sakai, and Minoru Mori$^{(\boxtimes)}$

Kanagawa Institute of Technology, Atsugi 243-0292, Kanagawa, Japan
`mmori@ic.kanagawa-it.ac.jp`

Abstract. Front cover design of books like Manga is one of the most important factors for appealing contents to users. Fonts used for the title in the front cover are carefully selected among a lot of ones for fitting selected fonts to the content and the design. However, this task to select fonts, that increases attractions of the front cover and are appropriate for human characters pictured in the front cover, is not easy. Few experienced designers or editors can do well. In this paper we try to estimate and recommend appropriate typefaces of fonts that seem to be appropriate for title fonts from an image of front cover of Manga and Light novels. To evaluate our framework, we gathered front cover images of Manga and Light novels, and created database that containing five kinds of images; front cover images with/without title fonts, whole-body images with/without title fonts, and face images. Each image has two types of label encoded from the count number of 5 typefaces used for title fonts. Experimental results using our database show that about 70% of typefaces are correctly estimated and suggest a strong relationship between fonts used for title and front covers.

Keywords: Front cover page · Manga · Light novels · Typeface · Deep Neural Network

1 Introduction

Lots of new contents and books of "Manga", comics and graphic novels, and "Light novel", Japanese young adult novels, have been continuously produced and published not even in Japan but in the world. When buying a book of Manga or Light novels, we usually select one on the base of its story, reviews, prices, character designs, and others. At least we all see a front cover page of each book. If a book of Manga or Light novels to buy is decided before, its front cover has nothing to do with sales or selections. But, if not decided, the impression and design of a front cover page seem to be a very important factor for sales on not only Manga books but other many books. Especially many Manga contents feature some human characters and the design of their character influence the popularity. Therefore, the front cover page needs to be designed for drawing attentions of users. One of important elements of the front cover design is the title font. Editors and

© The Author(s), under exclusive license to Springer Nature Singapore Pte Ltd. 2023
I. Na and G. Irie (Eds.): IW-FCV 2023, CCIS 1857, pp. 149–162, 2023.
https://doi.org/10.1007/978-981-99-4914-4_12

designers carefully select kinds of fonts to bring out and appeal the charm of the Manga content. Fonts are not only medium of language but a piece of art and impressions. From a lot of fonts, designers select fonts to fit the targeted Manga content and deliver its attraction to readers. Recently, though the number of amateur Manga and Light novels writers is increasing, they without knowledges about fonts cannot select appropriate fonts to fit their contents and design. If more appropriate fonts for the targeted Manga content or design can be easily selected, more attractive front covers with suitable fonts as its title can be produced and published.

In this paper we propose a framework that estimates suitable typefaces of fonts that fits the design of a front cover of Manga and Light novels and a database that consists of several types of images for this task. In detail, a lot of sets of the front cover image and its font information used as the title are created as the database and we evaluate our framework that estimates typefaces of fonts that fit front cover image or human characters contained in the front cover using our database. For validating relationship between fonts used as the title and human characters, we create whole-body images extracted from the front cover images and face images obtained from the whole-body image. Figure 1 shows examples of front cover images of Manga and Light novels and fonts used as the titles in these images that we handle in this paper. Figure 2 shows the overview of our framework that estimates typefaces included in an image using DNN. The paper is organized as follows: Sect. 2 provides related works about relationships between fonts and design of books or signboards. Our database and proposed method are described in Sect. 3. Section 4 reports evaluation experiments and discusses experimental results. Section 5 summaries this paper and lists future works.

(a)   (b)

Fig. 1. Examples of front cover images of Manga and Light novels. (a) Typeface: Designed, Font name: Hasetoppo (for 17 Hiragana characters), Typeface: Designed, Font name: Taka-hand (4 Kanji characters) [1]. (b) Typeface: Mincho, Font name: A1 Mincho (for all characters) [2].

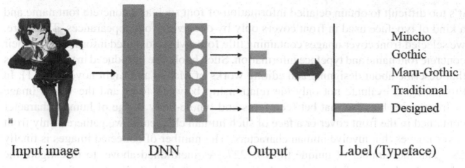

Fig. 2. Overview of our framework

2 Related Works

Shinhara et al. [3] analyzed that how genres of English books effect selections of colors of their front covers and fonts used as their book title. They split the genres of English books into 32 kinds of groups, and font types were split into 6 typefaces. They validated the performance of genre estimation from font typefaces. Their experimental results showed that there was the relationship between the genre and font typeface. Also, books with similar colored front covers are in the same or similar genres and font type groups. In [4], they validated a relationship between fonts used in signboards and impressions of shops with these signboards. 7 signboards with each different type of fonts were prepared as test images. Users selected genres of eateries or restaurants from the impression based on appearances of each font. Experimental results showed that users often imagined different genres of eatery from different types of fonts. The tendency on the font selection on the signboard of real eateries was very similar to that obtained in their experiments. From these researches, we can say that impressions felled from designed linguistic substance like front covers of books and signboards has a strong relationship between fonts selected in them. On books of Manga and Light novels, the design of front covers seems to have some degree of relationship with fonts used in these front covers. Therefore, as one of design analyses, the estimation result of font from front cover pages enables us to easily select fonts that suit human character pictured in front cover pages for automatic or semi-automatic book design.

3 Proposed Method

This section describes our database that consists of front faces from Manga and Light novels, typefaces used in front faces, several kinds of label information for each data. And we explain a DNN model as our estimation framework used in our experiments.

3.1 Database of Front Cover Images

For validating the typeface estimation on front cover images from Manga and Light novels, we gathered hundreds of front cover images from many books of them. Here, it's too difficult to obtain detailed information of font such as a concrete font name and a kind of typeface used in front covers only by observing font appearances. Therefore, we selected front cover images containing title fonts whose detailed information as their concrete font name and typeface information. Such books are introduced in several books that describe about designing and editing works of Manga and Light novels [6–11]. In this paper, to evaluate not only the relationship between fonts and the whole image of front cover but also that between fonts and whole-body image of human character contained in the front cover or a face of such human characters, we gathered only front cover images that involve human characters. The number of collected images is finally 581, and the number of unique titles is 227. As mentioned above, to investigate the relationship between fonts used in the front cover and whole bodies or faces too, we extracted a part of human characters and a part of faces from each front cover image. On front cover images and whole-body images from human characters, we erased font parts by using Adobe Photoshop. No Face images involve font images. Finally, we created five types of dataset that are front cover images with/without fonts, whole-body images with/without fonts, and face images. Figure 3 shows examples of each type of images.

3.2 Typefaces of Fonts Used in Title

This paper discusses only Japanese fonts as targets. Japanese fonts consist of more than 1,000 kinds. And designers sometimes originally adjust the shape of existing font design for suiting fonts to the design of front covers. Therefore, numbers of kinds of Japanese fonts exist. Moreover, some different kinds of fonts have very similar shape. From such reasons, estimating the concrete font name seems to be impossible. In this paper, we try to estimate not the detailed information such as concrete font name but the typeface name of each font as the general information. On the basis of Japanese font analysis in [12, 13], we classify each font into 5 typefaces; "Mincho", "Gothic", "Maru-Gothic", "Traditional", and "Designed". And we estimate a class of typefaces of fonts used from each image such as front cover, whole body, and face. Figure 4 shows examples of 5 typefaces mentioned above.

3.3 Label

A label information of each image contains the name of typeface used as title fonts and their number of counts. Here, some titles have multiple fonts and typefaces as shown in Fig. 1. Therefore, the label of several image has counts on multi typefaces among five typefaces mentioned above. To clarify such conditions on title fonts used in front cover of books, we investigated 581 images we gathered. Table 1 shows the number and ratio of images including only one typeface and that containing multiple typefaces for their labels. Table 2 provides the number and ratio of images on the main typeface of title fonts used in each image. Table 1 gives that there is a certain number of images.

with multiple typefaces and we cannot ignore such images. Table 2 indicates that designed typefaces are often selected for the front cover of Manga and Light novels and traditional typefaces rarely are used. They seem to be common and acceptable because of characteristics of such genres. On the other hand, the count number of images containing

(a) Front cover image
with title fonts

(b) Front cover image
with no title fonts

(c) Body image
with title fonts

(d) Body image
with no title
fonts

(e) Face image
(enlarged)

Fig. 3. Examples of front cover and several part images. JTC Janken font (designed typeface) is used [5].

(a) Mincho   (b) Gothic   (c) Maru-Gothic

(d) Traditional   (e) Designed

Fig. 4. Examples of each typeface. Each character expresses Japanese Hiragana.

the Mincho typeface as main title fonts is more than the sum of images including Gothic or Maru-Gothic. This is unexpected at least for us.

Table 1. Number of front cover images containing single or multiple fonts

Num. of font typefaces	Num. of images	Ratio [%]
Single	505	86.9
Multiple	76	13.1

Table 2. Number of images for each typeface

Typeface	Num. of images	Ratio [%]
Mincho	211	36.3
Gothic	91	15.7
Maru-Gothic	76	13.1
Traditional	20	3.4
Designed	183	31.5

On the basis of labels mentioned above, we encode each label information into two other types of label and adopt our evaluation method for each type of label. The first one is so-called one-hot encoding; a typeface with the most counts has one and the other typefaces have zero. This label has one-hot vector and this type of label are usually used for the multi-class classification task. In this paper we call this type of label "hard label". In the evaluation step, when a typeface with the highest probability in an output is same as that with one hot value, the estimation of typeface is regarded as correct. The other type of label consists of ratio values for each typeface; each ratio is computed by dividing count number of each typeface by the total count number among all the typefaces. So, if an original label has counts for multiple fonts, this kind of label has values on multiple positions. We call this type of label "soft label" in this paper. In the evaluation, we compare a typeface of the highest probability in an output with that with the highest label value. If it's same, the estimation is regarded as correct. Table 3 shows an original label information and 2 kinds of label that are encoded from the original one in our experiment.

3.4 Estimation Model

As a framework for estimating typefaces used in each front cover image, we use Deep Neural Networks (DNN). In this paper, we exploit a pre-trained DNN model trained by using many data and fine-tune such a model because few training images tend to obtain a model that over-fits training images. As a pre-trained DNN model, we use the VGG16 model [14] that were trained by the ImageNet dataset that contains 14 million images

Table 3. Examples of original label and 2 kinds of labels used in our data

Typeface	Origin	Hard	Soft
Mincho	0	0	0
Gothic	6	1	0.6
Maru-Gothic	0	0	0
Traditional	0	0	0
Designed	4	0	0.4

of 1,000 classes. We exploit only convolution layers of this pre-trained DNN model as a feature extraction part and trained new dense layers as a classification part by the use of training data mentioned in 3.1 in the training process. Moreover, 3 convolution layers in VGG16 are re-trained in the fine-tuning process. In the training using data with hard or soft labels, dense layers with the Softmax function were used in the final output layer. Figure 5 shows the structure of the DNN model used in our experiments.

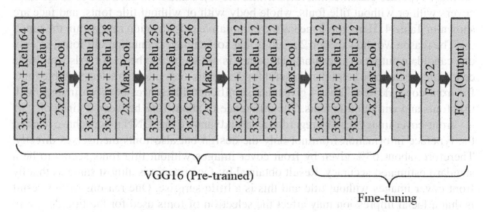

Fig. 5. The structure of our DNN model

4 Experiments

In this section we describe evaluation experiments for validating and analyzing the performance of our approaches to estimate typefaces of title fonts in the front cover of Manga and Light novels.

4.1 Experimental Set-Up

As experimental data, we split each data of front cover, whole body, and face 581 images into 4 sets. 436 images from 3 sets were used as training data and 145 images from another set were used as test one. We adopted cross-validation; therefore, each set were used as test data once in the rotation and 4 tests were totally carried out. Each result shown below was calculated as the average value among 4 tests.

Each data with hard or soft label were trained and tested as a multi-class classification problem. Thus, the cross entropy was used as their cost function for their training.

On the basis of preliminary experiment results, we set several experimental set-ups as follow. The number of epochs is 300. The batch size is 1 because of few training data. The initial learning late is 2.0e-5. Adam was used as the optimizer. The number of dense layers is 3, and the numbers of units in each dense layer are 512, 32, and 5, respectively. The cross-entropy was used as the loss function. As data augmentation, basic techniques as rotation, horizontal shift, vertical shift, and horizontal flip were adopted.

Each image is normalized into 256 x 256 pixels as a default size. Front cover images and body images are normalized into several sizes and details are described later.

4.2 Experimental Results

First of all, we describe experimental results using data with hard labels and default settings. Typeface classification rates within the top 1 and 2 for each image of the front covers with or without title fonts, whole body with or without title fonts, and face are shown in Table 4. Here, top 2 means the cumulative classification rate within the top 2.

The reason we show the top 2 result is that some images contain multi fonts, so only one candidate output as an estimated typeface is not seemed to be so fair. Also, multiple candidates seem to be helpful and useful for designers and editors to select suitable fonts for front cover design. Table 4 gives that significant differences between images with title fonts and without title fonts. The difference of about 10% between 2 kinds of.

front-cover images can be regarded as the advantage that DNN models have learned the typeface information from not only the design but also fonts themselves directly. Therefore, about 63% given by front cover images without title fonts seems to be a standard estimated accuracy. Result obtained by face images is almost same as that by front cover images without title and this is a little surprise. One reasons of this result is that a facial impression may affect the selection of fonts used for the title design in front covers. Figure 6 shows an example that the typeface used as title font was correctly estimated from an only face image. This example seems to provide the impression of font shape is similar to that derived from the human character's face. Other reason seems that front cover images was normalized into too small ones. In the next experiment, we validate accuracies using images with another size or aspect ratio. On the other hand, the estimation using whole-body images gives lower rates than other types of images. The lower results obtained by whole-body images seem to be caused by variations of composition in whole-body images (See Appendix Fig. 9 and Fig. 10). The difference between 2 kinds of whole-body images, about 4%, is smaller than that between front cover images, about 10%. This reason is that some original whole-body images have no title fonts. Also, as shown in Table 1, several data used in the experiment have multiple typefaces. Therefore, obtaining high rates is very difficult. The fact that all the rates within the top 2 are under 90% despite of a 5 class-classification problem indicates that this task is not very easy.

Table 4. Estimation rates [%] on hard labels

	Front cover w/ title	Front cove w/o title	Body w/ title	Body w/o title	Face
Top 1	72.5	62.8	62.3	58.5	63.0
Top 2	87.9	84.3	79.9	78.8	80.7

(a) Face image (enlarged)   (b) Original whole image

Fig. 6. Example of a face image that a typeface of title fonts used in front cover is correctly estimated [15]. Typeface: Mincho. Font name: Marumei Old.

Next, as mentioned above, we validate other image sizes or ratios that are different from default sizes. Table 5 shows estimation rates for every type of images with several image sizes or ratios. On the basis of image sizes in our database, 1.0, 1.5 and 2.0 as ratios of an image height to an image width were used for front cover images. 1.0, 2.0, and 4.0 as ratios of an image height to an image width were assessed for whole-body images. Only face image was normalized with keeping an image ratio is 1.0. Table 5 provides that bigger images have obtained better results. In particular, the increase of rates for front cover images, about 10%, are significant. This suggests that the default size is too small for such images and often lose important information including font one. And normalized images with similar ratio to original's one have almost same rates as enlarged square images. This gives that the characteristics as crucial information for each font class are retained if an original ratio of each image is changed.

Then, we compared experimental results using images with hard labels and soft ones. Table 6 shows estimation rates for 5 kinds of image with each label. Rates with soft labels are obtained using same image sizes/ratios that provided the best rates on hard labels. Compared to results with hard labels, all the results on soft labels are a little lower than those on hard labels. These results suggest that the expression by soft label encoding is not appropriate to our experimental data that have multi classes.

Table 5. Estimation rates [%] on hard labels in several image sizes and ratios

Image height	Image width	Front cover w/ title	Front cove w/o title	Body w/ title	Body w/o title	Face
256	256	72.5	62.8	62.3	58.5	63.0
384	256	76.9	67.1	-	-	-
384	384	78.5	65.6	64.9	63.3	62.5
512	128	-	-	60.4	58.7	-
512	256	79.0	70.6	63.3	62.3	-
512	512	**81.8**	70.1	65.2	62.5	**65.4**
768	512	80.0	68.0	-	-	63.5
768	768	80.4	**72.6**	**68.5**	**65.2**	63.5
1,024	256	-	-	68.3	64.2	-
1,024	512	81.4	70.4	65.9	64.4	-

Table 6. Estimation rates [%] on hard and soft labels

Label	Front cover w/ title	Front cove w/o title	Body w/ title	Body w/o title	Face
Hard	81.8	72.6	68.5	65.2	65.4
Soft	78.1	72.1	66.3	63.9	64.6

Finally, we analyzed error results and causes. Main mis-estimations are that Gothic or Maru-gothic typefaces were classified into Designed one. Some kinds of Designed fonts are very similar to Gothic or Maru-Gothic fonts. To solve this kind of errors, we need to introduce another scheme or information.

5   Conclusions

In this paper we have created the database that consists of about 580 images of front cover of Manga and Light novels books, and have proposed the framework for estimating typefaces of title fonts designed in such images for recommending the selection of suitable fonts for the title design. Our database contains five types of images; two kinds of whole front cover images of each books, two kinds of whole-body images extracted from a human character pictured in front cover images, and a character face image that are a part of a human character one. The difference between two kinds for front cover images and whole-body ones is with/without title fonts. In our experiments, we have estimated a kind of typeface of title fonts used in front covers from each type of images. We have exploited the pre-trained DNN model for the font typeface estimation and criteria for each label. Experimental results have shown that the design of front cover of books and human characters contained in the front cover have strong correlation with font typefaces selected for their front cover. The top rate of estimating kinds of typefaces using images without title fonts was about 72% on front cover image and about 65% for whole-body and face images. From these results we can say that estimating typefaces of title fonts in the front cover will enable us to ease the selection of suitable fonts for front cover design by providing candidates in the near future.

Future works are to gather more samples of cover front pages of Manga and Light novels for increasing training samples, correct the imbalance of data size among typefaces, and estimate not only kinds of typeface but concrete font names.

Appendix

Other examples of 2 kinds of front cover images, 2 kinds of whole-body images, and face images in our database are shown below (Fig. 7, 8 and 11).

Fig. 7. Examples of front cover images with title fonts

(a)   (b)   (c)   (d)   (e)

(f)   (g)   (h)   (i)   (j)

Fig. 8. Examples of front cover images with no title fonts

(a)   (b)   (c)   (d)   (e)

(f)   (g)   (h)   (i)   (j)

Fig. 9. Examples of whole-body images with fonts

Fig. 10. Examples of whole-body images with no fonts

Fig. 11. Examples of face images (enlarged)

References

1. Suzuki, D., Uru, D.: OniAni (in Japanese), vol.1, Media Factory (2010)
2. Haruba, N.: The Quintessential Quintuplets (in Japanese), vol.7, Kodansha (2019)
3. Shinhara, Y., Karamatsu, T., Harada, D., Yamaguchi, K., Uchida, S.: Serif or sans: visual font analytic on book covers and online advertisements. In: Proceedings of International Conference on Document Analysis and Recognition (2019)
4. Imakawa, S., Kodoi, T.: What kind of restaurant does the characters on the signboards conjure up? Graduate School Educ. Bull. Hiroshima Univ. **65**, 249–256 (2016)

5. Akime, J., Morisawa, H.: Otome-Ge no Koryakutaishou ni Narimashita (in Japanese), vol. 2, Ascii Media Works (2012)
6. BNN Editorial Department: The design of Light Novels. BNN Shin-sha (2018)
7. Sannoumaru, S., Yuzuki R.: Logotype!. Ritto-sha (in Japanese), A5 edn. (2015)
8. MdN Editorial Department: The Graphics Design of Manga & Anime (in Japanese) MdN EXTRA, vol.1, MdN Corporation (2014)
9. MdN Editorial Department.: The Graphics Design of Manga & Anime (in Japanese), MdN EXTRA, vol. 2, MdN Corporation (2015)
10. Nichibou Editorial Department.: The New Comics Design (in Japanese). Japan Publicaitons Inc. (2020)
11. Nichibou Editorial Department.: The New Comics Design 2 (in Japanese). Japan Publicaitons Inc (2021)
12. Morisawa + DESIGNNING Editorial Department.: Type and Font Book (in Japanese). Mainichi Communications (2010)
13. Date C.: Moji-no-Kihon (in Japanese). Graphics-sha (2020)
14. Simonyan, K., Zisserman, A.: Very deep convolutional networks for large-scale image recognition. In: Proceedings of International Conference of Learning Representation (2015)
15. Natsumi, K., Shizuki, M.: Hazakura ga Kita Natsu (in Japanese). Ascii Media Works (2008)

Human Face Detector with Gender Identification by Split-Based Inception Block and Regulated Attention Module

Adri Priadana[1]([✉]) [iD], Muhamad Dwisnanto Putro[2][iD], Duy-Linh Nguyen[1][iD], Xuan-Thuy Vo[1][iD], and Kang-Hyun Jo[1][iD]

[1] Department of Electrical, Electronic and Computer Engineering, University of Ulsan, Ulsan, South Korea
{priadana3202,ndlinh301}@mail.ulsan.ac.kr, xthuy@islab.ulsan.ac.kr, acejo@ulsan.ac.kr
[2] Department of Electrical Engineering, Universitas Sam Ratulangi, Manado, Indonesia
dwisnantoputro@unsrat.ac.id

Abstract. Smart digital advertising platforms have been widely arising. These platforms require a human face detector with gender identification to assist them in the determination of providing relevant advertisements. The detector is also prosecuted to identify the gender of a masked face in post-coronavirus situations and demanded to operate on a CPU device to lower system expenses. This work presents a lightweight Convolution Neural Network (CNN) architecture to build a gender identification integrated with face detection to respond to these issues. This work proposes a split-based inception block to efficiently extract features at various sizes by partially applying different convolution kernel sizes, levels, and regulated attention module to improve the quality of the feature map. It produces slight parameters that drive the architecture efficiency and can operate quickly in real-time. To validate the performance of the proposed architecture, UTKFace and Labeled Faces in the Wild (LFW) datasets, modified with an artificial mask, are utilized as training and validation datasets. This offered architecture is compared to different lightweight and deep architectures. Regarding the experiment results, the proposed architecture outperforms masked face gender identification on the two datasets. In addition, the proposed architecture, which integrates with face detection to become a human face detector with gender identification can run 135 frames per second in real-time on a CPU configuration.

Keywords: Human Face Detector · Face Gender Identification · Convolutional Neural Network (CNN) · Split-based Inception Block · Regulated Attention Module

1 Introduction

The advancement of information technology has stimulated the rapid development of smart digital advertising, not only in online media but also in offline

© The Author(s), under exclusive license to Springer Nature Singapore Pte Ltd. 2023
I. Na and G. Irie (Eds.): IW-FCV 2023, CCIS 1857, pp. 163–177, 2023.
https://doi.org/10.1007/978-981-99-4914-4_13

media. It is proven because these platforms appear in many public places, such as airports, stations, and markets [4]. Practically, smart digital advertising platforms are handily personalized and customized. Therefore, it can display dynamic contents as determined by the provider. Nevertheless, the market demands effective mechanisms that make these platforms can provide targeted advertising [1]. This mechanisms will offer more advantages in the digital advertising strategy [20].

Providing targeted advertising can be accomplished by personalizing the audience facing the platform. The audience's gender, which is an essential attribute, can be used in segmenting the readers. These platforms can provide better appropriate advertising for each reader by recognizing their gender [15]. This scheme can be achieved with the reader's face detection and classification.

Nowadays, Convolutional Neural Network (CNN) has verified a bunch of victories in image-based detection and classification tasks. The common direction in designing CNN architectures is to develop deeper architectures to reach higher accuracy [7,25]. However, it tends to generate architecture with a large number of parameters. It makes the architecture inefficient to operate, especially on low-cost devices in real-time. In the case of advertising platform implementation, it requires a low-cost device, such as a CPU device, to minimize the implementation expense [3,13]. Hence, it requires an efficient face gender detector, which can be suitably operated on a CPU in real-time.

A new challenge arises after the spread of the COVID-19 virus extensively. It makes people required or used to wear masks on their faces when they are traveling. It makes part of the face area occluded, such as the mouth, which is one of the essential features for recognizing gender through the face. Therefore, it needs an efficient human face detector with gender identification ability that can detect and recognize the gender of a masked face. This work presents an efficient human face detector with gender identification by a few parameters that can efficiently detect and identify a masked face gender while maintaining its performance.

An efficient CPU-based human face detector with gender identification called GenderMask-CPU proposed a lightweight architecture with a split-based inception block and regulated attention module (SiramNet). The split-based inception block is offered to efficiently extract features at various sizes by partially applying different convolution kernel sizes and levels. The regulated attention module, which consist of the channel and spatial, are employed to enhance the feature map grade. It produces scant parameters and guides the detector to work efficiently and fast. In summary, the main contribution of this work is twofold, i.e.,

1. An efficient architecture with a split-based inception block and regulated attention module (SiramNet) is proposed, which generates slight parameters. The split-based inception block can efficiently extract multi-size feature areas of the feature maps. The attention module can maintain the essential features of the face area, which can increase the gender accuracy of the classification.

2. A fast human face detector with gender identification is introduced, which can operate in real-time on a CPU device efficiently and fast. The performance of the offered architecture is proven to compete with other deep and light CNN architectures on UTKFace [30] and Labeled Faces in the Wild (LFW) [10] datasets, modified with an artificial mask utilized from [2].

2   Related Work

In recent years, CNN architectures, designed for face gender recognition work, have progressed with impressive improvement, especially in performance. Various modified versions of CNNs have been developed to optimize face gender recognition. HyperFace-ResNet [21], a CNN architecture, was proposed to perform gender recognition from a face. The architecture develops and adjusts ResNet [5] architecture and reaches good performance on LFW datasets. In [4], a CNN architecture has been employed to recognize gender and implemented in the monitoring system. The architecture utilized MobilenetV2 [22] architecture and generated 3.5 million parameters.

Nowadays, efficient face gender detectors emerge specially designed for CPU devices to encounter market demand which can reduce implementation costs. MPConvNet [17] based on the CNN architecture was developed and generated 659,650 parameters. The architecture proposed a multi-perspective convolution used to capture various feature regions of the object. The architecture reaches good performance on UTKFace and LFW datasets. SufiaNet [16] based on the CNN architecture was developed and only generated 226,574 parameters. Sufi-aNet [16] is a shallow architecture supported by a global attention module. The architecture gains sufficient performance on UTKFace and LFW datasets.

3   The Proposed Method

This work proposes a CNN architecture to recognize a gender of a masked face, as shown in Fig. 1. This architecture is structured as a backbone and classification module, generating 441,460 parameters.

3.1   The Backbone

CNN-based feature extraction has shown excellent performance. However, this extractor tends to generate enormous parameters [6]. Therefore, an efficient backbone module is proposed to develop a fast architecture, especially one that can run on the CPU in real time. This architecture employs three main convolution layers with same 3×3 kernel size, managed sequentially by three times the number of kernels growing, i.e. 16, 32, and 64. This mechanism seeks to acquire more information on the latter layers. Following each convolution layer, a batch normalization (BN) method and Leaky ReLU (Leaky Rectified Linear Unit) activation are applied to deal with the vanishing gradient. A dropout strategy puts previous to the final convolution operation is also used to impede overfitting. Three max-pooling operations are assigned in this backbone to down-sample the feature maps. One layer of 4×4 and two layers of 2×2 sizes max-pooling with two strides are applied.

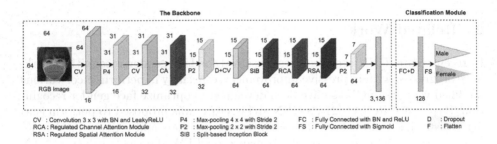

Fig. 1. The proposed architecture of the gender identification of masked faces contains a backbone with a split-based inception block and regulated attention module.

3.2 The Split-Based Inception Block

To improve the feature extractor on the backbone module, this work proposes a split-based inception block and applies the block after the last convolution layer. Inspired by the inception block [26], this module employs four branches of convolution layer with different levels and kernel sizes, as shown in Fig. 2. They are convolution layers with 1×1, 3×3, two times 3×3, and 5×5 kernel sizes. Unlike the original inception block that applies the convolution layer with the same number of a kernel as the input, this block divides the input feature map $\mathbf{X}$ become four components $[\mathbf{X_1}, \mathbf{X_2}, \mathbf{X_3}, \mathbf{X_4}]$. Then, it applies convolution operation with different levels and kernel sizes mentioned before, which is represented as follows:

$$
\begin{aligned}
SIB(\mathbf{X}) = \mathbf{X} + (SELU(BN(C1(D(\mathbf{X_1})))) \oplus SELU(BN(C3(D(\mathbf{X_2})))) \\
\oplus SELU(BN(C3(D(SELU(BN(C3(D(\mathbf{X_3}))))))))) \quad (1) \\
\oplus SELU(BN(C5(D(\mathbf{X_4}))))),
\end{aligned}
$$

where $C1$, $C3$, $C5$ are convolution layers with 1×1, 3×3, and 5×5 kernel sizes, respectively. $SELU$ is Scaled Exponential Linear Units (SELU) activation [12], D is dropout operation, BN is batch normalization operation, and $\oplus$ is the concatenate operation. This block will extract more information from different levels and area sizes efficiently. At the last stage, a residual mechanism [6] is applied to combine the concatenate operation result with the input feature map $\mathbf{X}$ by an addition operation.

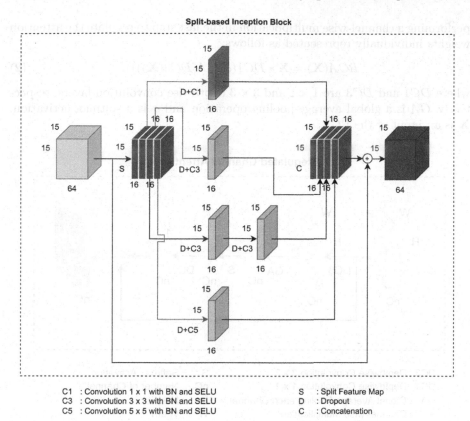

C1 : Convolution 1 x 1 with BN and SELU   S   : Split Feature Map
C3 : Convolution 3 x 3 with BN and SELU   D   : Dropout
C5 : Convolution 5 x 5 with BN and SELU   C   : Concatenation

Fig. 2. The proposed Split-based Inception block.

3.3   The Regulated Attention Module (RAM)

A backbone with few parameters feebly discriminates interest features of the face. Therefore, the Regulated Attention module (RAM) is proposed and applied to improve essential facial features. This module consists of a regulated channel attention module (RCA) and a regulated spatial attention module (RSA). Inspired by the attention module in [9], RCA performs a global average-pooling operation to aggregate each feature map based on channel. However, we do not use fully connected layers but apply softmax activation directly after the pooling operation to calculate the probability of channel importance level. A softmax activation is used rather than the sigmoid activation because it can establish long-range channel dependency [29]. Imbued from the attention module [18], this architecture puts a 3×3 depthwise convolution layer before the pooling operations to allow the individual channel to expand learning efficiently, as shown in Fig. 3. Different from [18], this architecture only applies global average pooling to squeeze the number of operations. Further, we proposed a 1×1 depthwise convolution layer located after softmax activation and before performing a channel-wise multiplication in the last step to regulate the attention weights individually represented as follows:

$$RCA(\mathbf{X}) = \mathbf{X} * DC1(\sigma(GA(DC3(\mathbf{X})))), \tag{2}$$

where $DC1$ and $DC3$ are 1×1 and 3×3 depthwise convolution layers, respectively. GA is a global average-pooling operation and σ is a softmax activation. $\mathbf{X}$ is an input of the RCA.

Regulated Channel Attention

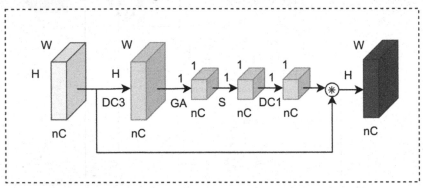

DC3 : Depthwise Convolution 3 x 3   S   : Softmax Activation
DC1 : Depthwise Convolution 1 x 1   nC : Number of Channel
GA   : Global Average Pooling each Channel   H   : Height
✳   : Channel-wise Multiplication   W   : Width

Fig. 3. The proposed Regulated Channel Attention module.

Motivated by [28], a global average-pooling operation is assigned on RSA to aggregate spatial features across the channel. This operation renders a feature vector and describes the feature overview of the corresponding channel. However, a softmax activation is voted than a sigmoid activation to calculate the spatial importance level. This activation can establish spatial dependency. A 1×1 depthwise convolution layer is also applied after softmax activation and before performing a spatial-wise multiplication to regulate the attention weights with a shared parameter, as shown in Fig. 4. It is represented as follows:

$$RSA(\mathbf{X}) = \mathbf{X} * DC1(\sigma(GA(\mathbf{X}))), \tag{3}$$

where $DC1$ is a 1×1 depthwise convolution layer and GA is a global average-pooling across the channel. σ is a softmax activation and $\mathbf{X}$ is an input of RSA.

RCA is assigned following the second convolution layer and the split-based inception block. This module will enhance the grade of the intermediate and latter features. On the other hand, RSA is only assigned following the last RCA, which drives the architecture to focus on the location of informative spatial features after it extracts the high-level features.

Regulated Spatial Attention

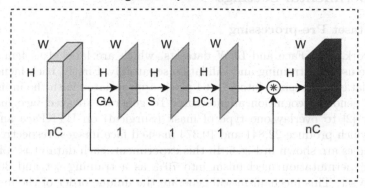

GA   : Global Average Pooling across Channel
DC1 : Depthwise Convolution 1 x 1
S   : Softmax Activation
nC   : Number of Channel
H   : Height
W   : Width
✳   : Spatial-wise Multiplication

Fig. 4. The proposed Regulated Spatial Attention module.

3.4   Classification Module

The backbone module is tasked to extract features from masked faces. Then, the results will be fed to the classification module employed to reckon the probability of each gender class. This operation leads to deciding whether the masked face is male or female. This classification module is composed of two dense layers with 128 and 2 units, respectively. A batch normalization and ReLU (Rectified Linear Unit) activation are applied after the first dense layer, and the Sigmoid activation is applied after the second dense layer. The Sigmoid activation will render the input into scenarios that could describe the prediction decision of whether the masked face is male or female. In order to discourage overfitting, it applies a dropout operation after the ReLU activation.

3.5   Face Detector

In this work, face detection is required for integrating with masked face gender recognition to build a masked face gender detector. It is employed to locate and get the region of the face or masked face referred to as a Region of Interest (RoI). An efficient face detection model with cheap operation is required to operate brief in the real-time. Hence, a face detector named LWFCPU [19] is utilized. It employs only several convolutional layers that generate slight parameters. The RoI, which comes from the face detection operation, will become an input of the proposed gender recognition architecture. It will be resized and cropped to a particular size appropriate for the architecture input.

4   Experimental Settings

4.1   Dataset Pre-processing

In this work, UTKFace and LFW datasets, which are labeled as females and males, are used for training and validation separately. Firstly, each facial image of these datasets is resized into 64×64 pixels appropriated with the input of the proposed gender recognition architecture. To generate masked face instances, we follow [2] to overlay one type of mask (Surgical) on UTKFace and LFW images, which produce 22,841 and 10,374 masked face images, respectively, and the examples are shown in Fig. 5. In this experiment, each dataset is split using a random permutation mechanism into 70% as a training set and 30% as a validation set. This mechanism will generate the unique order of the instances.

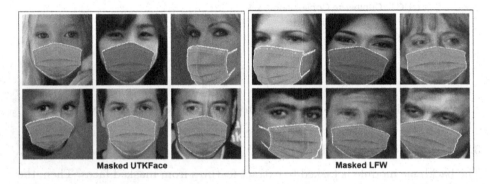

Fig. 5. The examples of the UTKFace and Labeled Faces in the Wild (LFW) datasets, modified with an artificial mask utilized from [2].

4.2   Implementation Details

The experiment is executed on the NVIDIA GTX 1080Ti 11GB to accelerate the training on the proposed architecture by using Tensorflow and Keras framework libraries. UTKFace and LFW datasets modified with an artificial mask referenced from [2] are used as training and validation to ratify the performance of the proposed architecture, which trains with three hundred epochs. The Adam optimizer is employed to optimize the weight on the Binary Cross-Entropy loss. The datasets are trained by using 10^{-2} initial learning rate, which will reduce to 75% if the accuracy does not improve in every 20 epochs. Intel Core i7-9750H CPU@2.6 GHz with 20 GB RAM is used to investigate the speed in frame per second (FPS) of the proposed architecture and the detector.

5   Results

5.1   Evaluation on Datasets

UTKFace. A face dataset labeled in gender, age, and ethnicity, is used for training and validation to ratify the performance of the proposed architecture. This dataset consists of 23,708 instances with various positions, expressions, resolutions, and lighting. This dataset also covers age variations ranging from 0 to 116. This dataset was modified with an artificial mask utilized from [2] and generated 22,841 masked face images. The proposed architecture, which only employs 441,460 parameters, gains 91.17% of validation accuracy. The proposed architecture outperforms deep CNN architectures [7,24,27], as sown in Table 1. Moreover, the proposed architecture reaches accuracy surpassing the three lightweight architectures, SqueezeNet [11], SufiaNet [16], and MPConvNet [17], which differed by 2.4, 1.16, and 0.98, respectively.

Table 1. Evaluation results on UTKFace dataset, modified with an artificial mask utilized from [2].

Architectures	Number of Parameters	Validation Accuracy
MobileNetV2 [23]	2,260,546	87.93
ResNet50V2 [7]	23,568,898	87.99
VGG13 [24] with BN	34,467,906	88.07
SquezeeNet [11] with BN	735,306	88.77
VGG16 [24] with BN	39,782,722	89.23
VGG11 [24] with BN	34,413,698	89.26
InceptionV3 [27]	21,806,882	89.64
SufiaNet [16]	226,574	90.01
MPConvNet [17]	659,650	90.19
SiramNet (ours)	**441,460**	**91.17**

LFW. A face dataset labeled in gender consists of 13,234 instances with unbalance proportion between males and females, about 77% and 23%. This dataset was also modified with an artificial mask utilized from [2] and generated 10,374 masked face images. The proposed architecture, which only employs 441,460 parameters, gains 95.64% of validation accuracy. The proposed architecture also outperforms deep CNN architectures [7,24,27], as sown in Table 2. Moreover, the proposed architecture also reaches accuracy surpassing the three lightweight architectures, SqueezeNet [11], SufiaNet [16], and MPConvNet [17], which differed by 1.38, 0.38, and 0.27, respectively.

Table 2. Evaluation results on LFW dataset, modified with an artificial mask utilized from [2].

Architectures	Number of Parameters	Validation Accuracy
MobileNetV2 [23]	2,260,546	79.93
VGG13 [24] with BN	34,467,906	91.18
InceptionV3 [27]	21,806,882	92.58
ResNet50V2 [7]	23,568,898	92.96
VGG16 [24] with BN	39,782,722	93.35
VGG11 [24] with BN	34,413,698	93.88
SquezeeNet [11] with BN	735,306	93.99
SufiaNet [16]	226,574	95.13
MPConvNet [17]	659,650	95.37
SiramNet (ours)	**441,460**	**95.64**

5.2   Ablation Study

This work performs the ablation study to investigate how much the proposed split-based inception block and attention module will impact the validation accuracy result. This ablative study conducts by repealing the block or module and then calculating the validation accuracy on the UTKFace dataset. As can be seen in Table 3, utilizing the proposed split-based inception block and applying this block after the last convolution layer can increase the accuracy by 0.12%. The proposed RCA can escalate the accuracy by 0.38%. Moreover, the proposed RSA module can also escalate the accuracy by 0.2% by adding only two parameters.

Table 3. Ablation study on UTKFace dataset, modified with an artificial mask utilized from [2].

Group Split Inception Block	Regulated Channel Attention Module	Regulated Spatial Attention Module	Number of Parameters	Validation Accuracy
			426,338	90.47
✓			440,306	90.59
✓	✓		441,458	90.97
✓	✓	✓	441,460	91.17

5.3   Runtime Efficiency

The proposed architecture recognizes gender from a masked face using only 441,460 parameters. The architecture operates in real-time at 272.80 and 135.02 frames per second for gender identification and gender identification integrated with face detection [19], respectively. The proposed efficient architecture becomes the second fastest compared to other deep and lightweight architectures, as shown in Table 4. Even though SufiaNet [16] has become the fastest architecture, the validation accuracy is not better than our proposed architecture, with a difference of 1.16 and 0.38 on the UTKFace and LFW datasets, modified with an artificial mask utilized from [2], respectively. Figure 6 shows the recognition result of the GenderMask-CPU, in which the green bounding box means a male face and the magenta bounding box means a female face. Although this detector is specially designed for faces with mask shown in Fig. 6(a), it can also work on faces without mask shown in Fig. 6(b).

Table 4. Runtime efficiency on an Intel Core i7- 9750H CPU.

Architectures	Number of Parameters	GFLOPs	Gender Recognition (FPS)	Gender Recognition integrated with Face Detection (FPS)
VGG16 [24] with BN	39,782,722	2.2900	43.28	37.15
VGG13 [24] with BN	34,467,906	1.6100	51.14	42.76
VGG11 [24] with BN	34,413,698	1.2700	55.49	45.71
ResNet50V2 [7]	23,568,898	0.5710	57.19	46.79
InceptionV3 [27]	21,806,882	0.4050	64.43	51.47
MobileNetV2 [23]	2,260,546	0.0501	118.71	81.20
SquezeeNet [11] with BN	735,306	0.0833	231.40	122.75
MPConvNet [17]	659,650	0.0670	269.86	132.04
SufiaNet [16]	226,574	0.0218	327.29	145.37
SiramNet (ours)	**441,460**	**0.0293**	**272.80**	**135.02**

5.4 Attention Modules Comparison

The proposed regulated attention module (RAM) is also compared with other common attention modules, as shown in Table 5. This module compares with Squeeze-and-Excitation (SE) [8], Bottleneck Attention Module (BAM) [14], and Convolutional Block Attention Module (CBAM) [28]. These attention modules are applied at the same place, i.e. after the second convolution layer and the split-based inception block on the UTKFace dataset, modified with an artificial mask utilized from [2], to perform a fair comparison. The validation accuracy of the proposed architecture with RAM is higher than the proposed architecture with BAM, SE, or CBAM, which differ by 0.48%, 0.39%, and 0.12%, respectively.

Table 5. Comparisons of Different Attention Modules applied on the Proposed Architecture on UTKFace dataset, modified with an artificial mask utilized from [2].

Attention Modules	Number of Parameters	GFLOPs	Validation Accuracy	Gender Recognition (FPS)	Gender Recognition integrated with Face Detection (FPS)
BAM [14]	449,736	0.0348	90.69	238.19	125.40
SE [8]	440,946	0.0284	90.78	307.44	145.18
CBAM [28]	441,084	0.0286	91.05	273.84	135,84
RAM (ours)	**441,460**	**0.0293**	**91.17**	272.80	135.02

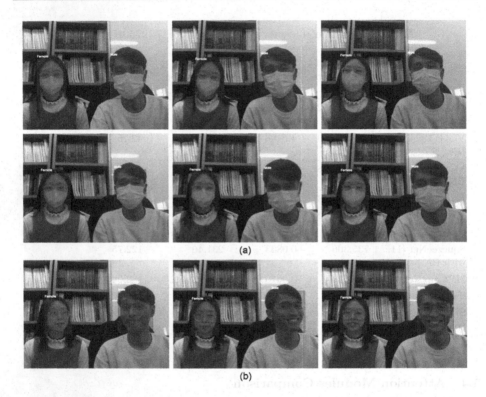

Fig. 6. The correct detection results of the GenderMask-CPU detector for masked (a) and non-masked (b) faces.

6   Conclusion

An efficient CPU-based human face detector with gender identification called GenderMask-CPU is proposed and offers a lightweight architecture with a split-based inception block and regulated attention module. This lightweight architecture assigns a few convolution operations that make the architecture only generates 441,460 parameters. This work offered a split-based inception block to efficiently extract features at various sizes by partially applying different convolution kernel sizes and levels. The regulated attention module is also proposed to improve the quality of the feature map. This architecture acquires competitive performance compared to other lightweight and deep CNN architectures on the UTKFace and Labeled Faces in the Wild (LFW) datasets, modified with an artificial mask utilized from [2]. Accordingly, when operating on a CPU device in real-time, GenderMask-CPU is capable of running at 135 frames per second while identifying the gender of masked faces. This detector outperforms other lightweight and deep competitors' architecture. In a forthcoming study, other mechanisms, such as Transformer, can be conducted to improve the identification accuracy. The augmentation strategy can also be explored to improve the dataset varieties that can increase the performance of masked face gender recognition.

Acknowledgment. This result was supported by "Regional Innovation Strategy (RIS)" through the National Research Foundation of Korea (NRF) funded by the Ministry of Education (MOE) (2021RIS-003).

References

1. Alhalabi, M., Hussein, N., Khan, E., Habash, O., Yousaf, J., Ghazal, M.: Sustainable smart advertisement display using deep age and gender recognition. In: 2021 International Conference on Decision Aid Sciences and Application (DASA), pp. 33–37. IEEE (2021)
2. Anwar, A., Raychowdhury, A.: Masked face recognition for secure authentication. arXiv preprint arXiv:2008.11104 (2020)
3. Bandung, Y., Hendra, Y.F., Subekti, L.B.: Design and implementation of digital signage system based on Raspberry Pi 2 for e-tourism in Indonesia. In: 2015 International Conference on Information Technology Systems and Innovation (ICITSI), pp. 1–6. IEEE (2015)
4. Greco, A., Saggese, A., Vento, M.: Digital signage by real-time gender recognition from face images. In: 2020 IEEE International Workshop on Metrology for Industry 4.0 & IoT, pp. 309–313. IEEE (2020)
5. He, K., Zhang, X., Ren, S., Sun, J.: Deep residual learning for image recognition. In: 2016 IEEE Conference on Computer Vision and Pattern Recognition (CVPR), pp. 770–778. IEEE (2016)
6. He, K., Zhang, X., Ren, S., Sun, J.: Deep residual learning for image recognition. In: 2016 IEEE Conference on Computer Vision and Pattern Recognition (CVPR), pp. 770–778 (2016). https://doi.org/10.1109/CVPR.2016.90
7. He, K., Zhang, X., Ren, S., Sun, J.: Identity mappings in deep residual networks. In: Leibe, B., Matas, J., Sebe, N., Welling, M. (eds.) ECCV 2016. LNCS, vol. 9908, pp. 630–645. Springer, Cham (2016). https://doi.org/10.1007/978-3-319-46493-0_38
8. Hu, J., Shen, L., Albanie, S., Sun, G., Wu, E.: Squeeze-and-excitation networks. IEEE Trans. Pattern Anal. Mach. Intell. **42**(8), 2011–2023 (2019)
9. Hu, J., Shen, L., Albanie, S., Sun, G., Wu, E.: Squeeze-and-excitation networks. IEEE Trans. Pattern Anal. Mach. Intell. **42**(8), 2011–2023 (2020). https://doi.org/10.1109/TPAMI.2019.2913372
10. Huang, G.B., Mattar, M., Berg, T., Learned-Miller, E.: Labeled faces in the wild: a database for studying face recognition in unconstrained environments. In: Workshop on Faces in 'Real-Life' Images: Detection, Alignment, and Recognition (2008)

11. Iandola, F.N., Han, S., Moskewicz, M.W., Ashraf, K., Dally, W.J., Keutzer, K.: SqueezeNet: AlexNet-level accuracy with 50x fewer parameters and <0.5 mb model size. arXiv preprint arXiv:1602.07360 (2016)
12. Klambauer, G., Unterthiner, T., Mayr, A., Hochreiter, S.: Self-normalizing neural networks. In: Advances in Neural Information Processing Systems, vol. 30 (2017)
13. Mishima, K., Sakurada, T., Hagiwara, Y.: Low-cost managed digital signage system with signage device using small-sized and low-cost information device. In: 2017 14th IEEE Annual Consumer Communications & Networking Conference (CCNC), pp. 573–575. IEEE (2017)
14. Park, J., Woo, S., Lee, J.Y., Kweon, I.S.: BAM: bottleneck attention module. arXiv preprint arXiv:1807.06514 (2018)
15. Priadana, A., Maarif, M.R., Habibi, M.: Gender prediction for Instagram user profiling using deep learning. In: 2020 International Conference on Decision Aid Sciences and Application (DASA), pp. 432–436. IEEE (2020)
16. Priadana, A., Putro, M.D., Jeong, C., Jo, K.H.: A fast real-time face gender detector on CPU using superficial network with attention modules. In: 2022 International Workshop on Intelligent Systems (IWIS), pp. 1–6 (2022). https://doi.org/10.1109/IWIS56333.2022.9920714
17. Priadana, A., Putro, M.D., Jo, K.H.: An efficient face gender detector on a CPU with multi-perspective convolution. In: 2022 13th Asian Control Conference (ASCC), pp. 453–458 (2022). https://doi.org/10.23919/ASCC56756.2022.9828048
18. Priadana, A., Putro, M.D., Vo, X.T., Jo, K.H.: An efficient face-based age group detector on a CPU using two perspective convolution with attention modules. In: 2022 International Conference on Multimedia Analysis and Pattern Recognition (MAPR), pp. 1–6. IEEE (2022)
19. Putro, M.D., Nguyen, D.L., Jo, K.H.: Lightweight convolutional neural network for real-time face detector on CPU supporting interaction of service robot. In: 2020 13th International Conference on Human System Interaction (HSI), pp. 94–99. IEEE (2020)
20. Putro, M.D., Priadana, A., Nguyen, D.L., Jo, K.H.: A faster real-time face detector support smart digital advertising on low-cost computing device. In: 2022 IEEE/ASME International Conference on Advanced Intelligent Mechatronics (AIM), pp. 171–178 (2022). https://doi.org/10.1109/AIM52237.2022.9863289
21. Ranjan, R., Patel, V.M., Chellappa, R.: HyperFace: a deep multi-task learning framework for face detection, landmark localization, pose estimation, and gender recognition. IEEE Trans. Pattern Anal. Mach. Intell. **41**(1), 121–135 (2017)
22. Sandler, M., Howard, A., Zhu, M., Zhmoginov, A., Chen, L.C.: MobileNetV2: inverted residuals and linear bottlenecks. In: 2018 IEEE/CVF Conference on Computer Vision and Pattern Recognition, pp. 4510–4520 (2018). https://doi.org/10.1109/CVPR.2018.00474
23. Sandler, M., Howard, A., Zhu, M., Zhmoginov, A., Chen, L.C.: MobileNetV2: inverted residuals and linear bottlenecks. In: 2018 IEEE/CVF Conference on Computer Vision and Pattern Recognition, pp. 4510–4520. IEEE (2018)
24. Simonyan, K., Zisserman, A.: Very deep convolutional networks for large-scale image recognition. arXiv preprint arXiv:1409.1556 (2014)
25. Szegedy, C., et al.: Going deeper with convolutions. In: 2015 IEEE Conference on Computer Vision and Pattern Recognition (CVPR), pp. 1–9 (2015). https://doi.org/10.1109/CVPR.2015.7298594

26. Szegedy, C., Vanhoucke, V., Ioffe, S., Shlens, J., Wojna, Z.: Rethinking the inception architecture for computer vision. In: 2016 IEEE Conference on Computer Vision and Pattern Recognition (CVPR), pp. 2818–2826 (2016). https://doi.org/10.1109/CVPR.2016.308
27. Szegedy, C., Vanhoucke, V., Ioffe, S., Shlens, J., Wojna, Z.: Rethinking the inception architecture for computer vision. In: 2016 IEEE Conference on Computer Vision and Pattern Recognition (CVPR), pp. 2818–2826. IEEE (2016)
28. Woo, S., Park, J., Lee, J.-Y., Kweon, I.S.: CBAM: convolutional block attention module. In: Ferrari, V., Hebert, M., Sminchisescu, C., Weiss, Y. (eds.) ECCV 2018. LNCS, vol. 11211, pp. 3–19. Springer, Cham (2018). https://doi.org/10.1007/978-3-030-01234-2_1
29. Zhang, H., Zu, K., Lu, J., Zou, Y., Meng, D.: EPSANet: an efficient pyramid squeeze attention block on convolutional neural network. In: Proceedings of the Asian Conference on Computer Vision, pp. 1161–1177 (2022)
30. Zhang, Z., Song, Y., Qi, H.: Age progression/regression by conditional adversarial autoencoder. In: Proceedings of the IEEE Conference on Computer Vision and Pattern Recognition, pp. 5810–5818 (2017)

Author Index

© The Editor(s) (if applicable) and The Author(s), under exclusive license
to Springer Nature Singapore Pte Ltd. 2023
I. Na and G. Irie (Eds.): IW-FCV 2023, CCIS 1857, p. 179, 2023.
https://doi.org/10.1007/978-981-99-4914-4

Printed in the United States
by Baker & Taylor Publisher Services

Printed in the United States
by Baker & Taylor Publisher Services